Contesting Symbolic Landscape in Jerusalem

Contesting Symbolic Landscape in Jerusalem

Jewish/Islamic Conflict over the Museum of Tolerance at Mamilla Cemetery

YITZHAK REITER

sussex
ACADEMIC
PRESS
Brighton • Chicago • Toronto

Jerusalem Institute for Israel Studies

2 4 6 8 10 9 7 5 3 1

First published 2014, in Great Britain by
SUSSEX ACADEMIC PRESS
PO Box 139
Eastbourne BN24 9BP

Distributed in North America by
SUSSEX ACADEMIC PRESS
Independent Publishers Group
814 N Franklin St, Chicago, IL 60610, USA

British Library Cataloguing in Publication Data
A CIP catalogue record for this book is available from the British Library.

Library of Congress Cataloging-in-Publication Data
Applied for.

Hardcover ISBN 978-1-84519-655-4
Paperback ISBN 978-1-84519-661-5

Typeset & designed by Sussex Academic Press, Brighton & Eastbourne.
Printed and bound by CPI Group (UK) Ltd, Croydon, CR0 4YY
This book is printed on acid-free paper.

Contents

Acknowledgments

This book is an updated edition of the Hebrew edition of 2011 (published by the Jerusalem Institute for Israel Studies). I am grateful to the Institute for funding the study and for assigning Ms. Galit Hazan to assist me in the research. Her thorough approach and instructive comments were of great help to me and contributed significantly to the final product, and I wholeheartedly thank her for this. Merav Datan edited and indexed the English edition and, as always, she did a great job. I am also indebted to Hamutal Appel, the Institute's Director of Publications, who masterfully handled everything related to the production of the Hebrew edition and the translation.

I am indebted to the Truman Institute for Research of the Hebrew University and Ashkelon Academic College, where I have taught since 2005, for their great support. This research was also supported (in part) by The Israel Science Foundation.

Finally, this book would not see light without the love and support of my beloved partner Dr. Nancy Kobrin.

YITZHAK REITER

Introduction

In February of 2010, 15 Palestinian organizations and 60 well-known Palestinian East Jerusalemites initiated a public media campaign against an Israeli initiative to construct the Museum of Tolerance (MoT) in the heart of West Jerusalem. The museum was to be built on a plot of land that in the past had been part of the Muslim Mamilla Cemetery and since the 1980s has served as a municipal parking lot.[1] The campaigners appealed to UN institutions and other international organizations demanding that the Israeli initiative be investigated and Israel be instructed to cease the work, that the cemetery be preserved as a site of antiquities, and that the human remains that had already been disinterred be reburied. The campaign succeeded in generating articles in the world's leading newspapers. It also achieved a resolution of the United Nations (UN) Human Rights Council, adopted 24 March 2010, against Israeli actions in the Occupied Territories, which called for the Israeli government to cease construction of the MoT in Jerusalem, describing the work as illegal.[2] The reason behind the elevation of activities directed against construction of the Museum – from the local Israeli level to the international arena – was the rejection by Israel's High Court of Justice in late 2008 of a petition that had been submitted by the Northern Islamic Movement in Israel against the construction of the museum on that specific plot of land. Moreover, Israeli authorities also intended to establish a "Compound of Justice" in Jerusalem (incorporating local and magistrate courts) on a nearby lot that had also been part of the Mamilla Cemetery and contained a school Israel had built during the 1970s. The Jerusalem Planning Committee decided to reject this plan, fearing that the excavation of additional human remains during the work would precipitate a new wave of protest. Perhaps the Hebrew-language publication of this study in 2011 had an impact on that decision.

When work began on construction of the MoT, the Al-Aqsa Corporation,[3] which is administered by the Northern Islamic Movement in Israel, petitioned the High Court of Justice, demanding cessation of the work. Five days later an international conference entitled "Confrontation and Coexistence in Holy Places" was held at both Haifa University and Al-Qasemi College.[4] Some of the parties to this dispute participated in the conference, and as one of the three organizers, I had a first-hand opportunity to learn about this particular dispute. I realized that the conflict over construction of the MoT in Mamilla embodies several questions of principle regarding the status of the Arab Muslim minority in Israel and its relationship with the Jewish majority as well as the role of a judicial court as a venue for conflict resolution with respect to holy places. The combination of these special issues was a strong motivation in my decision to investigate this affair.

Major Questions and Methodology

Very few in Israel know that until 1964 the disputed land was part of a Muslim cemetery named Ma'man-Allah, meaning Allah's Safe Haven, more commonly known as Mamilla (the name will be further discussed below). The Arabic name of the cemetery, implying a safe haven under God's protection, did not prove accurate in modern times. Since the late nineteenth century, as Jerusalem developed and spread beyond its walls, the cemetery was gradually encroached upon, and parts of it were allocated for housing, roads, and other public utilities such as a park and a parking lot.

This process of encroaching upon the territory of a cemetery is not unique to Mamilla. Generally speaking, modern societies have two contradictory approaches to ancient cemeteries. The first is shaped by the processes of modernization and economic development, resulting in the belief that the needs and interests of the living override the sanctity of the dead, and hence, graves should not pose an obstacle to vital urban development. The second approach, or attitude, centers on religious belief and tradition regarding the sanctity of the dead and prioritizes the preservation of heritage sites as part of the modern process of constructing a national, ethnic, or religious collective identity.

Along these lines, the Mamilla affair sparked an internal Israeli debate over the question of whether the construction of a museum dedicated to tolerance and human dignity on land that had in the past been a huge Muslim cemetery is important enough to justify the possibility of offending the Palestinian-Arab, predominantly Muslim minority in Israel. Moreover, during the thirty years prior to allocation of the land for the MoT, it had contained an underground parking structure that included surface parking as well. Whether this fact is enough to override the historical past of the land as a burial site and as part of the historical Muslim cemetery is a matter of cultural outlook and interpretation. Another question that has been raised is how to handle the huge number of human remains discovered during the excavation work prior laying the foundation of the MoT: Shall we view this discovery as an incidental exposure of graves during the course of work that in the case of Jewish graves in Israel, usually ends with a solution in accordance with *halacha* (Jewish religious law), enabling the resumption of work, or should we treat this case differently, as an important historical cemetery that requires protection?

Responses to the above questions inevitably embody ideological and national-political considerations. The establishment of the MoT in Jerusalem is a Jewish Zionist project initiated by the Simon Wiesenthal Center (SWC) in Los Angeles. The MoT of Los Angeles focuses, among other things, on the lessons of the Jewish Holocaust in Europe. Establishing a satellite museum in Jerusalem could be viewed as an expression of the mainstream Jewish Israeli concept of a "unified" Jerusalem under Israeli control. This is the ideological position of one side. On the other side is the Northern Islamic Movement's demand that the disputed land be preserved as a Muslim cemetery, a demand that expresses an Arab-Islamic counterstrategy. In Israel in general, and in Jerusalem in particular, there is competition over the identity of space and over sovereignty and physical control in the context of the Israeli–Palestinian conflict. The Northern Islamic Movement strives to renovate thousands of sites within Israel that in the past had been cemeteries, mosques, or Muslim saints' tombs and today lie ruined and abandoned. Its goal is both religious and national: to rejuvenate and restore the Arab-Islamic landscape of the country to the way it was during the long Muslim rule in Palestine.

On the Jewish side, other voices could also be heard. A group of academics and civil society organizations (including rabbis) voiced a different Jewish Zionist position. They advocated relocating the MoT to another site in Jerusalem, citing human rights' issues as well as concerns about negative ramifications of the affair for Israel's interests.

A personal disclaimer is appropriate in this context: In the early days of the legal dispute I assisted the museum's entrepreneurs. During the course of my research and writing, however, I gradually came to understand that the dispute could be viewed differently and in a more complex manner, as the chapters of this book explain. I made an effort to seek the objective truth without sparing criticism when it was warranted.

The study conducted for this book is based on a historical analysis, combining interdisciplinary research involving identity politics, historical approach, and conflict resolution. The sources for the study are documents collected from the *Shari'a* (Islamic law) Court of Jerusalem and Israel's High Court of Justice ("High Court") as well as the literature of Islamic law, Israeli civil law, reports of experts submitted to the courts, and personal participation of the author, including discussions with key players and informants.

The main issues addressed in this book are analyzed at three levels:

1. The individual case of a conflict over the location of the Museum of Tolerance in Jerusalem, including the internal Israeli public debate over a building project with an *a priori* inherent contradiction between its objectives – teaching the values of human dignity and tolerance – and its possible outcome – an act of insensitivity to the Muslim minority in Jerusalem specifically and in Israel generally.
2. The political level in the context of majority-minority relations. This case has raised a number of issues regarding the standing of the Arab-Muslim minority in Israel in the following contexts: the right of representation in the public domain and the symbolic landscape; the right of equal treatment by the state with respect to rights relating to

places of heritage and holy places; and the right to administer holy properties (*waqf*) according to religious law and the rulings of shari'a courts. In this context, the shari'a regarding a non-operational cemetery is also examined, and factual and interpretational precedents are discussed. This issue, in addition, has raised the question of the treatment of Muslim and Jewish cemeteries within Israel: Is this treatment fair or discriminatory?

3. The universal level, which poses the question of whether a conflict over a holy place that reflects "identity politics" can be addressed objectively and separately from the ideological and political positions that the place symbolizes. Specifically, the following questions are posed: Is a (secular) civil court competent to discuss issues that have a religious element and relate to other religious communities? Is the court the appropriate venue to adjudicate conflicts over holy places?

This book deals with all of the above questions. It presents the public and legal dilemmas raised during the dispute and their political context. The research for this book is based on a case analysis integrating a multi-disciplinary approach involving history, identity politics, and conflict resolution. The sources for the study are mainly the documents submitted to the High Court and the Sharia Court, as well as legal literature, both Muslim and Israeli, and the expert reports that the parties submitted to the High Court. Additional sources include the protocols of court hearings and personal discussions of the author with key informants and the press, as well as internet sites.

Structure of the Book

The first chapter reviews the history of the Mamilla Cemetery and the construction of memory and identity, as well as the chronology of the dispute regarding the location of the MoT.

Chapter 2 analyzes the conflict over locating the MoT in Mamilla as part of Jewish–Muslim struggle over the symbolic landscape of Jerusalem and Israel in general.

Chapter 3 deals with the argument of Muslim plaintiffs that because the cemetery's original status is a holy Islamic endowment – waqf – the proper jurisdiction for resolving its fate is the Shari'a Court. One can also view this process as a struggle by Israeli Muslims to restore the glory of the waqf institution and assets.

Chapter 4 elaborates on the status of the Muslim Shari'a Court and the tensions between the shari'a system and the Israeli High Court, and it examines the authority of the High Court to investigate an issue that is a Muslim religious matter under the jurisdiction of a shari'a court.

Chapter 5 deals with another central argument, that is, the shari'a law on changing the use of a cemetery. It elaborates on the ambivalent approach of shari'a to this question and on the positions expressed by academic experts in light of their cultural background. Beyond this theoretical aspect stands practice, to which Chapter 6 is devoted. In this chapter I investigate the precedent of the Palace Hotel, which was built on land that had also been part of the Mamilla Cemetery, in addition to other, similar precedents from Arab towns in Israel and Muslim countries.

Chapter 7 deals with an important moral and legal issue entailing a comparative perspective, which was raised in the High Court, that is, the accusation that Israeli authorities employ a double standard that discriminates between Jewish and Muslim cemeteries.

Chapter 8 analyzes the High Court's verdict, its framing of the dispute, and its characterization of the conflicting values of the case as well as its method of balancing among them.

Finally, Chapter 9 analyzes the entire affair using the tools of conflict resolution and queries whether a judicial tribunal is an effective tool for dealing with conflicts over holy places. I also use the Conclusion to update the reader on the media campaign directed against Israel that Palestinian civil society (including Arab-Israeli organizations) began in February 2010. This campaign marks a new phase of the struggle regarding Mamilla at the international level. The entire affair discussed in this book has acquired an international dimension, thereby increasing the importance of public engagement to deal with it and its implications.

Notes

1 The 60 renowned individuals represent the following families: Dajani, 'Akari, Duzdar, Hallaq, Husayni, Imam, Ja'uni, Khalidi, Kaluti, Kurd, Nusseibeh, Zayn, Sallah, and Sanduqa.

2 UN Human Rights Commission, 13th session, Agenda item 7, Res. A/HRC/RES/13/8 of 14 April 2010.

3 Registered in the Israeli Companies' Registrar. Al-Aqsa is the name of the mosque holy to Islam in Jerusalem.

4 International Conference, Haifa University and al-Qasemi College (with Catholic University of America), January 3–4, 2006. The conference yielded the following two volumes: M. J. Breger, Y. Reiter, and L. Hammer (eds), *Holy Places in the Israeli–Palestinian Conflict: Confrontation and Co-existence,* London and New York: Routledge, 2009; Idem., *Religion and Politics: Sacred Space in Palestine and Israel*, London and New York: Routledge, 2012.

CHAPTER

1

The Mamilla Cemetery and the Chronology of the Dispute

The History of the Mamilla Cemetery

In a sensitive location such as Jerusalem it is only natural that historical sites, including cemeteries, appear in mythological beliefs. Since ancient times, myths have been intertwined with the history of holy spaces, fueling and shaping the competition among holy cities seeking to attract pilgrims and public attention. In Islam, Jerusalem ("Al-Quds" or "Bayt al-Maqdis" in Arabic) competed for seniority with other cities such as Mecca, as reflected in the vast literature and praises (*fada'il*) of Jerusalem.[1] Myths and traditions regarding holy cities were constructed and disseminated in order to elevate the cities' importance within a given community.

Such a process also took place with respect to the importance of the Mamilla Cemetery. Present-day Palestinian Muslims believe that some 70,000 Muslims slain during the Crusader conquest of Jerusalem in the eleventh century and Saladin's warriors who liberated Jerusalem in the twelfth century are buried in this cemetery. They also believe that a number of notable companions of the Prophet Mohammed are buried in this cemetery.[2] The present-day narration is only partially supported by historical evidence. The Jerusalem Muslim historian of the sixteenth century Mujir al-Din (d. 1521) wrote the following about the Mamilla Cemetery:

The Mamilla Cemetery west of Jerusalem's walls is the largest cemetery of the city, containing the graves of notables, scholars (*ulama'*), righteous people, and slain people. As to the question of why this cemetery was called Mamilla, it is said that the origin comes from 'water from Allah' (ma' Allah), or 'the gate of Allah,' or 'the olives of al-Milla.' According to a traditional [popular belief] narrated by al-Hassan, anyone buried in Jerusalem in the Olives of al-Milla is regarded as buried in Heaven. The Jews call this cemetery 'Beit Milwa,' and its Christian name is 'Babilla.' However, the general public uses the name Mamilla. In the center of this cemetery there is a *zawiya* (Sufi lodge) named Al-Qalandariyya, containing a large building. This zawiya was in the past a Church, built by Christians and named Deir al-Ahmar, and the

Christians have a special attachment to this place . . . The greatest dignitaries who arrived to Jerusalem, as well as other people, were buried in Mamilla. The soil of this cemetery and most of the land of Mamilla is rocky, and digging graves in it is difficult . . . [3] This historical source teaches us that Mamilla is the most important cemetery of Jerusalem and that important people were buried therein. It does not specify the Prophet's companions or the slain soldiers of Saladin. However, the names of two important middle-rank people are mentioned: a sufi sheikh (al-Qalandari) and a military Mamluk Emir (al-Kabaki). The domed tomb of al-Kabaki who died in 1289 h. is still preserved.

Kamil Jamil al-'Asali, a Palestinian-Jordanian historian, dedicated a book to Muslim cemeteries of Jerusalem (published in 1981), and he believes that the modern name of the Cemetery Ma'man Allah is a recent variation on the name "Water from Allah" (perhaps because of the water pool that exists there). Another possibility for the origin of Mamilla is "the Water of Milo," a name of a place in Jerusalem.

Al-'Asali quotes a ninth century Christian traveler who wrote that Mamilla was the name of a Christian female saint after whom a place of worship in the cemetery was named. He tells us that this cemetery was used by Christians during the Byzantine period and that during the Persian conquest of Palestine in 614 AD, more than 60,000 Christians slaughtered by the Persians were buried in this cemetery.[4] During the Crusader conquest of Jerusalem in 1099, 70,000 Muslims were also slaughtered, according to Arab sources, and they were buried in Mamilla. Crusaders continued to bury their dead in this cemetery (apparently in another section closer to the city walls),[5] where later the slain soldiers of Saladin who defeated the Crusaders in 1187 were buried. Finally, drawing on various ancient Arab sources, al-'Asali compiled a list of 150 Muslim dignitaries from the post-Crusader period who were buried in the Mamilla Cemetery.[6] Contrary to what present-day Palestinian Muslims contend, no single companion of the Prophet Mohammed was buried there. From a polemic point of view, al-'Asali's argument that the Mamilla Cemetery began as a Christian cemetery (with 60,000 buried) is important for the dispute over the fate of the cemetery because Muslims who wish to preserve the cemetery could potentially consolidate support from the Christian world for their endeavor. Yet the current campaign underscores only the Muslim character of the site.

During the nineteenth century, towards the end of Ottoman rule, the south part of the Mamilla Cemetery was designated for construction, and a stone wall was built to protect the rest of the cemetery.[7] During the British Mandate in Palestine the cemetery was reduced to only 134 Dunams, and this space was registered in the 1938 land registry as waqf property, administered by the director of the General Waqf of Jerusalem (regarding the waqf, see chapter 3).

Al-'Asali tells us that in 1927, "The supreme Muslim Council ordered that burials in this cemetery cease following the development of Jerusalem surrounding the cemetery in the heart of the city, not to mention that there was insufficient space to contain more graves."

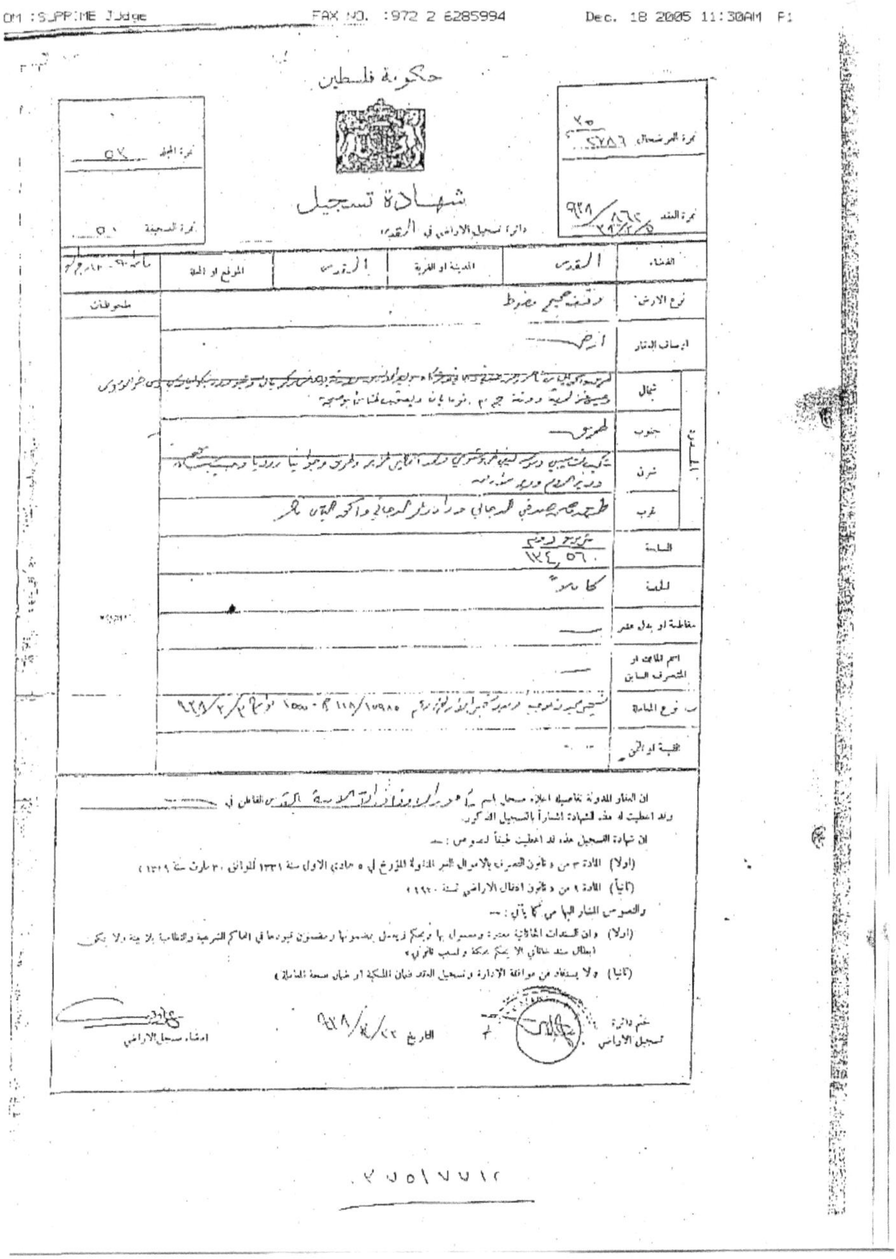
OM :SUPRIME Judge FAX NO. :972 2 6285994 Dec. 18 2005 11:30AM P1

حكومة فلسطين

شهادة تسجيل

Land Registry of 1938: 134.56 dunum of waqf land

Al-'Asali adds that the Palace Hotel (see chapter 5) was built in 1930 within the cemetery grounds, above the remains of the Qalandariyya Zawiya, indicating that the cemetery was originally larger than officially delineated in the 1920s. His narrative in fact embraces accusations leveled by the Palestinian opposition against Grand Mufti Haj Amin al-Husayni, the leader of the Palestinians at that time, for building the hotel on top of the graveyard. Al-'Asali, adds that the Mamilla Cemetery has been neglected in recent decades and that after 1948 Israelis continued to reduce the area of the cemetery by paving roads, a public park, and buildings, including a hotel, on its western part.[8]

Following the 1948 war, the Mamilla Cemetery, which is situated only a few hundred meters west of the Old City walls, came under Israeli rule and became part of West Jerusalem's downtown, bordering important Israeli national institutions such as the first Knesset building on King George Street, the Jewish Agency, the Great Synagogue (which is also the premises of the Chief Rabbinate), and the Jerusalem Municipality, located at the beginning of Jaffa Street in close proximity to the 1948 border with Jordan and Jaffa Gate ("Bab al-Khalil" in Arabic).

Article VIII of the 1949 armistice agreement signed between Israel and Jordan called for a special committee, composed of two representatives of each party, to direct its attention to the formulation of agreed plans and arrangements for, among other things, "free access to the Holy Places and cultural institutions and use of the [Jewish, YR] cemetery on the Mount of Olives . . . "[9] Yet this committee was never established, and both Israel and Jordan voiced complaints regarding the neglect of holy places under the control of the other side. The Mamilla Cemetery was the subject of one of these complaints. It appears that the Jerusalem Municipality and the government of Israel did not properly maintain the Mamilla Cemetery following 1948. It should be mentioned that during this period there were almost no Arab Muslim residents in West Jerusalem (with the exception of the nearby village Beit Safafa, located far from the cemetery), and no entity other than the Israeli Ministry of Religious Affairs bore responsibility for maintenance and preservation of this Muslim cemetery. In fact, most of the Muslim Cemeteries in Israel were neglected by both the Muslim residents and the Israeli government, and some of them were even sold for development purposes with the approval of Israeli civil servant shari'a court qadis.

In 1950, the government of Jordan officially protested "Israeli damage to the Mamilla Cemetery" and published its claim in the Arab Press.[10] In response, the Israeli Ministry of Religious Affairs promptly took action, cleaning the cemetery and planting some trees, while responding that no damage had been caused to the cemetery.[11]

After 1948, the central location of this old burial compound, in combination with its neglected condition and the near absence of preserved and intact gravestones, attracted several development initiatives. Initially the cemetery's land was used for provisional utilities (e.g., a circus tent). In the 1960s the

Mayor of Jerusalem, Mordechai Ish-Shalom, initiated development of the cemetery's land by rendering it a public park. He contacted the chief Muslim qadi of Israel, Sheikh Tahir Hammad, requesting that he nullify the holiness of this cemetery and issue a *fatwa* (a non-binding Islamic legal opinion issued by an expert on shari'a) allowing construction of a public park at this place. The park subsequently constructed is known today as Independence Park (Gan HaAtzma'ut). The qadi approved this action and the Mayor, for his part, promised to preserve part of the historical cemetery south of the Mamilla pool, where dozens of gravestones were still in good shape. Soon after the qadi issued his fatwa, the municipality utilized the land to construct not only a public park but also several buildings, among them a school, a hotel, and a parking lot, as well as a new paved road and other utility infrastructures for electricity and sewage. The plot that served as a parking lot was later reassigned for the building of the MoT.

In 1964, when Qadi Tahir Hammad issued his approval, no social, political, or religious body complained about damage to the cemetery. As mentioned above, West Jerusalem had no Muslim community. Moreover, most of the Arab minority of Israel was subject to restrictions on movement under the martial regime in force at the time, which was abolished only in late 1966.

At the same time, the government of Jordan endorsed the construction of a hotel on the Mount of Olives (the Intercontinental Hotel, later renamed the Seven Arches Hotel), which was built on land that the government expropriated from the waqf of the family of Abd al-Razzaq al-'Alami. During the works a road was paved leading to the hotel through the middle of the old Jewish cemetery of the Mount of Olives, causing damage to Jewish gravestones. Although most of the graves were not damaged, it was reported that some of the gravestones were used as a foundation for the road.[12] This affair has played and continues to play an important polemic role (to be discussed later).

During the Six Day War of June 1967, Israel captured the eastern part of Jerusalem, among other territories, and the city's municipal boundaries were expanded, resulting in the incorporation of 65,000 Palestinians into the city. The Palestinians' reaction to unilateral Israeli actions regarding religious issues and sites was the establishment of the Supreme Muslim Authority, which from time to time sent letters of protest to Israeli authorities regarding works conducted within the Mamilla Cemetery. The digging to construct the parking lot in the mid-1980s, where the Museum of Tolerance was planned to be erected, was the subject of a complaint submitted by diplomatic representatives of Jordan and the PLO. On 28 January 1986, two Jordanian ministers, the minister of foreign affairs and the minister of awqaf (the East Jerusalem Waqf Authority was affiliated with Jordan even under Israeli rule), submitted a complaint to the director-general of UNESCO, asserting that the Israeli authorities were demolishing the tombs and buildings of the Ma'man Allah cemetery and causing damage to graves of important Muslim dignitaries.[13] They wrote in their letter of complaint that they view these works as damaging to sites of Islamic heritage in Al-Quds (Jerusalem), which is among World Heritage in Danger sites.

The Jordanian delegate to UNESCO conveyed that the Jerusalem Municipality was building an underground parking lot and that human remains were exposed and scattered during the works. This complaint was one in a series of other complaints that the Muslim Waqf submitted regarding Muslim holy places in Jerusalem. The complaints focused in particular on the compound of Al-Haram al-Sharif and excavations around it. Following these complaints, the director-general of UNESCO sent an expert, Professor Raymond Lemaire, to investigate the facts. Lemaire insisted on arriving in Jerusalem within a couple of weeks, at the beginning of March 1986. In his report he notes that Israel responded that it could receive him only in July of that year. He reported that when he first visited the Mamilla site he did not see bones exposed by the digging works, but on a later visit to this site with Jerusalem Municipality archeologist Dan Bahat and Waqf representative Mr. Natshe, they discovered some ten human bones scattered around. He further concluded that the parking lot infringed somewhat on the northern part of the cemetery. Lemaire reported also that the Jerusalem Municipality officially informed him of its decision to abandon its plan to lay down a sewage pipe across the cemetery and promised to preserve and develop the fabric of the cemetery and some burial structures in the framework of an agreement with the Waqf.[14] Three months later, however, in November 1986, the PLO observer to the United Nations, Omar Masalha, submitted a complaint to UNESCO, asserting that municipality bulldozers had been digging in the cemetery (for the purpose of laying down a sewage pipe) and that Waqf representatives reported that many human remains were exposed during this process.[15] Another complaint was submitted to UNESCO by the Head of the Supreme Muslim Authority Sheikh Sa'd al-Din al-Alami, who accused Israel of damaging Islamic heritage and culture. The Jerusalem Mayor's Advisor on Arab Affairs Amir Cheshin responded to this complaint by saying that two graves containing bones had been exposed during the works and were reburied by Muslim employees of the municipality.[16]

The above complaints indicate that East Jerusalem Muslims as well as the leaders of Jordan and the PLO were not indifferent to what was happening in the Mamilla Cemetery. They were limited in their ability to preserve and maintain the cemetery, however, because it was under the control of Israeli authorities and the East Jerusalem Waqf had no authority to maintain a site located in West Jerusalem. Indeed, the responsibility for maintaining the cemetery belonged to the Israeli government, which declared the area "Absentees' Property" under the law (among other pre-1948 waqf properties) and took possession of it. In another report by Professor Lemaire in 1990, he indicated that the cemetery is "severely neglected and in crucial need of preservation and beautification".[17]

Since the first Palestinian uprising – the Intifada that erupted in 1987 – the center of Israeli–Palestinian tension has shifted to the most holy place in Palestine that is, the Temple Mount/Al-Haram al Sharif, which is known today by Muslims as the Al-Aqsa compound. Hence, the Mamilla Cemetery did not make headlines and was seemingly forgotten by the public.

The municipal parking lot constructed in the northern part of the cemetery served the city's residents, including many Muslims, and there were no further complaints that it was constructed over a historic cemetery. In the late 1990s the Jerusalem Municipality decided to designate the area of the parking lot for the construction of the Museum of Tolerance. During at least five years of the planning review process, which included a public display of the MoT model designed by the American Jewish Architect Frank Gehry, there was no notable opposition from the Muslim community to this project. This lack of opposition posed an obstacle later for those who opposed building the museum at this location, when the dispute was the subject of a petition to the High Court. The museum entrepreneurs argued – and this argument was underscored by the justices of the High Court – that the delay exhibited by opponents to the MoT location indicates that the Muslim community did not view the particular land in dispute as bearing the special status of a holy cemetery and that it was indifferent to the museum project.

Chronology of the Dispute

The dispute discussed in this book broke out on 28 December 2005, when three activists of the Northern Islamic Movement in Israel appeared at the excavation site for the planned construction of the foundation of the MoT, sponsored by the Simon Wiesenthal Center (SWC) of Los Angeles. They were received as respected guests by those in charge of the site, who explained to them that archeologists from the Israel Antiquity Authority (IAA) were excavating the site and when they found human remains they transferred them to a special facility. They invited the Islamists to participate in a committee that would be responsible for the removal of the bones, to be respectfully reburied in the nearby visible part of the cemetery. The surprise visitors were informed that the Simon Wiesenthal Centers of both Los Angeles and Jerusalem were assigned the land from the State and the Jerusalem Municipality for the construction of the Museum of Tolerance, and they were proceeding with an urban plan approved in 2002 and a building permit issued by the Israeli authorities in 2004.

After receiving this explanation, the three visitors observed human remains in the excavation site, which they photographed, and they left the location without confrontation. That same day, the Al-Aqsa Corporation petitioned the High Court, demanding the cessation of work and the termination of the planned construction. The Al-Aqsa Corporation is affiliated with the Islamic Movement, which strives to identify and preserve Muslim holy places.[18]

The Al-Aqsa Corporation defines itself as "a corporation that develops

Muslim endowment properties in Israel with the goal of preserving and maintaining Christian and Muslim Holy Places within the State of Israel." Its demand that digging and construction work cease was based on the argument that the site is a Muslim cemetery and that the work there involves the desecration of graves and damages a Muslim holy place, and therefore is absolutely forbidden. Before the High Court decreed a temporary cessation of construction, the remains of 400 bodies had already been excavated and removed from the site. The archeologist responsible for the digging and excavation of this plot on behalf of the IAA estimated that some 600 additional graves were yet to be unearthed.[19]

During the High Court hearing, the history of using the Mamilla Cemetery for development purposes was publically exposed. Beginning in 1960, the Jerusalem Municipality had approved a series of urban plans to develop the site for housing, business, and public facilities, as well as open spaces for public and private use, including Independence Park, the Experimental School, the Engineers' House, the Agron House, and more. Furthermore, in 1979, the plot later allocated for the MoT had been approved for construction of a parking lot (completed in 1986). In 1991, another plan was approved to pave a road across the center of the cemetery, and in 1998 the parking lot's planning status was changed to "business zone" after the municipality, headed by Ehud Olmert, offered the parking lot as a venue for the MoT instead of another plot of land that the Museum entrepreneurs had identified in the French Hill. In 1999 Frank Gehry was hired to plan the Museum, and in 2000 the Municipality approved the addition of two stories to the Engineers' House as well as two new buildings to be built within the compound that had been part of the cemetery in the past.

The architectural design of the MoT by Frank Gehry is reminiscent of his special artistic approach and signature. The building was designed as a sculpture that integrates different materials and gives it a special appearance, salient within its environment. The plan received contradictory reactions, ranging between enthusiasm and strong criticism. Critics claimed that the building is grandiose, reflecting a form of megalomania that disconnects it from the surrounding context and from the Jerusalem landscape. Gehry denies this criticism and argues that the design intertwines with the immediate landscape and even connects with the Muslim cemetery to its south.[20] According to the MoT entrepreneurs, the museum structure will contain five buildings that are harmoniously connected. At their center will be a round hall decorated with 16 tall titanium columns rising to the height of five stories (according to the SCW these columns will be inscribed with donors' names, visible to all who enter the museum).[21] The five surrounding buildings will serve as a gallery, a conference center, an educational center, a theatre, and a children's museum.[22]

The Museum of Tolerance plan was advertised in four newspapers (two in Hebrew, *Ma'ariv* and *Yerushalayim*, and two in Arabic, *Al-Ittihad* and *Al-Quds*) as well as in the Official Gazette,[23] and the plan was finally approved in March of 2002. (Following Frank Gehry's resignation from the project planning endeavor, the museum entrepreneurs decided in 2010 to seek an alternative plan more modest in its size and budget that was prepared by the Israeli Chyutin Architects firm that also resigned afterwards).

On 24 November 2002, the unveiling ceremony for the Museum's model took place at the residence of Israeli President Moshe Katsav. In the same year, the model was displayed for architects and the general public in the main hall of the Jerusalem Municipality. The ceremony for laying the cornerstone took place on 2 May 2005, with the participation of the Governor of California Arnold Schwarzenegger, as well as President Katsav, Deputy Prime Minister and Minister of Industry and Trade Ehud Olmert, Minister of Foreign Affairs Silvan Shalom, Minister of Defense Shaul Mofaz, and many other high ranking officials. The Islamic movement claims, apparently incorrectly, that the ceremony's speakers drew a connection between the establishment of the museum and the rebuilding of Solomon's Temple. The Islamic Movement claimed in an Arabic publication that Islamic institutions in Jerusalem denounced the decision to locate this project within a cemetery and warned against it.[24] I could not find any record of or support for this claim.

A building permit for the MoT in Mamilla was issued in 2004, and the local SWC Museum Corporation started work in late 2005 by digging the area intended for placement of the building's foundation. Once human remains were unearthed during this work, the IAA came in to conduct salvation excavations, following which some 400 graves were interred and archaeological artifacts were exposed. The IAA determined that from a historical and archaeological point of view, there is no obstacle to continued construction of the MoT on the main portion of the designated plot, subject to a few restrictions aimed at preserving the small portion that still contains human remains.

On 28 December 2005 the Al-Aqsa Corporation for Developing Muslim Endowment Properties in the land of Israel filed a petition with the High Court[25] against eight defendants: the Simon Wiesenthal Center Museum Corporation in both Israel and Los Angeles; three Israeli government authorities (the Israel Land Administration, the District Planning and Building Committee for Jerusalem, and the IAA); and three municipal authorities (the Jerusalem Municipality, the local Jerusalem Planning and Building Committee, and "Moriyah," a company dedicated to the development of Jerusalem).

Advocate Muhammad Sulayman Aghbariyya, representing the Al-Aqsa Corporation, claimed in his case to the High Court, that the excavation works were being conducted within the actual boundaries of the Ma'man Allah Cemetery.[26] According to him, "Throughout history the entire cemetery had been completely preserved" and was registered under the name of the Islamic Waqf of Jerusalem. As noted above, however, after 1964 some sections of this cemetery had been rendered for use as public parks and roads, and only a small segment of the greater cemetery was preserved. Against this background he claimed that construction of the museum on the small remaining section poses "additional and significant damage to what remains of the Cemetery (remnants). The Al-Aqsa Corporation further argued that according to shari'a, "it is ultimately impermissible to dig or rummage inside a grave, to unearth graves, or to cause harm of any kind to the sanctity of the deceased." This claim was backed by two fatwas, one issued in 1991 by Qadi Tawfiq Asaliya, former president of the Shari'a Court of Israel and the second in 2004 by Qadi Ahmad Natour, who succeeded him as president of the Sharia Court and still holds this position. The Muslim plaintiffs also argued that the Museum's purpose of "promoting amicability among the different peoples in the Holy Land" could never be realized through the infliction of damage to the deceased and the sentiments of the Muslim community within the country and throughout the world. The excavation and construction works, according to them, are a severe violation of the law of human dignity and freedom and the values of the State of Israel as a Jewish and democratic state, as well as in the principles of Judaism.[27]

On 2 February 2006 three Muslims from notable families in East Jerusalem, Muhammad Khayr al-Dajani, Muhammad Zaki Nusseibeh, and Muhammad Badr al-Zayn, represented by the Karama Association, an Israeli Arab human rights organization, filed a petition with the Shari'a Court requesting that the qadi issue a temporary restraining order suspending work at the MoT compound. The objective of this petition was to transfer decision making from the High Court to the Shari'a Court, which was the Muslims' "home town" judicial court. The Israeli qadi of Jerusalem, Muhammad Zibde, issued the requested decree, but the police refused to assist in enforcing it. The plaintiffs reacted by filing another petition with the High Court, requesting that it compel the police to enforce the decree issued by the Shari'a Court.[28] In parallel, the museum entrepreneurs and the relevant state authorities filed another petition with the High Court against six defendants: the Shari'a Court of Jerusalem, the three above-cited Muslim dignitaries, and two government authorities – the Custodian of Absentees' Properties in the Ministry of Finance and the Development Authority, which is an organ of the Israel Land Authority.[29] The Development Authority holds all absentee properties that were handed over to it by the Custodian of Absentees' Properties, including the Mamilla Cemetery after its holiness was nullified. The entrepreneurs requested that the Shari'a Court decrees be overruled, claiming that this court has no authority over land not possessed by the Waqf.[30]

Later, in April 2007, when the High Court hearing was in its final stages, a group of some 70 senior Israeli academics headed by Professor Shimon Shamir, including five Israel Prize laureates and seven civil society and human rights organizations that objected to the construction of the museum in Mamilla, took the initiative of applying to the High Court, seeking to join the legal case as "Friends of the Court." Their opposition to the location of the museum was based on the ramifications of construction of this particular project on a Muslim cemetery in Jerusalem and the way it reflected on the relationship between state institutions and the Jews of Israel, on the one hand,

and the Arab Muslim minority and other Arab and Muslim countries, on the other, as well as the implications for preservation of Jewish cemeteries abroad. The High Court decided not to accept them as an official party to the legal case. However, the justices agreed that they would have the right to voice their opinion during the hearings and to submit expert reports challenging the reports of the local SWC Museum Corporation. The museum, for its part, responded by organizing an alternative group of elite academics and public figures, headed by the former head of Mossad Shabtai Shavit, with the participation of 182 members. They also submitted expert reports as counter-testimony.

In all, the parties involved submitted a large number of expert reports to the High Court, which were subsequently consolidated into one file. The court plenum of three members included Justice Ayalah Procaccia (Chair), Justice Edna Arbel, and Justice David Cheshin. The High Court refrained during the first stage of the dispute from issuing a restraining order against the works and decided to refer the entire affair to mediation, to be conducted by the former president of the High Court, Meir Shamgar.

During the hearing of the three cases, the High Court issued three temporary injunctions. The first ordered the cessation of excavation works in the compound until the case was adjudicated. The second prohibited the Shari'a Court from taking any parallel procedures regarding the museum. Then, when the High Court realized that the excavation works in two of the three subsections of land designated for the museum had already been completed, it issued a third injunction, ordering the cessation of work on the third plot, which contained only 12% of the entire space designated for construction of the museum. This section was numbered 3 on the map submitted to the court and was painted in purple, and was therefore was termed the "purple section" and contained most of the human remains, according to the archeological report. The injunction ordered the museum entrepreneurs and the state authorities to explain to the High Court why they should not change the construction plans.

The mediation process, facilitated by Justice Meir Shamgar, lasted seven months but ultimately failed. The Muslim plaintiffs refused any compromise that would result in construction of the museum in Mamilla. Following this, the museum entrepreneurs were asked by the High Court to suggest a technical solution to the problem regarding the purple section. The latter presented to the court two alternatives. The first option was to remove the human remains at own their expense and rebury them in another Muslim Cemetery. They suggested that this transfer would "be conducted in a professional, respectful, and proper way, according to the Muslim religious guidelines, and under the supervision of Muslim clerics." They also proposed various technical ways of removing the human remains without causing damage to the graves themselves. The second alternative was to build over the "Purple Section" but to refrain from digging deep into the earth, thus minimizing damage to the graves. The entrepreneurs also promised the court that

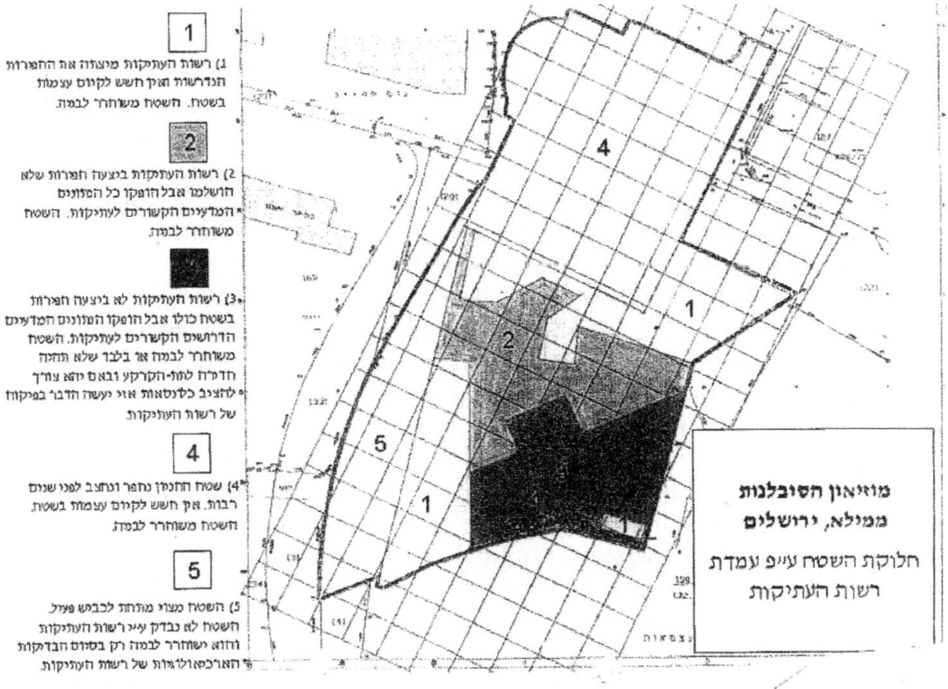

Sketch of the Israel Antiquity Authority ("purple section" = section 3, black)

they would build a floating floor over this section in such a manner that there would be a space between the surface of the ground and the building itself, preventing physical contact between the two. According to them, this was a method regularly employed to resolve similar disputes, such as the construction above a huge Muslim cemetery in Cairo, known as the "City of the Dead." The entrepreneurs agreed that the Al-Aqsa Corporation would have the right to choose among alternatives, but the latter rejected all of the alternatives proffered.

The Al-Aqsa Corporation, which is the major plaintiff and opponent of construction of the MoT, is affiliated with the Northern Islamic Movement, a movement whose leaders actively supported the Palestinian Intifada and the Hamas organization. In August 2008, Israel's minister of defense issued a decree under the Mandatory Defense Regulations (state of emergency 1945), declaring the Al-Aqsa Corporation an illegal organization and ordering the confiscation of its properties. It is unclear whether the campaign of the Islamic Movement against the MoT had the effect of accelerating action against this corporation.

In December 2008 the High Court issued its verdict, which will be analyzed thoroughly in Chapter 8. This verdict introduced a precedent for Israeli law regarding change in the status of graveyards, including those that in the past had been part of a historical cemetery but whose status the state had changed.

Three years after the petition was submitted to the High Court, the verdict that was finally issued rejected the claim of the Al-Aqsa Corporation and enabled the museum entrepreneurs to resume the project, subject to the condition that they take appropriate care of the human remains in that part of the land that was designated for the museum (which, according to the estimate of an IAA archeologist, might contain about 600 graves). The court permitted the entrepreneurs to act in accordance with one of the alternatives that they themselves had proposed: to relocate the graves in their entirety and reinter them elsewhere. Then they would be permitted to build an underground parking lot for the MoT, but they would still have to submit a change of plan or, alternatively, conduct minimal excavation in this section in order to position columns that support a floating floor for the museum.

After the legal dispute ended, academics and civil society organizations who objected to the project attempted to take action against the museum in the public sphere, but they failed. Apparently the public protest against the MoT's location in Mamilla had some impact, particularly on potential donors who had committed themselves to funding the museum. I conclude this from that the museum entrepreneurs ordered a new planning design that would be less ambitious and less costly. Perhaps this is why architect Frank Gehry resigned in early 2010 from the planning of the museum. In parallel, Palestinian civil society organizations initiated an international campaign against Israel's policy, portraying the Mamilla dispute as part of Israel's policy to erase Muslim cultural heritage sites.

When Gehry resigned from this project and when the donations did not flow as expected, the SWC announced a competition to re-design the MoT in Mamilla. In September 2010 the architectural firm Chyutin from Givatayim won the competition. According to this new design, presented in October 2010, the MoT would comprise 46,000 square meters and six stories, three underground and three aboveground. The project, scheduled to be completed in 2015, is to include a theater, an academic center, and an exhibition hall. The entrepreneurs estimated its cost at $100,000,000, as compared to $250,000,000 for the original plan.

In 2009 the Mamilla affair took on greater proportions when the government announced its intention of erecting the Jerusalem Judicial Compound (Heikhal HaMishpat, integrating Jerusalem's district and magistrate courts) on an adjacent plot of the historical cemetery, where the Experimental School stands today. The Israeli press revealed that the president of the High Court at the time, Justice Dorit Beinish, had hesitations regarding the proper location of this project within Jerusalem. As of the time of this publication, I have been informed that the authorities withdrew from this location and that perhaps the Hebrew publication of this book contributed to the decision.

Notes

1 On the literature of the praise of Jerusalem see: M. Sharon, "The 'Praises of Jerusalem' as a source for the early history of Islam," *Bibliotheca Orientalis*, 49:1/2 January–March 1992.

2 See for example the website of the Israeli Islamic Movement, www.islamic-aqsa.com.

3 Mujir al-Din, *Al-Ins al-Jalil bi-Ta'rikh al-Quds wal-Khalill*, Amman: Al-Muhtasib, 1973, II, pp. 63–5 (Arabic).

4 He also found it important to write that the Persians were assisted by the local Jewish community but he does not provide references for this.

5 See the article by archaeologist R. Reich, "The cemetery in the area of Mamilla in Jerusalem," *Qadmoniot* 26, 1994, 103–9 (Hebrew). In this area today a large shopping mall (Alrob), housing units, a hotel, and a parking lot were erected.

6 Kamil Jamil al-'Asali, *Ajdadna fi Thari Bayt al-Maqdis*, Amman: Royal Council for the Study of Islamic Civilization, 1981, pp. 117–32, 159–96 (Arabic). On the history of the semetery see also: Fahmi al-Ansari, *Maqbarat Ma'man Alla (Mamilla). Dirasa*. Jerusalem: PA's Ministry of Information, 2010.

7 See expert report by Professor Yehoshua Ben Arieh, 20 March 2007, submitted to the High Court, file 52/06 ("HCJ 52/06") (Hebrew).

8 Al-`Asali, op. cit.

9 UN doc. S/1302/Rev. 1, June 20, 1949.

10 *Filastin*, 25 March 1950 (Arabic).

11 Article by Yaakov Yehoshua, the Director of the Department of Muslims of the Ministry, *HaYedion HaMuslemi*, April 1950 (Hebrew).

12 Z. Vilnai, *Sacred Gravestones in Eretz Israel*, Jerusalem: Ahiever, 1996, vol. 2, p. 329 (Hebrew).

13 Letter of 28 July 1986 from the Permanent Delegate of the Hashemite Kingdom of Jordan to the Director-General of UNESCO. See: http://unesdoc.unesco.org/images/0006/000695/069594eo.pdf#xml=http://www.unesco.org/ulis/cgi-bin/ulis.pl?database=&set=4F9969CE_1_258&hits_rec=21&hits_lng=eng, p. 6.

14 Ibid., Addendum I.[Lemaire's report is in Addendum I of the above link.]

15 See http://unesdoc.unesco.org/images/0007/000761/076196eo.pdf.

16 S. Berkovits, *The Wars on Holy Places*, Jerusalem; Maariv – Hed Artzi, 2000, p. 83, citing Haaretz, 11 July 1986 and 10 November 1986 (Hebrew).

17 Berkovits, op. cit., p. 84.

18 Al-Aqsa is the name of the Mosque mentioned in Quran 17:1, identified as Haram al-Sharif of Jerusalem. This same site is viewed by the Jews as the spot where the Jewish Temple existed and is the primary issue of contention in the struggle over sovereignty in Jerusalem between Israel and the Palestinians. The Northern Islamic Movement, headed by Sheikh Raed Salah, has since 1996 been conducting a campaign under the banner of "Al Aqsa is in Danger," aiming to employ religious symbols for political ends.

19 " . . . 250 skeletons were unearthed out of 200 graves, including second burial in the same grave. Another 200 graves were exposed that were not excavated yet, and according to my understanding of the burial layers I am estimating that there are about 1,000 graves in the project's area" wrote Gideon Sulimani in his report dated 9 April 2009, sent to the IAA archaeologist in charge of the Jerusalem

district. See also Sulimany's interview at: N. C. Gross, "Grave thoughts," The Jerusalem Report, 5 January 2009, pp. 21–4.

20 See *Critical Inquiry* 36:3, 2010, 517–94.

21 Ibid., 543.

22 Ibid., 569.

23 Local zoning plan 8030 was published in the Official Gazette 5023 of 16 October 2001 after advertisement in *Maariv,* 16 September 2001; *Yerushalayim,* 21 September 2001; *Al-Ittihad* and *Al-Quds*, September 2001.

24 www.islamic-aqsa.com an item dated 9 May 2006.

25 HCJ 52/06 Al-Aqsa Corporation for Developing Muslim Endowment Properties in the land of Israel LTD vs. the Simon Wiesenthal Center Museum Corp.(Hebrew).

26 Ibid.

27 Ibid.

28 HCJ 1331/06 Muhammaed Khayr al-Dajani vs. Israel's Police, submitted 12 February 2006 (Hebrew).

29 HCJ 1671/06 The Simon Wiesenthal Center Museum Corp. vs. the Shari'a Court of Jerusalem (Hebrew).

30 Ibid.

CHAPTER

2

The Struggle over the Symbolic Landscape: Zionization versus Palestinization and Islamization

The conflict over construction of the MoT in Mamilla embodies a series of tensions and clashing interests between Israel's Jewish majority and its Arab minority. The first conflict is a national and cultural struggle between two identity groups over design of the symbolic space and landscape using the politics of identity. I will begin by explaining the following terms: identity, landscape, symbolic landscape, and identity politics.

Identity is a set of categories internalized within human cognition from the surrounding culture. Identity determines how a person conceives the events of his life and gives it meaning: the intellectual and emotional content of a human being's existence. In every society the lives of its members are conducted in accordance with a series of cultural systems, and hence the human being is in fact a multi-cultural creature. His identity is multi-faceted, divided, and incoherent. The culture attaches normative weight, be it positive or negative, to the values and categories that represent it. Ascribing several identity characteristics to a large number of people creates a group's collective identity that is based on affiliation to the group, even though the members of the group do not personally know most of the other group members.[1] With regard to the conflict discussed in this book, we refer to two main identity groups: Jewish Israelis and Palestinian Muslims.

Identity politics is the political activity of affiliates of identity groups aiming to change the normative method in which the dominant culture perceives the identity group members. It seeks to influence the dominant culture in a society, causing it to attribute a positive normative weight to people with a particular identity and in this way to change the way in which the identity group members perceive themselves.[2] The term "politics of identity" or "identity politics" expresses a discursive framework, a strategy of action and a political practice that underlines the particularity of different identity groups within a society and aspires to promote the interests of these identity groups. The theory of identity politics is generally focused on the need of the minority, which reacts to the challenges posed by the majority.[3] In the case of the struggle over the landscape of Jerusalem, the Jewish majority and state institutions also use the politics of identity with reference to their existence as a minority within the Arab Muslim region of the Middle East.

Landscape is an outcome of struggle and compromise within human societies and among them. As such the landscape incorporates elements of politics, identity, memory, suppression of memory, resistance, and other aspects that combine to create comprehensive spatial expressions of the human activity therein. Landscape is interpreted differently by groups and individuals, and it embodies the competition over legitimacy of expression. What one group perceives as legitimate, normative, right, and rational could be seen by another group, particularly a minority group, as threatening, discriminatory, and oppressive. The above situation results in different geographies and processes of landscape creation.[4] The landscape usually expresses the hegemonic identity of the ruling majority.[5] Hence, challenging the hegemonic landscape is the special social expression of a minority group in shaping its identity. The minority will search for measures to cope with the control of the hegemonic majority and with the processes of exclusion that the majority operates. The alternative landscape that the minority group seeks to create is guided by a competing historical narrative that challenges the official history of the state and the narratives of the majority. The Palestinian lawyer and writer Raja Shehadeh, for example, maps his passion to the Palestinian landscape that in his eyes is disappearing quickly under the wheels of the Israeli settlement machine and the momentum of Palestinian development.[6]

Mitchell writes that the imperial landscape of the land, which he terms "holy landscape" in this context, could turn into an idol that demands human sacrifice and into a "place where symbolic, imagined and concrete violence crash into a current social space."[7] According to him "The face of the sacred landscape is so scarred from the war, from archeological excavation and from uprooting until one cannot hold either for a moment any delusion of innocent and original nature."[8] Hence, the landscape "is not only a sign or a symbol for power relations; it is a tool of cultural power."[9] In a manner that will appear as bias to Israeli Jews, Mitchell critiques the selectivity of memory and history that Israel imposes on the holy landscape. According to him, "the most refined concentration of holiness in the symbolic landscape of Palestine is not surprisingly embodied in the landscape of the city of Jerusalem and particularly in the sight of the Dome of the Rock."[10]

During the 1960s, a period of martial law in the population centers of the Arab minority of the Galilee, the "Triangle" (Wadi 'Ara area), and the northern Negev in Israel, the Israeli authorities succeeded in changing the landscape of the Mamilla Cemetery of Jerusalem. Most of the cemetery was rendered a public park named Gan HaAtzmaut (Independence Park), to which most of the Arabs in Israel had no free access. Earlier, during the 1950s, a

Jewish holy place named Me'arat HaArieh (the Lion's Cave) had been established within the cemetery by the director-general of the Ministry of Religious Affairs, Shmuel Zanvill Kahana (1905–1988). In 1950 Kahana attempted to link this cave (apparently the same cave that Muslims call "the Cave of the Shuhadah") with a medieval Jewish legend about a lion that collected the human remains of slain Jews who had defended Jerusalem during the Second Temple period and heroically protected them in the cave.[11] The Ministry of Religious Affairs and the Jerusalem Municipality inaugurated the cave as a "heritage site" and made an effort to encourage Jewish pilgrimage to this place.[12]

The landscape in Israel and particularly in Jerusalem bears the imprint of thousands of years of different civilizations and cultural entities. Since 1948 the processes of shaping the landscape have been influenced primarily by the Jewish Zionist hegemonic majority in Israel. The shaping of the landscape in Israel has entailed a major endeavor aimed at obliteration and denial of past landscapes and particularly the one that represents the Arab and Islamic past of the country.[13] Hence, the struggle of the Arab minority in Israel to preserve islands of Islamic and Arab landscapes wherever they can is an expression of resistance to the Jewish hegemony and of demands for proper representation in the public space. Specifically, the minority has striven to incorporate into the public landscape their own particular spaces of activity, such as mosques, cemeteries, and saints' tombs.[14] The social sensitivity attributed to holy places makes such sites effective tools in the strategy of resistance characteristic of Israeli Palestinian society's political and cultural development in recent years.[15]

The MoT project in the center of Jerusalem is not an ordinary public facility. It has strong symbolic meaning. This museum was planned as a symbol of identity embodying the Zionist project and even reinforcing the Zionist paradigm of "a reunited city" where two nations comprising three religions live side by side in a state of peace and tolerance. The museum's initiators from the SWC described their vision for the project as follows:

> The Simon Wiesenthal Center's new Israel Project — The Center for Human Dignity in Jerusalem — attempts to give institutional substance to the popular injunction that we should 'think globally, but act locally'. The Center will take the broad lessons about tolerance promotion that we have learned over the past decade in the United States and tailor them to the distinctive realities of a diverse Israel and the Middle East values crucible . . . A moral and ethical beacon light for tree of the world's great religions, *Jerusalem is the contested ground where a shared faith in the sacredness of human dignity took shape, and where common ground in shared values of human rights must be reclaimed. Our ultimate hope is that The Center for Human Dignity, Museum of Tolerance, Jerusalem, will develop into a global hub that will promote civility and mutual respect among the multiplicity of peoples of the*

> *Middle East as well as international visitors of all faiths and origins.* [Emphasis added.]

The High Court justices, accepting the narrative of the MoT entrepreneurs, presented the museum's vision in the following words:

> The Museum of Tolerance embodies the idea of establishing a spiritual center from which a message will spread of human tolerance among peoples, among population sectors, and among individuals. The construction of the museum can make an important national contribution to the entire state, which to date has had no center whose purpose is to deal with the substance of tolerance in its various aspects and to act to disseminate this value amidst the general public. This center ought to serve as a point of reference both within Israel and with respect to the states of the entire world. It ought to attract visitors from all over the country and the world who while visiting will have the special architectural and artistic experience that the museum provides. There is a special significance to the location of the museum in the center of Jerusalem, a city that has a special valuable meaning for three religions as well as a long history and a special place in human civilization. The existence of the Museum of Tolerance in the capital of Israel, against the background of the ongoing Israeli–Palestinian conflict, also has special weight regarding the dynamics of dialogue and efforts to bridge between the conflicting parties. The construction of the Museum in the center of the city of Jerusalem is aimed at making an important contribution to the development of Jerusalem as the capital of Israel and to advance the urban development of the center of the town as a city center that has an important significance both in the local and national realms . . . To restore Jerusalem's ancient crown, which it has lost over the years.[16]

Moreover, the original architect, Frank Gehry, is famous for planning monuments that have salience within their environmental landscape. In other words, the structure will become a symbol in itself of what it represents.

The museum was also linked to the Holocaust because it was initiated by the Wiesenthal Center. This is how Justice Ayalah Pocaccia began her verdict:

> The idea of establishing a center of tolerance in Jerusalem was a vision of the late Simon Wiesenthal, who belongs to the generation of the Holocaust of the Jews in Europe. His special and individual way of drawing the lessons to be learned from the Holocaust was by locating Nazi criminals all over the world and bringing them to justice through the court system; in the framework of this commitment, the late Simon Wiesenthal wanted to establish a spiritual center whose subject matter and activities would focus on transmitting the message of tolerance to

> humankind. No wonder he chose Jerusalem, the capital of Israel and the Jewish people, which is also the world center of the three great religions of humanity, to implement this idea. The Museum of Tolerance was planned to reflect the lessons of the past and to disseminate these lessons into the future through the values of tolerance and amicability. It is intended to link past, present, and future in upholding the basic rights of the individual as a supreme value of human life and in the regimes of peoples and states.[17]

The discourse of the museum entrepreneurs, which was adopted in its entirety by the Supreme Court justices, is thus a Jewish national narrative centered on "Jerusalem as the capital of Israel and the Jewish people" and "center of the three great religions of humanity." It makes no mention whatsoever of the two parts of the city, its Palestinian residents who have an opposing vision, or the reality of a socially and politically divided city. The MoT has a mission of promoting the image of Jerusalem as a (one unified) city and a city of interfaith tolerance under the current situation of a complete Israeli control.

We can better understand the Mamilla dispute if we view it as a struggle over the character of and symbolic representation in the public space and as a competition for power between the state and the minority.[18] Lefebvre, who wrote about the shaping of urban spaces, referred to social groups who produce a space in order to be included in the society, noting that, whoever finds himself discriminated against and excluded from urban space will find legitimacy for actions of resistance.[19]

Another expression of the conflict over representation within the symbolic landscape appears in an article strongly criticizing the MoT project in Mamilla, written by Saree Makdisi, a professor of English and comparative religion at the University of California Los Angeles, and published in *Critical Inquiry*.[20] In his article Makdisi presents a Palestinian position that compares the museum's design to the "Separation Wall" that Israel built in Jerusalem to exclude Palestinians, claiming that constructing the museum on a historical Muslim cemetery reflects the Zionist policy of erasing the Palestinian presence. According to him, this act is the second erasure (erasing the past act of erasure). After the Palestinian landscape was first erased in the post-1948 period, the next step is to "deny the denial." Makdisi views this trend as a "form of racism."[21] He claims that in general the monuments planned or designed by architect Frank Gehry are detached from their local context and intended to underline the global context. He argues that the MoT entrepreneurs seek to erase memories of the local context and to reshape Zionism as a universal value of tolerance.[22] Otherwise, asks Makdisi, why not simply name the MoT "the Museum of Jewish History and the History of Zionism?"[23] According to him the MoT suits the political trend of Zionism and therefore draws so little criticism in Israel and among Zionists.[24] Makdisi goes on to cite from SWC publications regarding the MoT's clearly internal

Jewish orientation rather than as an institute aimed at representing the different cultures of Jerusalem. According to the cited publication, the purpose of the museum is to offer "a social laboratory that speaks to the world and confronts today's important issues – like global antisemitism, terrorism and hate. A place that will remind us that greater than any external threat is the internal divide that seperates us. A place that will reinforce the idea that Jewish unity is not a slogan, but an essential recipe for survival in the 21st century." [25] In order to underline the Jewish approach of the MoT Makdisi italisuzed twise the word *us* in the above quotation.

The volume of *Critical Inquiry* that published Makdisi's article also contains articles written in response by Gehry and by representatives of the museum, namely, Professor Rafael Israeli, Dr. Shmuel Berkovits, Dr. Jacques Neria, and Rabbi Marvin Hier of the SWC in Los Angeles.[26] These responses underline the ideological dimension of the competition over the symbolic landscape. Gehry begins his article with the ideological aspect, thereby attributing some merit to Makdisi's claim that the museum project is a one-dimensional and Zionist endeavor. Gehry writes that during his childhood in Canada he personally suffered from anti-Semitism and that 33 of his family members and relatives were exterminated in the Holocaust. He therefore concluded that Israel is a safe haven for Jews.[27] Responding to Makdisi's claim that the museum represents only the Zionist narrative, Gehry writes that the museum entrepreneurs promised him that the exhibitions therein would provide "complete representation to all parties" and absolute freedom of expression.[28] Makdisi reacted to this response by writing that Gehry's article overlooks the voices of Muslims who protested the erection of the Museum over their relatives' graves and, therefore, Gehry's response only reinforces his criticism.[29] In any event, it is clear that Gehry's article overlooks the reality in Jerusalem with respect to freedom of expression in a city that stands at the core of a national struggle and is controlled by one party.

The article by Rabbi Marvin Hier and experts on behalf of the museum also underlines the ideological and symbolic aspect of the MoT project and the essence of the dispute regarding its construction in Mamilla. This aspect is expressed in two matters in particular: first, the museum content, which according to the MoT will comprise two major parts, a historical department and a social laboratory. The historical section will contain multi-media displays entitled "The Long Way Home: A People's Journey to Freedom," which "will take visitors on a virtual journey through time and space to experience epochal moments of the history of the Jews and, consequently, the developments of modern of civilization."[30] The second symbolic matter is the role of the historical narrative regarding the antiquity of the land where the museum is to be constructed. According to Dr. Jacques Neria, during the salvation excavations prior to laying down the foundations of the museum, three water chutes from Jewish periods were discovered: one from the Iron Age (the period of Hezekiah), another one from the Hellenistic period, and the third from the Herodian period (the time of the Second Temple). Hence the respondents, on behalf of the museum, argue that before the site became a Muslim cemetery it was a Jewish site and thus part of the Jewish history of Jerusalem.[31] The combination of this last argument with another argument of the MoT, according to which the land designated for building the museum had not served as a Muslim cemetery for decades, could be interpreted as part of the denial of Muslim attachment to the site.

Another expression of the way in which the MoT in Mamilla reflects political competition over the character of Jerusalem can be found in a 2009 letter that the ambassador of Yemen to the UN, Abdallah Al-Sa'idi, delivered to the Security Council on behalf of the League of Arab States. In this letter and in another letter sent by his successor as representative of the League of Arab States to the UN, the ambassador of Kuwait, Mansur al-Utaibi, in April 2010, the two ambassadors describe the project in Mamilla as " . . . a criminal attacks being carried out by the Israeli occupation authorities against the important Islamic antiquities in and features of the city of Jerusalem . . . Such attempts to Judaize the holy city and change its Arab and Islamic character."[32]

The Zionist vision of the museum entrepreneurs, which was supported by the Supreme Court justices, is the polar opposite of the Muslim plaintiffs' vision. The Palestinian residents of East Jerusalem were represented in the legal dispute by three members of distinguished families from Al-Quds who in themselves symbolize Jerusalem under Muslim rule in the context of identity politics.

The Northern Islamic Movement, headed by Sheikh Raed Salah, has been challenging the Jewish Zionist landscape of Jerusalem, underscoring their Muslim-Arab vision of Al-Quds of the past. Over the past two decades, Salah and his followers have actively worked to expose, preserve, rebuild, and reinstitute Muslim cemeteries and monuments within the country's landscape: the mosques, saints' tombs, and Muslim cemeteries that were obliterated and abandoned during the 1948 War, which Jews define as the War of Independence and Arabs refer to as the catastrophe, or "Nakba," of Palestine.

The State of Israel, which was established during that war in order to realize the goal of self-determination for the Jewish people in their historic homeland, did its utmost to promote the Jewish character of the state, including through the symbolic landscape. This objective was implemented through a number of methods, two of which are of particular importance: first, the demolition of Arab towns and villages that had been abandoned during and following the 1948 War (418 villages and hamlets[33]). In many cases, however, mosques and cemeteries were not erased from the landscape, even when new Jewish towns and villages were erected on the spot and settled by Jewish newcomers. The second method was the assignment of Hebrew names to the geographic and topographic markers of the land, including towns, villages, streets, and facilities. Within the Prime Minister's Office Israel established a special Government Naming Committee (*Va'adat HaShemot HaMemshaltit*) aimed at reviving the ancient Hebrew names of the land and its landmarks.[34]As an example, this committee renamed the demolished Arab village of Safuriyya, restoring its former Hebrew, first-century name, Tzipori, which is today the name of a moshav and a national park that were erected on the former lands of Safuriyya.[35]

The Islamic Movement has been working to reverse these developments in one major area: holy places. From an Islamic point of view, if the movement is able to preserve and renovate demolished Muslim mosques and cemeteries, it will revive the pre-1948 Arab-Muslim landscape of the country. In this-context, mosques and cemeteries serve as the cornerstone of restitution of pre-1948 Arab towns and villages, from which Palestinian Arabs were uprooted during the war.

The Islamic Movement as a political formation is not a nationalist organization in the classical sense. It is a religious and political movement representing about one fifth of the 1.4 million Arab citizens of Israel (in 2014). However, the strategy of this movement serves what we view as the agenda of a national movement, that is, restitution of the Arab and Muslim character of the Palestinian homeland. The leaders of this movement initiated a plan to survey and inspect the land throughout the entire country in search of remnants of ancient Muslim monuments, particularly mosques, saints' tombs, and cemeteries.[36] Sheikh Raed Salah once asserted that every Muslim Arab settlement demolished in 1948 had approximately four cemeteries and four mosques and that his movement was acting to unearth them in order to preserve, revive, and reactivate them. According to his calculation, there are some three thousand such holy places to be restored within the country's landscape.[37] Since the Islamic Movement split into two factions in 1996, the two movements compete in their search for holy places to be revitalized.[38]

The Northern Islamic Movement's website highlights the historical narrative of the Mammilla Cemetery in a way that underscores the Arab Islamic symbolic identity of the place:

> King Suleiman (Solomon) was anointed in the Cemetery of Mamilla in the year 1015 BCE. In this place camped the army of Assyrian King Sennacherib when he arrived in Jerusalem in 1017 BCE. Many of the Prophet's Companions (*sahaba*) who conquered Jerusalem in 636 AD are also buried here, as well as the soldiers of Saladin's army who arrived to liberate Jerusalem from the Crusaders in 118 [1187]. In this cemetery are buried sahaba and their followers, as well as many saints and dignitaries. When the Crusaders conquered Jerusalem, some 70,000 [Muslim] men, women, and children were killed, and the Crusaders ordered those who remained alive to bury the dead in the Mamilla Cemetery. Saladin also ordered that his army Martyrs be buried in this cemetery, among whom was one of his famous advisors, the Emir 'Issa bin Muhammad al-'Akari.[39]

Interestingly, the Islamic Movement completely ignored the historical account holding that tens of thousands of Christians were buried in this cemetery during the Persian conquest of Jerusalem in 614. Some say that the Jews of Jerusalem assisted the Persians because the Byzantines placed restrictions on where the Jews could reside.[40] By denying this important historical record, the heads of the Islamic Movement are treating Christians in the same way that, according to their complaints, Jews treat Muslims in Mamilla. They make use of the site exclusively for their own interests. All the parties to the conflict, as well as all the experts who submitted reports to the High Court, overlooked the historical Christian connection to this cemetery. From the point of view of those opposed to construction of the MoT at this site, ignoring this historical connection hinders consolidation of potential opponents to the project within the Christian world. Perhaps the need of the Islamic Movement to Islamize the symbolic landscape of Jerusalem is more important than recruiting the support of the Christian world for their struggle and engaging Christians in what they see as an Islamic heritage site.

In addition, the Islamic Movement links the ancient historical context of the cemetery and its contemporary historical context, which gives the cemetery symbolic meaning in current times. The following excerpt from an article published on their website on 9 May 2006 illustrates how the Islamic Movement portrays the contemporary history of the place:

> These days we are commemorating the 58th year since the Nakba of Palestine according to the Palestinian Calendar, which is the right calendar. The Nakba testifies to the atrocities and attacks against the Palestinian people, against human beings, against a land, and against the history and the holy places. Hundreds of villages were demolished and destroyed, over 1200 mosques were demolished in 1948, and hundreds of cemeteries were plowed and destroyed. Since that day there has been a systematic policy regarding holy places, aimed at erasing their remnants because they stand as a living memory of the identity of the land from the point of view of history and civilization . . . The [Israeli] occupation is vigorously acting to obliterate all Arab and Islamic remains in the Holy City [Jerusalem] using all means . . . This is an attack against the history and the culture of the Arab and Islamic nation that began in 1948 and has never halted since then . . . [41]

This excerpt makes clear the political significance of the Islamic Movement's activity. This is a struggle to halt the erasure of the land's Arab-Muslim identity, on the one hand, and to reinstitute the landscape that preceded the establishment of the State of Israel.

This activity was summarized as follows by the Or Commission of Inquiry, which investigated the clashes between Arabs and Jews in October 2000:

> The Islamic Movement took upon itself the struggle to reinstitute the holy places of the Muslim community. To achieve this end, during the 1990s an organization was established named "The Al-Aqsa

> Corporation for Preserving Islamic Endowments and Holy Places" (against the background of conflict between the two factions of the Islamic Movement over this association, the Northern Movement formed in parallel the "Al-Aqsa Corporation to Develop and Preserve the Islamic Endowment Properties in Israel"). The Islamic Movement opted to map and document Muslim sites throughout the entire country. The Movement's lawyers submitted complaints to the Ministry of Religious Affairs and to the police, and they even applied to the court demanding the cessation of damage to Muslim holy places, but their demands were rejected. In late 1996, the Movement's people applied to the High Court demanding a halt to the construction of a sports hall over a Muslim cemetery in Netanya. The High Court ruled that the building is already an irreversible fact on the ground. The Islamic movement [activists], whose demands were consistently rejected, were frustrated with the legal and political state systems, and therefore they sought a more assertive method of protest. The members of the Movement, in particular the radicals among them, tended to escalate disagreements into heated political struggle, employed radical systems for creating facts on the ground, and attempted to raise awareness within the Muslim community surrounding their struggles and stir them up. These patterns of activity contributed to political radicalization of the Arab street during the second half of the 1990s.[42]

These activities of the Islamic Movement have generated tension between Muslims and Jews in Israel. The case of the Mosque in Tiberias is one such example. Tiberias was a mixed city of Arabs and Jews prior to the 1948 War, and its Arab residents had to leave the city during the war. After 1948, two Mosques remained as a living memory of the Muslim community of Tiberias. One of them was the focus of a dispute, summarized by the Or Commission in the following way:

> Following a news item conveying that the structure of the Al-Bahr Mosque, which formerly served as a city museum, was occupied by a homeless man who also used it to make fire inside, the Islamic Movement began arranging mass Friday prayers in front of the two abandoned mosques in this city, while inciting the Muslims by saying that the Mosque had been 'burned.' Many of the Jewish residents of the city, which today has no Muslim community, viewed the weekly mass presence of hundreds of Muslims as political provocation that had nothing to do with real religious needs. One day in March 2000, young [Jewish] gangs from Tiberias confronted the Muslims who arrived in the city, and violent clashes erupted between the two groups, which were dispersed by the police.[43]

Finally, the mayor of the city reached an agreement with the Islamic

Movement, according to which the two mosques would be repaired. The Movement activists realized, however, that they would be incapable of successfully confronting the people of Tiberias at that time because the latter were furious about Hezbollah's detention in Lebanon of a city youngster, whose fate was unknown. The Islamic Movement therefore abandoned their activism in Tiberias.

Efrat Ben-Ze'ev and Issam Aburaiya [44] coined a term for the Islamic Movement's efforts to preserve holy places, borrowing from the vocabulary of nationalism rather than religion: "Re-Palestinianization," meaning activity aimed at consolidating the popularity of a political religious movement within the general Arab public. In analyzing another case in which the Northern Islamic Movement was involved in reinstituting an old mosque located at the demolished village Sarafand (near Moshav HaBonim today), they describe how fifty years after the Nakba, the Islamic movement provided the meaning re-fusion of the Palestinians with their lost land. For many of them their presence in the space is an expression of their rejection of Judiazing these places. The Islamic Movement framed its activity as protecting the holy places instead of using a comprehensive nationalist strategy of 'Right of Return', a matter that enable them to avoid confrontation with the state and its Jewish majority.[45]

The activities of the Islamic Movement with respect to holy places contribute to the activities of Palestinian organizations that endorse the right of return of Palestinian refugees to their original residential areas prior to 1948. For example, the Palestinian Markaz al-Awdah – the Palestinain Return Centre, a London-based organization that deals with the Palestinian refugee issue – published a list of Muslim holy places that Israel does not protect or respect. This publication, posted on the organization's website, aimed to bring these places to public awareness.[46]

In Tiberias, Sarafand, and other places throughout Israel, the Islamic Movement failed to achieve its goal. However, a similar claim for representation in the urban landscape of Tel Aviv–Jaffa during the 1970s and 1980s was very successful. This was a struggle that the Arabs of Jaffa conducted in order to prevent the sale of the Hasan Bey Mosque and to re-operate the mosque. It is a unique case in which Israeli Muslims succeeded in rebuilding and re-operating an abandoned Mosque in a non-Muslim residential area, specifically in the commercial center of Tel Aviv.

Nimrod Luz showed that this success was grounded in the Muslim community's uniting around its identity symbols, making the mosque a symbol of the struggle for their rights as a minority in Israel. When the Hasan Bey affair began in the 1970s, the Islamic Movement did not yet exist. The campaign was conducted by Arab activists of Jaffa (Muslims and Christians alike). Luz maintained that "for the Muslim community of Jaffa, this [Mosque] was a symbol to be preserved in the urban landscape because it represents Palestinian-Arab identity and history."[47] The Arabs of Jaffa, who had been excluded from public space, used this protest to rebuild the mosque as a test case for the promotion of equal and just representation in the urban space. The Hasan Bey Mosque was a center of resistance and challenged the prevailing interpretation of space and life within the space of the majority. Perhaps this first successful case served to inspire the Islamic Movement to pursue the preservation of holy places as an overall strategy.

The dispute over the Mamilla Cemetery and construction of the MoT is another manifestation of identity politics between the minority and majority in Jerusalem, and between the two rival parties to the Israeli–Palestinian conflict, in which each party represents an opposing religious community of believers. However, the case of Mamilla differs from the above-mentioned case. In this case the minority is represented by the Islamic Movement in its attempt to employ the Mamilla dispute as a flagship of an ideological and political struggle, while the state institutions representing the dominant Jewish majority group, for the most part, are driven by the same motivation. The Jews, even though they comprise the majority in Israel, feel like a minority in the predominantly Arab-Muslim Middle East. Hence, the necessity of constructing a Jewish identity for Jerusalem and the Land of Israel in general is an expression of a Jewish national communal identity and of the need of Jewish Israelis to unite around foundational identity symbols. The politics of identities in our case means that the dominant Jewish majority group constructs a framework of discourse that serves its interests (unified Jerusalem, which the museum serves to promote) while excluding and marginalizing the interests of the Muslim-Palestinian minority group. The minority's reaction is represented by the Islamic Movement, which struggles to preserve the entire space of the Mamilla Cemetery, beyond the small section that the State of Israel permitted to be preserved to date, as well as to prevent the establishment of the MoT on this site.

Returning to the case of Mamilla, the politics of identity was clearly reflected during the High Court hearing, as well as in the verdict written by Justice Ayalah Pocaccia and her colleagues, Justice Edna Arbel and Justice David Cheshin. The Al-Aqsa Corporation emphasized the historic symbolism of Mamilla in both the national and religious realms, as cited in the verdict:

> The construction of the Museum on the cemetery compound, which embodies historical, national, and religious importance, severely damages the dignity of those who are buried in this place and offends the sentiments of the Muslim community in Israel, and as such contradicts the basic law of human dignity and freedom. According to the [Al-Aqsa Corporation's] approach, any construction in this compound, even if legal under the procedures of land ownership and planning, is actually devastating to the dignity of the deceased and the sentiments of the Muslim public, for whom this cemetery represents a historical symbol.[48]

The museum entrepreneurs, as well as the state institutions that were the defendants in the High Court proceeding, also underlined the symbolic meaning of the museum as a national (i.e., Zionist) project that will contribute to the image of Jerusalem in attracting international visitors, as cited above. In addition, as part of their defense they submitted expert testimonies emphasizing the nationalist Arab-Muslim confrontational challenge underpinning the efforts of the Islamic Movement.

Professor Joseph Ginat, vice-president of Netanya Academic College, submitted an expert opinion on behalf of the Museum Corporation, in which he maintained the following: "To the best of my knowledge and assessment, the main force behind the plaintiffs' petition is Sheikh Raed Salah. In applying to the Court, he seeks to undermine the construction of the Museum of Tolerance; this effort emanates from a political goal: to create strongholds in West Jerusalem in order to turn back the wheel of history."[49]

Shalom Goldstein, who had served as political advisor on East Jerusalem and the Arab population to the mayor of Jerusalem between 1995 and 2004, testified as an expert for the museum entrepreneurs that "the uproar against this construction is in fact a political move generated behind the scenes by Sheikh Raed Salah, who strives through political and ideological actions to restitute the entire cemetery compound to the Islamic Waqf."[50]

Goldstein also emphasized the strong collaboration of Sheikh Salah with the Palestinian Mufti Sheikh Ikrima Sabri,[51] who asserted in a press interview that, "We reclaim West Jerusalem together with East Jerusalem because Muslims have waqf properties there, public waqf, family waqf properties, and private properties, cumulatively totaling more than 70% of the space of West Jerusalem."[52]

Professor Yehoshua Porath, a Hebrew University historian of the Middle East, presented the activities of the Islamic Movement in his report in a broader and more threatening context:

> In the past decade the Islamic Movement has systematically attempted to strengthen the Islamic character of the State of Israel as much as possible by reinstituting and re-operating demolished Islamic sites that had served Muslim communities before 1948 but are today deserted because there are no Muslim communities around. For example, the movement attempted to revive religious activities in the site of the tomb named Sayyiduna 'Ali in Herzliya, which is not near any Muslim community. They also attempted to prevent the pavement of a road in the town of Nesher where Sheikh Izz a-Din al-Qassam, leader of the gang that murdered Jews during the first half of the 1930's, is buried; they attempted to reopen the Uqasha Mosque in West Jerusalem near the Histadruth building on Straus Street. The main motivation behind the efforts of Sheikh Raed Salah to undermine construction of the museum emanates from his intention to establish Islam in the land of Jerusalem in preparation for his political plan to reinstitute the Caliphate . . . Preventing construction of the museum will undoubtedly

> reinforce the Islamic movement's standing among Israeli Arabs and increase the power of Arab Palestinian nationalists who strive to reinstitute the Islamic-Arab character in Eretz Yisrael.[53]

The museum entrepreneurs cooperated with the state institutions in emphasizing the subversive character of the Islamic Movement before the High Court. Towards this end they also submitted an expert opinion by David Klein, who had held various positions within the General Security Service in the past , including director of the unit in charge of preventing political and fundamentalist subversion among the Arab citizens of Israel. Klein's document highlights a link among the Northern Islamic Movement headed by Sheikh Raed Salah, the affiliated Al-Aqsa Corporation, and Hamas:

> The Islamic Movement has served for years as an important channel of funding to organizations in the [Palestinian] Territories connected to the Hamas movement. The involvement of the Islamic Movement in assisting Hamas with money and other materials such as food, clothing, and equipment emanates mostly from the ideological connection between the two movements because they affiliate with the Muslim Brotherhood, the major fundamentalist movement in the region.[54]

Klein used quotations from the Or Commission report, which referred to Salah as one of the inciters of violence:

> The head of the northern faction of the Islamic Movement, who was also the mayor of Umm al-Fahm and a public figure, was responsible during the period prior to the events of 1 October 2000 events and during the years of 1990 to 2000 for the repeated dissemination of messages encouraging the use of violence as well as threatening to use violence as a way to achieve the goals of the Arab sector in Israel. These messages also included the goal of liberating the Al-Aqsa Mosque. In addition, he organized massive conventions and used inflammatory propaganda methods to fuel the public atmosphere surrounding this delicate issue. Through all of the above acts, he significantly contributed to the inflaming of sentiments and to the widespread outbreak of violence in the Arab sector in the beginning of October 2000.[55]

Klein also emphasized the identification of the Northern Islamic Movement with Hamas:[56]

> My personal observation is that the politics of identity as expressed in the testimonies submitted by experts on the Middle East were a salient issue during the High Court hearings. For example, during the hearings on 29 April 2007, Advocate Abu Hussein, representing the plaintiffs, claimed, "There are some things that you never buy with money –

> history and the geography of people you cannot buy with money. The cemetery is a part of the history of the city."

In response to these words, Advocate Renato Yarak, representing the SWC, asserted, "Somebody is threatening us in this court with incitement. In fact, these are political considerations." Advocate Durgham Sayf, representing the Karama Association, then responded to this assertion, stating, "These are not extreme Muslims; there are also Jews who oppose construction of the museum."

A review of the High Court verdict leaves no doubt that the discourse on identity moved the justices and that they identify themselves with the Zionist goals that the museum aims to symbolize. This partiality is apparent not only in the way the Justices cited the above-mentioned assertions of the parties, but also in their phrasing and description of the importance of the MoT project, particularly its location in the center of the city of Jerusalem rather than anywhere else. Justice Procaccia stated:

> The choice of the particular location emanates from a national and municipal concept that vests a special importance in this project, not least because of the planned location of the structure. Jerusalem as the capital of Israel is a point of interest for the entire world, for many visitors from around the globe, and for pilgrims to a city that is a religious and spiritual center for the three major religions of the world. The location of the Museum of Tolerance in the heart of Jerusalem carries a special significance, which is intertwined with the cosmopolitan character of the city as a religious and spiritual center that unifies the peoples of the world. Moreover, in recent years there has been a special effort underway to develop the urban center of Jerusalem through integrated planning that combines various plans to render this area a cultural, spiritual, economic, and tourist focal point, thereby creating a natural spatial continuum between the old city and the new city. The goal is to transform the center of the city of Jerusalem into an appropriate focal point as the capital of Israel, which will attract both domestic and foreign visitors.[57]

This description by Justice Procaccia presents the MoT project as a Zionist national project aimed at strengthening the legitimacy of Jerusalem as a unified city and as the capital of the state under complete Israeli control. The eastern part of the city is mentioned in this verdict in only one sentence – "creating a natural spatial continuum between the old city and the new city" – meaning that the Old City is part of a unified city that is the capital of the state of Israel. Neither the Palestinian residents of the city, represented by three members of distinguished families who served as plaintiffs in this process, nor their identity interests received any attention from the court.

The reaction to the court's verdict by one of the lawyers representing the

Muslim plaintiffs, Advocate Durgham Sayf, reflects this ideological identity struggle: "The verdict is political and biased in favor of the Jews. Another tribunal with non-Jewish justices would have decided in our favor."[58]

The High Court dismissed the suggestion of a group of academics and civil society organizations to move the location of the future museum to another spot, outside the center of Jerusalem, because this "would undermine the chances of establishing such a center with all its symbolic meaning in Jerusalem."[59]

The High Court rejected the arguments of civil society organizations and a group of mostly Jewish academics who claimed that the extraordinary architectural design of the museum by a leading architect, in combination with the public Muslim opposition to the project, would transform the museum building, which will dominate the landscape and eternalize this dispute, into a symbol of non-tolerance and lack of cooperation from the Muslim side. According to them, this scenario could undermine the very reason for establishing the museum. The court, despite having heard and read the reports by experts, including Jewish academics and particularly the opinion of Professor Yehoshua Ben-Arieh, did not embrace this argument.

It should be noted in this regard that the state and the museum entrepreneurs exploited an insinuated argument of the Muslim plaintiffs and Jewish academics, according to which construction of the museum might lead to acts of violence by Muslims who could not accept this construction. The defendants provided the court with expert opinions asserting that, based on former precedents, if the authorities respond positively to the demands of extremist movements such as the Islamic Movement, the situation will escalate. However, they argued, a steadfast policy to protect the state interests reinforces moderate elements among the Arabs of Israel, effectively granting permission to resume construction of the MoT and excavation in areas that have not been the subject of violent actions, protests, or special complaints.

In addressing this issue, the High Court justices underscored the court's policy that threats of violence should never influence rulings:

> During court hearings as well as in arguments and expert testimonies submitted to the court, one of the arguments presented was that implementation of the construction plans could inflame sentiments and polarize emotions and sectarian hostility, resulting even in violent acts by a few segments of Israeli society who oppose implementation of the plan in the area where the remains of old graves are located. These arguments were not disregarded by us. It is important to emphasize clearly in this regard that fears of an outbreak of illegal violence in response to a court ruling enabling the building of the museum under certain conditions should not be given consideration in our judicial work. While the question of offending people's sentiments because of implementation of the plan is a legitimate consideration, the threat of violence and illegal behavior is not a consideration in the context of a

> judicial decision . . . Toleration and consideration of the sentiments of the other in the context of judicial work does not mean surrender to the external pressure of illegal demonstrations or other violent acts by extreme elements who seek to impose their will on state authorities. The claims regarding fear of outbreak of violence and public disorder following the museum plan's implementation, therefore, were not among the relevant considerations in reaching a decision. It is expected that all factions and sectors of the Israeli public will respect the court ruling and behave accordingly, within the framework of law.[60]

Even though the court did not name the Islamic Movement, the above statements indicate that the High Court viewed the movement as "extreme elements," and consequently the insinuation of the plaintiffs regarding possible future violence only undermined the position of opponents to construction of the museum in Mamilla.

The state's defense against the Islamic Movement's activities in general, and in the realm of the struggle over the symbolic landscape in particular, reached a peak in August 2008 when the minister of defense issued a decree under the Emergency Defense Regulations of 1945, outlawing the Al-Aqsa Corporation and confiscating all of its properties. This decree was issued on the basis of information indicating a close relationship between the Al-Aqsa Corporation and Hamas. For the justices of the High Court this only reinforced what they had already concluded regarding the radical image of the Islamic Movement, which challenges the State of Israel and its Jewish citizens. They indicated in their verdict that although the museum entrepreneurs had requested that the High Court reject the petition in light of the plaintiffs' illegal activities, they believe that the case of the MoT presents a matter of principle to be examined by the court regardless of illegal status of the key plaintiff.[61]

In sum, in Israel, which has continuously sought legitimacy as a Jewish State in the Middle East, even liberal justices cannot ignore the motivation of a plaintiff who affiliates with a fundamentalist Islamic organization. The verdict of the High Court of Justice, which will be analyzed in depth in Chapter 8, adopted the national ideological discourse, and my impression is that this explains why the petition was rejected.

Shifting the venue of the struggle to the international domain emphasizes and reinforces the ideological aspect of the dispute and tests the various positions regarding the character of Jerusalem and the right of representation of peoples and religions in the public sphere.

Another aspect of the identity struggle refers to the institution of the Muslim waqf and particularly to the attempt of the Islamic Movement to restitute general waqf properties, including the Mamilla Cemetery, to Muslim administration. Waqf assets were nationalized by the State of Israel under the 1950 Absentees' Properties Law, but the Muslims of Israel never recognized the legitimacy of this law. The next chapter deals with this issue.

Notes

1 M. Mautner, *Law and Culture in Israel*, Oxford: Oxford University Press, 2011, p. 229.

2 Ibid.

3 See A. Levy, "Towards politics of identities," *Panim*, 10, 1999, 31–40 (Hebrew); C. Calhoun (ed.), *Social Theory and the Politics of Identity*, Oxford: Blackwell, 1994.

4 N. Luz, "Metaphors of resistance – holy places in the Palestinian society of Israel: The case of Maqam Abu al-Hija," (Hebrew) available at: virtualnew.haifa.ac.il/users/www/12990/courses/ . . . /Luz,fordganit.doc.

5 On the link between landscape and ideology, see A.R.H. Baker and G. Biger, *Ideology and Landscape in Historical Perspective: Essays on the Meanings of Some Places in the Past*, Cambridge: Cambridge University Press, 2006.

6 Larry Abrahams, *Sacred Landscape* (Resling, 2009) [Hebrew], p. 188 quoting Raja Shehadeh, *Palestinian Walks: Notes on a Vanishing Landscape* (London: Profile Books, 2007). W.J.T. Mitchell, "Holy Landscape: Israel, Palestine, and the American Wilderness," *Critical Inquiry*, 26:2, 2000, 193–223.

7 Mitchell, *Sacred Landscape*, p. 116.

8 Ibid., p. 106.

9 Ibid.

10 Ibid., p. 67.

11 D. Bar, *Sanctifying a Land: The Jewish Holy Places in the State of Israel 1948–1968*, Jerusalem: Yad Yitzhak Ben-Zvi and Ben Gurion University, 2007, p. 120 (Hebrew). See Kahana's *Legends of Zion* (1974).

12 The legend about the lion's cave developed in the context of the Christian tradition pertaining to the Christians who were massacred in Jerusalem in 614 A.D. The Ministry of Religious Affairs inaugurated the new Jewish site in a modest ceremony, including a presentation by Jewish Yemenite immigrants to Israel and Chief Rabbi Yitzhak Isaac Herzog. When the Ministry realized that one of the two Chief Rabbis challenged the authenticity of the cave, it was decided to recognize it as a traditional site and not as a holy place. Nonetheless, the Ministry attempted to organize a pilgrimage to the cave every year during the Hebrew month of Elul. In 1954 the Ministry excavated the cave and re-inaugurated it in a ceremony in which representatives of the Jerusalem Municipality participated. The Ministry and the Jerusalem Municipality intended to develop the site as a memorial to Jewish heroes and built a visitors' center, including a museum, shops, and a garden with symbolic elements from the cave. At the end of the 1960s the cave was abandoned because it did not attract the Jewish public. See Bar, op. cit., pp. 120–3.

13 M. Benvenisti, *Sacred Landscape: The Buried History of the Holy Land 1948–1998*, Berkeley: University of California Press, 2000.

14 N. Luz, "Metaphors of Resistance" citing the following references: J. Duncan and N. Duncan, "Re(reading) the landscape," *Environment and Planning D: Society and Space* 6, 1988, 117–126; D. Harvey, "Monument and Myth," Annals of the Association of American Geographers 69, 1979, 362–81; D. Haynes and G. Parkash, 1991). "Introduction: the entanglement of power and resistance", in D. Haynes and G. Parkash, (eds.) *Contesting Power: Resistance and Everyday Social Relations in South Asia*, Delhi: Oxford University Press, 1991, 1–22; L. Kong,

"Ideological hegemony and the political symbolism of religious buildings in Singapore" *Environment and Planning D: Society and Space* 11, 1993, 23–45; D. Mitchell, *Cultural Geography: A Critical Introduction*, Oxford: Blackwell Publishers, 2000; S. Pile, "Introduction: opposition, political identities and spaces of resistance," in S. Pile and M. Keith (eds), *Geographies of Resistance*, London, New York; Routledge, 1997, pp. 1–32; J. C. Scott, *Weapons of the Weak*, New Haven, London: Yale University Press, 1985; Y. Tuan, "Thought and landscape," in D. W. Meinig (ed), *The Interpretation of Ordinary Landscape*, New York, Oxford: Oxford University Press, 1979, pp. 89–102.

15 On the symbolic meaning of sacred landscape within the Israeli–Palestinian conflict, see Mitchell, "Holy Landscape."

16 Article 239 of the High Court Verdict 52/06 (HCJ 52/06) (Hebrew).

17 Ibid., Article 1.

18 See W. J. T. Mitchell, "Imperial Landscape," in W.J.T. Mitchell (ed) *Landscape and Power* Chicago: University of Chicago Press, 1994, 2nd edn, 2002.

19 H. Lefebvre, *Writing on Cities*, Oxford: Blackwell, 1996, p. 195, quoted by E. Ben-Ze'ev and I. Aburaiya, "'Middle-ground' politics and the re-Palestinization of places in Israel," *International Journal of Middle East Studies* 36, 2004, 639–55 and by N. Luz, *The Arab Community of Jaffa and the Hassan Bey Mosque*, Jerusalem: The Floersheimer Institute for Policy Studies, 2005 (Hebrew).

20 S. Makdisi, "The Architecture of Erasure," *Critical Inquiry*, 36:3, 2010, 519–59. Makdisi is an American of Lebanese and Palestinian extraction and nephew of Professor Edward Said, who was considered among the stronger critics of Israel and Zionism.

21 Ibid., 555.

22 Ibid., 542.

23 Ibid., 553.

24 Ibid., 557.

25 Ibid., 551.

26 R. Israeli, S. Berkovits, J. Neriah, and M. Hier, "The architecture of erasure: Fantasy or reality?" *Critical Inquiry*, 36:3, 2010, 563–94.

27 After he immigrated to the United States, he changed his family name from Goldberg to Gehry, according to him to appease his wife, who is Catholic, and his sons were baptized.

28 F. Gehry, "Critical response I," *Critical Inquiry*, 36:3, 2010, 560–2.

29 *Critical Inquiry*, op. cit., 610.

30 *Critical Inquiry*, op. cit., 592.

31 Ibid., p. 584. The excavation artifacts have not been published yet. Responding to Makdisi's charges of a Zionist project, the respondents wrote that there is no connection between the museum as a private institution and the government of Israel.

32 See http://ccrjustice.org/files/Lettre%20Yemen%20et%20ol%C3%A9rance.pdf. The letter of the ambassador of Yemen is dated 4 March 2009. The letter of the ambassador of Kuwait is dated 20 April 2010. Both were published on the web site that campaigns against the project.

33 W. Khaladi, *All That Remains: The Palestinian Villages Occupied and Depopulated by Israel in 1948*, Washington DC: Institute of Palestine Studies, 1992.

34 M. Benvenisti, *Sacred Landscape: Buried History of the Holy Land Since 1948*, University of California Press, 2001, pp. 270–316.
35 Y. Reiter, *National Minority, Regional Majority: Palestinian Arabs versus Jews in Israel*, Syracuse University Press, 2009, p. VI.
36 R. Khamaisi, *General Survey The Islamic Waqf; Land. Mosques and Cemeteries within the Green-line*, Kufr Barra, Al-Aqsa Association for the Protection the Islamic Waqf, 2002).
37 See, for example, the assertion of Sheikh Raed Salah cited in I. Inbari, "Israel turns graves into pens," *Ma'ariv*, 4 August 2007 available at: www.nrg.co.il/online/1/ART1/617/382.html.
38 Internet websites of the two movements: www.aqsa-mubarak.org; www.islamic-aqsa.com accessed during 2006, the website was replaced with other websites.
39 Islamic Movement website.
40 E. Horowitz, "The vengeance of the Jews was stronger than their avarice: Modern historians and the Persian conquest of Jerusalem in 614," *Jewish Social Studies* 4, 1998.
41 www.islamic-aqsa.com accessed 9 September 2006. This Islamic Movement's website was removed since then.
42 *Or Commission Report*, vol. 1, sec. 1, Article 97 (Hebrew).
43 Ibid., Article 98.
44 E. Ben-Ze'ev and I. Aburaiya, "'Middle-ground' politics and the re-Palestinization of places in Israel," *International Journal of Middle East Studies* 36, 2004, 639–55.
45 Ibid. The same case was summarized by the Or Commission in the following way: "The people of the Islamic movement began renovating the mosque, but on July 25, 2000, during the night unknown people bulldozed the structure. The Islamic activists removed the ruins of the mosque floor, erected a prayer tent on its spot, and recruited hundreds of worshippers. The magistrate called for and accepted a request by the Israel Land Authority, and ordered the dismantling of the demonstration prayer tent. The legal attempts to rebuild the mosque failed. This case incited significant Muslim protest against the state authorities, which the Supreme Follow-Up Committee, the highest authority of Arabs in Israel, joined as well. It seems that the attempts to re-operate abandoned mosques triggered actions from Jews to prevent the possibility of rehabilitation of these mosques and resulted in a dynamic of escalation. The activities of the Islamic Movement intertwine with the activities of the Arab Cultural Association, which organizes tours to discover national roots in demolished villages, and with the activities of the Supreme Follow-Up Committee, which has initiated mass rallies in demolished villages on the Nakba Day of May 15 in recent years. See *Or Commision Report*, Article 99 (Hebrew).
46 www.Nakbainhebrew.com
47 N. Luz, *The Arab Community of Jaffa and the Hassan Bey Mosque*, Jerusalem: The Floersheimer Institute for Policy Studies, 2005 (Hebrew).
48 Article 35 of HCJ 52/06 (Hebrew).
49 Expert opinion of Joseph Ginat, who was the vice-president of Netanya Academic College and passed away in 2008 (Hebrew).
50 Expert opinion of Shalom Goldstein, dated 25 April 2007, quoted in Article 65 of HCJ 52/06 (Hebrew).
51 Interview with Dr. Mahdi Abd al-Hadi, published by Al-Quds, 21 July 2006,

quoted by Goldstein in his expert opinion dated 25 April 2007 (Hebrew translation from Arabic).

52 *Al-Sha'b* 11 October 1996 (Arabic).

53 Expert opinion of Yehoshua Porath, dated 25 April 2007 (Hebrew).

54 Expert opinion of David Klein, dated 18 January 2006. Klein goes on to mention that the Islamic Movement's newspaper, *Saut al-Haqq wal-Huriyya*, amplifies Hamas's messages. This newspaper was closed down in January 1990 by a decree of the minister of the interior, initially only for three months, for the above-mentioned reason. Klein presents a significant quote from an article written by Raed Salah and published in this newspaper on 18 August, 1992: "We want that the Flag of Allah will be raised again over an Islamic state and the voice of the Muezzin will be heard praising Allah all over . . . The Mediterranean Sea and the Red Sea should return to be Islamic lakes . . . We are equipped with a steadfast conviction and with souls searching for martyrdom for Allah." (Hebrew translated from Arabic).

55 *Or Commision Report*, vol. 1, sec. 5, Article 106 (Hebrew).

56 The expert opinion states, "The declared goals of the Muslim Brotherhood, Hamas, and the Islamic Movement are: To establish an Islamic theocratic state over the entire land of Palestine; great and even decisive weight to be granted to the activities of the Al-Aqsa Corporation in its 'war' against attempts to build and develop Israeli and Jewish projects in every spot that it has determined (not always according to the common Islamic law, but in their special interpretation) is sacred to Islam. They hold that the entire territory of Palestine is an Islamic waqf, regardless of whether the land is the ruins of a village, an old mosque, or a Muslim cemetery whose 'holiness' was long ago removed . . . The struggle is total and has one goal: The establishment of the great Islamic state" (Hebrew).

57 Article 11 of HCJ 52/06 (Hebrew).

58 N. C. Gross, "Grave thoughts," *The Jerusalem Report*, 5 January 2009, 21–4.

59 Article 242 of HCJ 52/06 (Hebrew).

60 Article 255 of HCJ 52/06 (Hebrew).

61 Articles 252–254 of HCJ 52/06 (Hebrew).

CHAPTER

3

The Waqf in the National-Religious Struggle of the Arab-Muslim Minority in Israel

In the dispute over construction of the Jerusalem MoT, the Muslim plaintiffs and the Shari'a Court qadis argued that the Mamilla Cemetery is a holy Islamic endowment – waqf – and hence under the exclusive jurisdiction of the Shari'a Court. The excavation of human remains of hundreds bodies during the work to lay down the foundation of the Museum building provided the Islamic Movement and the Shari'a Court a new venue to re-challenge the 1950 Absentees' Properties Law, under which the state expropriated the properties of the General Waqf Administration *(al-waqf al 'amm)*[1].

Nationalization of waqf properties by the state and the Muslim minority's struggle to restitute these properties are among the most emotionally charged issues between the Arab minority and the Jewish majority in Israel. Israeli Muslims have never accepted the state's takeover and subsequent sale of its waqf assets, including cemeteries. The cemeteries are their identity symbols, binding them to the land and history. Their struggle to restitute the waqf properties is aimed at rejuvenating their status as a homeland minority, that is, a group of people who became a minority in its native land. Hence the question of how to handle this delicate issue requires a review of the waqf institution and its transformation following Israel's formation in 1948.

The Waqf Institution and Its Development in Modern Times

From the Muslim standpoint, waqf is an endowment founded according to religious law and has religious meaning as a charitable act for which the endower is rewarded with eternal life in the afterworld.[2] Every individual or statesman can endow his privately owned property for charitable public or family purposes. The moment he announces his act of endowment before two witnesses, he loses ownership of the property. Endowed property is, theoretically, transferred to the ownership of God. The founder of the waqf can, through the founding deed, maintain the administration of and benefits deriving from the property for as long as he lives, but he is prohibited under shari'a from abolishing the waqf endowment or from selling an endowed property. Waqf in Arabic means "to halt" and it is interpreted as symbolizing the halting of ownership of the endowed property, preventing its being traded anew in the free market.

Since the nineteenth century it has been standard practice to distinguish between public (*khayri*) and family (*dhuri*) waqfs. Most of the endowments of the first type were transferred to the atate under the Ottoman reforms of the nineteenth century while the family waqfs remained mostly in the hands of private family members. The Ottoman state registered all mosques, cemeteries, and other Muslim places of warship as properties owned by a waqf administration under a special ministry. Following the dismantlement of the Ottoman Empire, the General Waqf Administration of Palestine was handed over to the Supreme Muslim Council, which had been established by the British Mandate government of Palestine. The Council became "a mini Palestinian autonomous authority" of sorts. In 1948, when Jordan assumed rule of East Jerusalem and the West Bank, the Hashemite government transferred the powers of the Council to a Ministry of Awqaf (plural of waqf). In 1967, after Israel took over East Jerusalem and applied Israeli law and administration, the General Waqf Administration remained under Jordanian rule. However, waqf properties in West Jerusalem, including the Mamilla Cemetery, were transferred under the Israeli 1950 Absentees' Properties Law to the administration of an Israeli government custodian (see below).

As I have shown elsewhere,[3] *the waqf asset is not holy and not eternal.* Under some conditions it is permissible to exchange and even to sell waqf properties in order to preserve its charity status. The same is not necessarily the case for Muslim cemeteries, which are also waqf properties, as I will discuss in chapter 5. This matter is highly significant in light of the false argument put forth by Muslim clerics that every waqf property is eternally sacred. Furthermore, there is also an incorrect counter-argument put forth by academic experts (former civil servants who drafted the 1965 Third Amendment to the Absentees' Properties Law) stating that the waqf institution is economically stagnant and inflicts damage on the state economy.[4] This last argument was rejected during the British Mandate in Palestine.[5] An analysis of the documents of the Supreme Muslim Council and of the Shari'a Court records (*sijillat*) reveals that qadis as well as the Supreme Muslim Council members were very flexible and open regarding exchange and economic development of waqf properties, including even the sale of such properties if necessary.[6]

Yet there is another important aspect concerning the preservation of waqf properties in their original form, and particularly those that provide religious, educational, and welfare services. These services, especially those that symbolize group identity, require social, economic, and political consideration.

The Waqf in Israel

The State of Israel, which is controlled by a Jewish majority, has a different set of interests and needs from the British Mandate, under which Palestinian Muslims had an institutional autonomy of sorts. With the establishment of Israel, a new era began. It was contended that the waqf was part of the old social order from a period when the (Ottoman) state did not provide religious, educational, and welfare services. Rather, these activities had been funded by private individuals or the community that founded waqf endowments.[7] It was further argued that today, when Israeli government ministries as well as public associations fulfill the functions of providing these services, the waqf becomes redundant. This approach, an expression of modernization, had generated earlier reform of the waqf institution in the mid-nineteenth century, resulting in transfer of the large public waqfs into a central administration under a special Ottoman ministry. Interestingly, following World War I the Ottoman model was also adopted by Muslim states, and some even abolished the waqf institution completely.[8]

In the name of modernization, senior civil servants argued that the modern state (Israel in this case) was responsible for the provision of social and religious services as well as the maintenance of holy places. Therefore the state can nationalize waqf properties whose revenues were used in the past for these purposes. This position could be morally justified in Israel if the state indeed provided a reasonable level of religious services to the Muslim community. However, as High Court deliberations revealed time and again, past Israeli governments have severely neglected Muslim holy sites. In addition, the quality and funding of religious services for the Jewish community significantly exceeded the quality and funding of religious services allocated to the Muslim sector.[9] Muslims in Israel have no religious councils and no state or government institution in charge of maintaining holy places such as the Jewish community presently has for the upkeep of at least 137 Jewish holy sites.[10] On the one hand the Israeli government took over vast areas of Arab Muslim land in urban centers as well as in the rural periphery, but on the other hand it resists allocating significant resources to fund the charitable purposes that in the past the expropriated waqf properties had supported. Thus, the Western model of modernization used by civil servants does not pass the test of social development in Israel. Today the government prefers to delegate these services to public non-governmental organizations (NGO)s funded completely or partially by the government.[11]

Two major interests motivated the takeover of the General Waqf properties by the government of Israel: the first was the need to designate lands in the center and the north of the country for development of Jewish settlement projects; the second was the interest in preventing reestablishment of a national Muslim council headed by someone such as the previous Grand Mufti al-Husayni from the British Mandate period. The state leaders feared that such a personality would exploit the economic might of the waqf for political purposes against the interests of the state and its Jewish majority.[12] Consequently, the government decided not to establish an overall Islamic body or appoint a mufti. The government preferred to de-centralize and reduce the authority for administration of mosques and cemeteries, dispersing it among local Muslim committees that were subject to the Ministry of Religious Affairs, which had a demonstrated policy of co-optation of the Arab minority.[13] The government refrained, however, from revoking the authority for internal administration of waqf properties that had been granted to the Shari'a Court during the British Mandate under Article 52 of the 1922 Palestine Order-in-Council (see chapter 4). Apparently, and somewhat ironically, the Israeli government was seeking to avoid violation of Islamic religious law even though such a measure was not necessary at the time because the Shari'a Court judiciary was composed of "yes men." In the long run, this policy resulted in a backlash, as we shall see below, because the authority retained by the Shari'a Court with regard to the founding and internal administration of waqf properties would later be used by Islamic activists, thereby undermining the government's policy.

In 1950 the government enacted the Absentees' Properties Law, enabling the state to seize the properties of Palestinian refugees, including the General Waqf assets, that is, those properties that had been administered by a central state administration or the Supreme Muslim Council and its regional waqf administrators between 1922 and 1948. The sophisticated wording of the law was intended to obscure the seizure and nationalization of waqf properties. Under this law, every resident or entity who owned land and was out of the country for a certain period of time following the establishment of Israel was declared legally "absent" and his properties were transferred to a government custodian who was entitled to use them for the country's development.

There was a catch in the law, however, as the government custodian was only considered a trustee who was supposed to administer and maintain the property for the benefit of its original owners. It is unclear, therefore, how in 1953 the government custodian sold some two million dunams (approximately half a million acres) of absentees' properties to the Jewish National Fund (JNF), which is an organization of world Jewry, not part of the State of Israel. These dunams included waqf properties.. Prime Minister David Ben-Gurion was apparently very concerned at that time that an international resolution would be imposed on Israel regarding the return of Palestinian refugees. He therefore wanted to create facts on the ground, namely, to ensure that the refugees would have no property motivating their return.[14] It also remains unclear what position was taken by the attorney general and other governmental legal advisors who approved such an action, in contradiction of the letter of the law. Indeed, under the 1950 law, the custodian was only a trustee who was granted authority to watch over *and maintain* the property, *not* to sell it to a third party (and certainly not the JNF). Let us examine the fate of waqf property in Israel under the Absentees' Properties Law.

Since the early 1950s, Muslim citizens of Israel have protested the Absentees' Properties Law, particularly the language of the law defining "absentee." [15] They claim that according to shari'a, when a property owner dedicated assets to the waqf, the property ownership transfers to God. This is how most Islamic schools of law define the action of endowment, emphasizing the eternal aspect of the waqf.[16] "Allah is not absent," the protesters insisted, but in vein. They initiated a campaign of slogans expressing resentment and of protests that were relatively moderate because they had not yet come to terms with the defeat of the 1948 war, their "Nakba" (catastrophe), and the nationalizing of General Waqf properties was part of this Nakba. Moreover, under Israeli military rule, which restricted movement, they could not organize an effective public campaign.

An immense Arab outcry was finally voiced regarding the less valuable assets – urban properties – while neglecting the rural waqf lands in the center and north of Israel, which were of enormous size and value. Arab protest has tended to focus mainly on the urban properties such as mosques, cemeteries, and saints' tombs in the big cities in which Arabs resided before and after 1948. Here their outcry was amplified because a Jewish government had taken holy places as well as historical sites, such as the Al-Jazzar Mosque in Acre, an action which they could not tolerate. Their symbolic landscape and identity was devastated by this action. Consequently, the labor government of the 1950s decided that the government custodian would transfer the "administration" (as opposed to possession and ownership) of religious monuments to the Ministry of Religious Affairs, which in turn nominated Muslim clerics to run these facilities on its behalf.[17] The result of this decision was that the government still controlled religious Muslim monuments and cemeteries that were outwardly run by Muslims.[18]

Political pressure was exerted on the ruling Mapai (Labor) party because during these years a majority of the Arab population tended to vote for Mapai and its satellite lists. Mapai was searching for an appropriate way to amend the Absentees' Properties Law, enabling some waqf property to be returned to the administration of Muslims, on one hand, while remedying the loophole in the Absentees' Properties Law in such a way that the Shari'a Court would have no legal power in the future to revoke the authority of the Israeli government custodian over waqf properties, on the other hand. There were three other motivations for amending this law as eventually approved by the Knesset in 1965:[19] first, that the Muslim trustees to whom waqf property was transferred would also be appointed by the government and subject to its supervision; second, that the property would be urban only and mainly religious monuments and sites; and third, that the law would free General Waqf properties from being subject to shari'a, that is, they could be sold and traded, with one exception – a Mosque could not be traded or sold. In other words, the 1965 amendment to the Absentees' Properties Law did not prohibit the sale of a Muslim cemetery. Thus if an abandoned cemetery was discovered in a developing urban zone, it could be sold and commercial buildings built in its place. Such was the case of the Hasan Bey Mosque, for example, which happened to be situated in a developing commercial area in southwest Tel Aviv, near the beach, where in the past the Arab neighborhood Manshiya had existed as part of the city of Jaffa. In 1973, in accordance with the above-mentioned amendment, the government nominated a Muslim board of trustees to which it handed over what was left of the collapsing mosque in a long-term lease to a well-known businessman, for the purpose of building shops for tourists while preserving a small part of the mosque in the center of the mall. In this case, the struggle of the Arabs of Jaffa (including its Arab Christians) to preserve and rebuild the mosque was exceptional.[20] After 1977, the Arabs of Jaffa were unexpectedly supported by the new government of Menachem Begin, which sought to detach itself from the corrupt actions of its predecessor, Mapai. In nearly all other similar cases, waqf properties that had been leased or sold by Muslim boards of trustees to private entrepreneurs were not reclaimable and the Muslim community lost them forever.

The 1965 amendment to the Absentees' Properties Law satisfied the three above-mentioned motivations of the government. The government appointed Muslim trustees to administer properties that the custodian released to them in five (mixed) cities: Tel Aviv–Jaffa, Ramla, Lod, Haifa, and Acre. By enacting this amendment, the government effectively granted retroactive approval for all past transactions of sale of absentee properties by the custodian (who had sold them to the government and to the JNF). The new law did not appease the Muslim community, however, nor did it yield any peace. In a study of the Muslim boards of trustees that I conducted in the 1980s, I found that the amendment to the law failed to achieve its purposes because of the way in which the government implemented it.[21]

The Struggle of the Islamic Movement to Restitute Waqf Properties

The waqf issue in Israel also has a political dimension of collective identity. Government policy and action revived the Muslim protest regarding waqf issues. As long as the waqf was in the possession of Arab Muslims, the Muslim public in Palestine benefitted from a religious and economic enterprise that controlled a multifaceted system of institutions and economic and social activity. The existence of waqf in Palestine vested the Muslim population with an important Islamic identity and symbol of national solidarity. The absence of the waqf institution in Israel, resulting from the state's seizure of most of the waqf properties, is a great loss to Arab-Muslim society in Israel.

The political conflicts regarding waqf in Israel are part of the struggle of the Arab, predominantly Muslim, minority to re-institute and restitute control over its institutions and historical properties, and part of its struggle over constructing the public space and landscape in a way that will grant legitimacy to the minority's culture and historical religious and national narrative. During the 1980s, a Muslim organization under the auspices of the Communist Party (Hadash) was active on this issue. It was headed by Fathi Furani, a party activist from Haifa who also published a booklet on the topic.[22] These were the years during which the Arab community of Jaffa emerged victorious from its long struggle to prevent the sale of the Hasan Bey Mosque and to renovate it following a lengthy period of neglect and abandonment, since 1948.[23]

During the 1990s the Islamic Movement also entered the picture. The process of privatization and liberalization that the Israeli community was undergoing created the impression that the Jewish public might tolerate the relinquishment of control over these holy sites. The method employed by the Islamic Movement was to take possession unilaterally of every cemetery or mosque where some remains were preserved, to maintain and rebuild it, and in some cases even to reactivate it. According to the Islamic Movement's estimate, every one of the approximately 400 Arab demolished villages had an average of four mosques and four cemeteries. In other words, potentially they had some 2,400–3,200 places to take over, even if the state were still the legal possessor. The Islamic Movement conducted a comprehensive survey of waqf properties in demolished villages and existing towns based on the Palestinian waqf archive (formerly the archive of the Supreme Muslim Council).[24] Once they started this process of restituting abandoned holy sites to their original use, they documented their actions on websites in the Arabic language.[25] Nevertheless, the state authorities ignored their demands and undermined most of the attempts of the Islamic Movement to take over abandoned holy places.

The Struggle over the Waqf Status of the Mamilla Cemetery and Its Control

The struggle against construction of the Museum of Tolerance in Mamilla intertwines with the strategy of returning General Waqf assets to Muslim control. The Muslims who were direct or indirect plaintiffs against the MoT in Mamilla claimed that the cemetery is registered in the Land Registry as owned by the General Waqf. This argument aimed to establish two points: first, in their opinion if the cemetery indeed belongs to the waqf, then its internal administration according to law (Israel's 1961 Qadis Law) comes under the sole jurisdiction of the Shari'a Court. Hence, the local qadi of (West) Jerusalem can *prima facie* appoint a trustee for the cemetery who is authorized to make a determination regarding any change of the land use. This claim was rejected by the state authorities and the Museum entrepreneurs. The second objective of the above argument was to employ Mamilla as a precedential case study within the ongoing struggle of the Muslim population of Israel against the government, demanding the restitution of all waqf assets that were expropriated after Israel was established. Thus the Mamilla affair is part of a broader Muslim struggle to re-glorify the waqf and restitute it to its former grandeur by taking control of waqf assets that had been nationalized and returning them to their original purpose as properties run by Muslims for the benefit of the Muslim community.

Indeed, the Muslims who were direct or indirect plaintiffs against the MoT in Mamilla framed their struggle in the broader context. They argued that Muslim cemeteries are not "absentees' properties" with which the state can do as it wishes without accountability, but waqf properties, and as such they are under the sole jurisdiction of the Shari'a Court. It should be stressed that the struggle to reclaim assets, and in particular Muslim cemeteries, is also part of the agenda of the Shari'a Court and especially its president, Qadi (Dr.) Ahmad Natour. This is why shortly after the case was appealed to the High Court, another case was filed with the Shari'a Court, ostensibly by a different body and different people. As we shall see in the following chapter, this affair had an added aspect, namely, the struggle over the status and authority of the Shari'a Court regarding waqf affairs. The West Jerusalem Shari'a Court attempted to disregard the government actions and to treat the disputed land in Mamilla as if still a waqf property under its own jurisdiction (prior to the 1965 amendment). The qadis of today followed in the steps of their predecessors of the 1950s and 1960s, who had issued appointments to the position of *mutawalli* (administrator) of General Waqf assets that were in the government custodian's possession. They ignored the above-mentioned fact that the 1965 amendment actually voided the "waqf" status of General Waqf properties and handed them over to a government custodian, i.e., to the state.

On 1 March 2006, the qadi of Jerusalem, Muhammad Zibde, appointed two *mutawallis* for a General Waqf asset entitled "the Mamilla Cemetery." He ordered them to take any action to protect the cemetery. The *mutawallis*, Sheikh Mustfafa Abu Zahra and Sameh Abu Mukh, were Islamic Movement activists. Immediately following their appointment, they organized two one-day campaigns to clean the cemetery with the participation of Islamic Movement supporters headed by Sheikh Raed Salah. Yet this was a one-time action with no follow-up, and the Islamic Movement did not carry out any additional actions on the cemetery's grounds (although on two occasions they added hundreds of new gravestones to the preserved part of the cemetery to make it look more important, but the Israeli authorities removed these immediately).

The major plaintiff against the MoT, the Al-Aqsa Corporation, challenged the legal status of the General Waqf properties in Israel. It claimed in the High Court that the Absentees' Properties Law is in fact illegal because waqf is not a regular social institution that can be expropriated, but an eternal religious charitable endowment. Al-Aqsa based its argument on a government resolution from November 1961 that stated that waqf properties that are not religious sites should be governed by the Ministry of Religious Affairs and removed from the custodianship of absentees' property. That resolution, however, had been passed by the government four years prior to the 1965 amendment of the Absentees' Properties Law, which voided the waqf status of absentees' properties. Through this argument the Northern Islamic Movement sought to convey that there is a distinct difference between religious and regular properties. The first, they claimed, should be administered by religious clerics.

The Al-Aqsa Corporation further argued that religious and holy assets could not be defined as absentees' property because the abstract ownership (*raqaba)* over these properties is not subject to human control but is controlled by God, and thus "absence" is impossible. The Al-Aqsa Corporation tried to benefit from the best of all worlds: shari'a as well as state laws. On the one hand, they claimed that under the state law of absentees' properties, one has to distinguish between holy places and waqfs of non-holy places. On the other hand, they argued that under shari'a all waqfs have a religious character. Alternatively, they claimed that even if we assume that a property could be regarded as belonging to an absentee, its very nature as a holy site does not allow its transfer to a third party even if its original formal owner is absent. They based this argument on Article 29(7) of the Absentees' Properties Law (the amendment of 1965), claiming that the reparation money from the sale of the Mamilla Cemetery should have been used for public purposes to benefit the Muslim community, and that because it was not used in this way, the sale was illegal.[26] The High Court justices did not accept the argument that the proceeds from every property that the custodian sells must immediately and directly be allocated for the benefit of the Muslim community. It should be noted in this context that, through a committee in the Prime Minister's Office, the custodian annually allocates a sum of money termed "reparation," derived from properties that he sold, for activities in the Muslim sector. The sum is low compared to the value of the sold assets, less than one million NIS annually (during the 1970s and 1980s, the sum was significantly lower). This amount is arbitrarily determined by the Finance Ministry, and it contravenes the Absentees' Properties Law. In my opinion, a professional accounting of the General Waqf properties that have been sold in addition to those that still remain under his administration could yield an appropriate budget for developing and preserving Muslim holy sites, in addition to funding sound and reasonable religious services for the Muslim community. If this had been the case, then one could have morally and substantively justified the policy of nationalizing public waqf property.

The justices of the High Court also rejected the Al-Aqsa Corporation's interpretation of the Absentees' Properties Law. They reasoned as follows:

Once the 1965 Absentees' Properties Law was amended, there is no doubt that a waqf property whose administrator is absent comes under the full ownership of the custodian, and this entails not only appropriation of the right to administer the waqf. Complete ownership is rendered to the custodian, free of any other claim, meaning that the property's waqf status is revoked. The property loses its special character as an endowment. The implementation of the amendment is retroactive to 1948, and therefore it also applies also to the land in dispute.[27]

The High Court verdict goes on to declare that the law does not distinguish between religious and other public properties. It states that it is doubtful that the cemetery is holy given the 1964 shari'a fatwa that removed this holiness. The justices also note that the use of the disputed land as a parking lot for a few decades is incompatible with the holy nature of the site, and most importantly, "even if the cemetery land is still recognized religiously as a holy space, in this case involving the allocation of rights [ownership and building rights] the applicable law is the civil not the religious law".[28] They added that the disputed land was registered in 1966 as owned by the Custodian of Absentees' Properties, who sold it in 1992 to the governmental Development Authority as a regular property. Consequently, the Shari'a Court lost any authority and jurisdiction to hear a case on this matter.

Ultimately, the Islamic Movement and the Shari'a Court failed to achieve their political goal. The High Court verdict set a precedent for the future and put an end to legal interpretations surrounding the questions of who owns General Waqf assets and whether old Muslim cemeteries could serve development projects. In addition, the Muslim plaintiffs failed to gain the support of the Muslim public for their struggle. Perhaps the general Muslim public, despite its opposition to government policy and strong preference for the return of General Waqf properties to Muslim administration, does not want to identify with an activist movement that operates against the ruling establishment of the state or to become involved in a protest activity that might result in a confrontation with security forces.

Notes

1 In 1950, Israel nationalized all of the properties belonging to this administration, while family waqfs and other small public waqfs, administered by Muslims who remained in the state of Israel after its establishment, remained intact under the supervision of the shari'a courts. The number and property value of these waqfs, however, are marginal compared to the properties of the General Waqf Administration.

2 On the waqf institution see Y. Reiter, *Islamic Endowments in Jerusalem under British Mandate*, London and Portland, Oregon: Frank Cass, 1996; M. Hoexter, "Waqf studies in the twentieth century: The state of the art," *Journal of Economic and Social History of the Orient* 41, 1998, 41, 133–65.

3 Hence, when the endowment is voided, the special reward is also seized. This principle of the waqf system resulted in a legal rule of the shari'a according to which a property once endowed for a particular purpose (beneficiary) is eternal and the property should not be traded or sold. The popular practice of Muslims was to preserve their original assets as a living memorial to the endower and his legacy. However, when some properties were threatened by dilapidation, Muslim jurists permitted the exchange of the original waqf properties for substitute ones, and in

some cases even the sale of the original properties in order to rescue the waqf institution from an economic catastrophe and at least preserve the purpose of the endowment, i.e., the beneficiaries of the waqf usufruct. One of the drafters of the Muslim waqf rules in shari'a, Al-Khassaf (Hanfite jurist, d. 874) offers the following example: A man dedicated a date plantation to charity; over time the land lost its fertility to the extent that the plantation was about to expire (to die), and with this, the waqf as an endowment and its charitable purpose could disappear. In such a case, al-Khassaf ruled, it is preferable to exchange the original land with a substitute property that will potentially yield fruit in order to restore the endowment's profitability. See Al-Khassaf, *Kitab Ahkam al-Awqaf*, Cairo: Ministry of Awqaf, 1902, p. 22 (Arabic). Put differently, there are shari'a methods for exchanging and sometimes even for selling waqf properties once the local Qadi finds that it is justified according to the principles of duress and benefit for the Muslim community. Another example is from the British Mandate period in Jerusalem: The Palestinian al-Nammri family owned non-agricultural land (rocky land) outside of Jerusalem as part of the family waqf. When the British Mandate government extended the building zone of Jerusalem many of al-Nammari's lands were incorporated into the southern part of the municipal zone. The lands had no income because they were non-irrigated, and irrigation demanded investment that the family waqf could not afford. Nevertheless, the government imposed a property tax on vacant lands in the city zone, again in values that the family could not afford.

The family waqf administrators found a solution under shari'a. They repeatedly appealed to the Shari'a Court of Jerusalem and demanded a legal permit to sell these lands (which in the meantime were parceled for housing plots). The qadis under the jurisdiction of the president of the Supreme Court Haj Amin al-Husayni permitted the sale of these waqf lands, on the condition that using the money they received in return, the family would invest in constructing new houses on other vacant lands belonging to the waqf in Jerusalem, and that the new constructed houses would be registered as part of the family waqf rather than the sold land. In this way the charitable purpose of the waqf could be preserved through the continuing income of rent from the newly built houses. This cooperation between the family waqf entrepreneurs and the religious establishment rendered the al-Nammari waqf (within several years) one of the richest endowments of Jerusalem and provided income for the family after they sold some thirty land plots and constructed houses that were profitable. As I have shown elsewhere in this book, Haj Amin al-Husayni, who was in charge of the General Waqf in Palestinian, himself initiated the sale of waqf lands in order to develop economically viable substitute properties by using reparation money from these transactions. One can conclude from the above examples, that the Islamic law and waqf perception holds that it is more important to preserve the charitable purpose of the waqf that the original properties' endowed status. In other words, the waqf asset is not holy and not eternal. See Reiter, *Islamic Endowments in Jerusalem*, op. cit., p. 172.

4 A. Layish, "The Muslim Waqf in Israel," *Asian and African Studies* 2, 1966, 41–76.

5 Reiter, *Islamic Endowments in Jerusalem*, op. cit.

6 Y. Reiter, "Waqf in Israel since 1965: The case of Acre reconsidered," in M.J. Breger, Y. Reiter and L. Hammer (eds), *Holy Places in the Israeli–Palestinian*

Conflict: Confrontation and Co-existence, London and New York: Routledge, 2009, pp. 105–28.

7 G. Baer, "Waqf as a prop for the social system (sixteenth-twentieth centuries)," *Islamic Law and Society* 4:3, 1997, 264–97.

8 For a survey of the reforms see Y. Reiter, *Islamic Institutions in Jerusalem: Palestinian Muslim Administration under Jordanian and Israeli Rule*, The Hague, London, and Boston: Kluwer Law International, 1997, p. 37.

9 See for example HCJ 240/98, Adalah, et al. v. Minister of Religious Affairs, et al.; Piskey Din [hereinafter P.D.] 52 (2) 167; Y. Reiter, "A twofold barrier – The case of religious services for the Muslims in Israel," in S. Hasson and M. Karayanni (eds), *Obstacles on the Development and Equality of the Arabs in Israel*, Jerusalem: the Floersheimer Institute for Policy Studies, 2006, pp. 166–82 (Hebrew).

10 See the website of the Ministry of Tourism: http://www.tourism.gov.il/other/other/seker_tashtiot.pdf.

11 Another argument that the Israeli government uses, which is justified in my opinion particularly regarding the Mamluk and Ottoman rules, is that the record of waqf administration in Palestine as well as in other places is a story of corruption, embezzlement, failed administration, and the exploitation of administrative authority for political ends and/or for personal and family interests. However, in a study that I conducted on waqf administration during British Mandate Palestine, I did not find any evidence of corruption or inefficient administration as far as the General Waqf was involved. During that period the problem was that only one man (Haj Amin al-Husayni) and one political entity under him had a monopoly over the waqf institution, which was a source of great political might. The situation was different with regard to small public waqfs and family endowments, which were outside the control of the Supreme Muslim Council but were under Shari'a Court supervision. The problem with these waqfs was that the regional qadi, even if he sincerely aspired to fair administration of waqfs under his supervision, did not have sufficient manpower or the tools to oversee these institutions, a fact that was exploited by the waqf administrators. As a result, I found many acts of embezzlement and the use of waqfs for personal gain, yet the corruption was not institutionalized, and it did not involve the senior religious system that oversaw the waqf. In spite of this, the image of corruption of private and family waqf administrators was widespread. See Y. Reiter, *Islamic endowments in Jerusalem under British Mandate*; idem., "The administration and supervision of waqf properties in 20th century Jerusalem," *Varia Turcica* 26, Istanbul: Institute Francais d'etudes Annatoliens, 1994, pp. 169–82.

12 B. S. Shitrit, *The Supreme Muslim Shari'a Council*, Jerusalem: Government Press, 1949 (Hebrew).

13 M. Dumper, *Islam and Israel: Muslim Religious Endowments and the Jewish State*, Washington DC: Institute for Palestine Studies, 1994; A. R. Peled, *Debating Islam in the Jewish State*, New York: SUNY, 2001.

14 A. Kedar and O. Yiftachel, "Land regime and social relations in Israel," *Swiss Human Rights Book*, vol. 1, 2006. Available at SSRN: http://ssrn.com/abstract=906336; cf. H. Sandberg, *Land Title Settlement in Eretz-Israel and The State of Israel*, Jerusalem: The Harry and Michael Sacher Institute for Legislative

Research and Comparative Law, Faculty of Law, The Hebrew University of Jerusalem & Land Use Research Institute, Israel National Fund (Keren Kayemeth LeIsrael), 2000.

15 See http://en.wikipedia.org/wiki/Israeli_land_and_property_laws#The_Absentees.E2.80.99_Property_Law.2C_5710-_1950:
[. . .] a body of persons which, at any time . . . [between 29 November 1947 and the day on which a declaration is published] . . . was a legal owner of any property situated in the area of Israel or enjoyed or held such property, whether by itself or through another, and all the members, partners, shareholders, directors or managers of which are absentees within the meaning of paragraph (1), or the management of the business of which is otherwise decisively controlled by such absentees, or all the capital of which is in the hands of such absentees . . .
This sweeping definition of an absentee included the General Waqf administrators – all of the members and workers of the Supreme Muslim Councils – and rendered them "absentees." That is how General Waqf properties were legally transferred to the Israeli government, namely to the government custodian in charge of absentee property, who was a legal government employee. Moreover, the fact that after 1948, Muslims who remained in Israel were legally potential "beneficiaries" from the General Waqf facilities, in other words, present rather than absent, did not prevent the government from taking over these properties, and through the law of 1950, depriving them of the benefits they had enjoyed prior to the establishment of the state.

16 See for example M. Abu Zahra, *Muhadarat fi al-Waqf*, Cairo: Dar al-Fikr al-Arabi, 1971, p. 41 (Arabic).

17 Reiter, "Waqf in Israel since 1965," op. cit.

18 Ibid. This situation soon generated private initiatives to take over waqf properties. Some of the Muslim clerics appointed by the Ministry of Religious Affairs were found to be corrupt. These people were involved in the attempt to sell cemeteries as well as other waqf property and to benefit personally, pocketing the reparation money. They applied to the qadis, the Shari'a Court judges, and succeeded in receiving permits in the form of a fatwa authorizing them to sell or rent Muslim cemeteries and in some cases, such as in Jaffa, even mosques (The Hasan Bey Mosque, for example). At the same time, industrious Muslim entrepreneurs found waqf that were not registered under the General Waqf Administration, and as such could not be identified as "absentee property", nor were their administrators' positions occupied. One of these entrepreneurs was Suhayl Shukri from Haifa. Suhayl was the son of Hasan Shukri, the Arab mayor of Haifa who died in 1940, and was known to have friendly relations with the Jews. In the 1950s Suhayl was a cleric at the Ministry of Religious Affairs, appointed as head of the Advisory Council for Muslim Affairs in Haifa, the body that oversaw Muslim religious monuments and cemeteries subject to the ministry's control. Shukri recognized that one of the largest waqf institutions of Haifa was independent (as indicated by its name, "*Istiqlal*," meaning "independence") or in other words, outside the administration of the General Waqf. He applied to the qadi of Haifa, who appointed him a *mutawalli* in charge of all of the waqf properties in Haifa. This appointment was possible because Waqf Istiqilal was run by a private administrator who had died prior to the 1948 war. Hence he could not be declared absentee. Shukri hired the services of a renowned Jewish advocate in Haifa and conducted a legal offense against the state,

demanding control of the waqf assets in his city. The friendly relations between the Shukri family and Jewish institutions contributed to the decision of the government's attorney general to accept the Shari'a Court's decision to appoint Shukri as the administrator of Waqf Istiqilal, but not of all waqfs in Haifa as he had demanded. The compromise served the interests of both parties. Shukri gained control of the largest waqf in Haifa, while the government succeeded in rejecting his demand to control all general waqf assets that were under the custodianship of absentee property. It did not take long for Shukri to hand over waqf assets under his jurisdiction, including two Muslim cemeteries in Haifa, to private entrepreneurs.

Although Shukri acted independently, the Muslim public viewed him as a government collaborator and his actions as representative of government policy. Ultimately, Shukri left the country, after embezzling the profits that he made from transactions of waqf properties. The precedent that Shukri created sparked the imagination of other Muslim activists. One day a businessman from the village of Dir al-Asad in the north of Israel named Bulous Hanna Bulous, who possessed a stone quarry that was part of the General Waqf, noticed – apparently following the advice of his Jewish lawyer – that there was a loophole in the Absentees' Properties' Law. He was advised by the secretary of the Shari'a Court of Acre, Sheik Muhammad Hubeishi (who later became a qadi of Haifa and Acre). Bulous succeeded in being appointed by the qadi at the time (Musa Tabari) as administrator of the waqf of his village. Houbashi and Bulous assumed that the government custodian is only a trustee and, because the internal administration of waqf properties under Israeli Shari'a Court law is in the hands of the Shari'a Court qadi, the qadi can appoint a trustee to replace the government custodian. The High Court upheld this assumption. Consequently, a growing number of letters of appointment of waqf administrators in urban and rural places were issued by the Shari'a Court qadis. Industrious "waqf entrepreneurs" succeeded in reclaiming urban property and subsequently selling Muslim cemeteries, all of which in turn resulted in public outrage erupting in mixed cities where Muslims live, particularly in Jaffa and Haifa.

19 The Absentees' Properties Law (Amendment No. 3) (Release and Use of Endowment Property) Law, 5725-1965.

20 N. Luz, "Self-empowerment through the sacred culture and representation in the urban landscape: The Mosque of Hassan Bey and the Arab community of Jaffa," in M. J. Breger, Y. Reiter and L. Hammer (eds), *Holy Places in the Israeli–Palestinian Conflict: Confrontation and Co-existence*, London and New York: Routledge, 2009, pp. 250–64.

21 See Y. Reiter, "Waqf in Israel Since 1965," op. cit. Genuinely devoted trustees, such as in Acre, never sold waqf properties although they could do so according to the amendment. However, the trustees of Jaffa, some of whom were fraudulent, sold off many properties and outraged the Muslim public, who therefore continued to be strongly critical of government policy. Israel's land authority, which controlled most of these properties, released only some of waqf properties in their city of jurisdiction to the new Muslim trustees. The result was that the trustees were in a bind if they wished to justify their position and even if they only wanted to properly maintain assets under their administration (let alone develop services for Muslims). They had to sell some properties simply to be able to invest their reparation money and demonstrate some activity that benefitted

the Muslim community, if only so as not to be mocked by the community as inactive puppets.

22 F. Furani, *Wathiqat Difa'an an al-Juzur an al-Awqaf al-Islamiyya fi Filastin al-Muhtalla 1948*, Amman: Dar al-Jalil, 1985 (Arabic).

23 Luz, "Self-Empowerment through the Sacred Culture."

24 R. Khamaisi, *General Survey: The Islamic Waqf: Land. Mosques and Cemeteries within the Green*-line, Kufr Barra: Al-Aqsa Association for the Protection the Islamic Waqf, 2002 (Arabic).

25 www.aqsa-mubarak.net.

26 See Articles 31–33 of HCJ 52/06 verdict.

27 Article 109 of HCJ 52/06 verdict.

28 They also argued that the custodian is permitted to release properties to the trustees but not to sell properties to others. The High Court rejected this argument because the 1965 Amendment explicitly permits the custodian to sell properties. Here the Islamic Movement also argued that the legal prohibition against the sale of mosques applies to other holy sites, such as cemeteries. This argument was also rejected in the High Court verdict (Article 117). The court cited a case from 1993 in which a Haifa court approved the custodian's sale of a cemetery in Haifa.

CHAPTER 4

The Struggle over the Jurisdiction of the Shari'a Court

The quasi-exclusive status that the State of Israel granted to the rabbinic courts regarding personal matters resulted in the state having to grant such vast jurisdiction to non-Jewish religious courts as well. The Shari'a Court apparatus in Israel therefore became the only preexisting Muslim institution that was not significantly affected by the establishment of the state in 1948. Israel permitted the Shari'a Court to retain the same jurisdictional authority granted by the British Mandate under Article 52 of the 1922 Palestine Order-in-Council, to be detailed below. In Israel as well as under British rule in Palestine, state law establishing the Shari'a Court overrides religious law and the qadis are appointed by the president of the state.[1]

The 1961 Qadis Law makes clear that qadis are subject to the laws of the state.[2] Qadis are not authorized to rule beyond the scope of the law (i.e., any rulings must be within the authority of the law). Thus, in adjudication the shari'a courts (like rabbinical courts) may not ignore the laws of the state.[3]

The High Court has the authority to override Shari'a Court rulings, but in practice such cases are rare, as with Rabbinical Court decisions. The High Court interferes in religious courts only when this intervention is essential to safeguard the basic values of society.[4] During the 1990s the Shari'a Court of Israel was socially transformed when a number of young qadis who had acquired their education in institutes of higher education in Israel were nominated. The leading reformist is Qadi Ahmad Natour.[5]

Qadi Natour has been warmly embraced by Israeli academia. He was a student of Professor Aharon Layish when he enrolled in the Hebrew University for his BA degree in Islamic Civilization and MA degree in Media and Culture Studies. He later received bachelor's and master's degrees from Tel Aviv University's Faculty of Law. In 2009 he received his doctoral degree (SJD) from Washington College at the American University in Washington, D.C. He tought Islamic law at Tel Aviv University, at the Interdisciplinary Center of Herzliya, and at Netanya Academic College, as well as in universities outside Israel. In the Mamilla affair, however, Natour has been criticized by the MoT entrepreneurs and in expert opinions written by his professors from the Hebrew University. Ironically, in 2014 Natour was appointed as professor of Law at this university.

Professor Aharon Layish, an authority on Islamic law, wrote in an expert opinion that the museum entrepreneurs submitted to the High Court that Qadi Ahmad Natour, President of the Shari'a Court of Appeals in Israel, practices as a "modernist" adjudicator, namely that he interprets the shari'a according to modern and western values in matters of personal status, yet in other matters, such as waqf and cemeteries, he is a staunch conservative. Layish hinted that Qadi Natour is not familiar with flexible rulings in the Muslim world regarding the use of cemeteries, or that his rulings are politically driven.[6]

Another expert who criticized Qadi Natour in his report to the High Court is Professor Yehoshua Porath, who wrote as follows:

> With all due respect, Qadi Ahmad Natour studied Islamic Law at the Hebrew University and not at al-Azhar (where they issued permits to accommodate Muslim Law regarding the removal of cemeteries for the needs of a modern society in accordance with the public interest). However, Qadis Tahir Hammad and Tawfiq Asaliya, who also served as presidents of the Shari'a Court of Appeals, issued legal opinions on this subject as authorities who graduated from Al-Azhar institution.[7] [The latter two qadis permitted the sale of Muslim cemeteries. Y.R.]

The criticism voiced by Layish and Porath about Natour's education is problematic in my view. It means that a graduate of a university in Israel, who took courses in Islamic law (including courses taught by Layish) is still not considered an authority in shari'a in their opinion.

Natour's position undoubtedly represents an ideological public agenda. When he served in the first instance of the Shari'a Court of Jaffa and Be'er Sheva, he issued a number of fatwas according to which a Muslim cemetery is eternally holy and cannot be rendered for any use other than burial. His opinion became the official opinion of the shari'a judicial system in Israel when he became president of the Shari'a Court of Appeals in 1996. In the process of safeguarding the independence of the Shari'a Court from the state authorities, Natour issued legal guidelines to all qadis stating that they should not allow a Muslim cemetery to be used for any purpose other than burial. His opinions and guidelines are detailed in the next chapter.

His ideological standpoint was made clear when he made the following statement in an appearance before the Knesset Committee of Internal Affairs and Environment:

> Dear friends, causing damage to Islamic holy places is one of the most severe tragedies affecting the relationship between the Muslim public

> and the Israeli public in general, and is one of the obstacles preventing amicable relations between Muslims and non-Muslims in the country. The damage inflicted on the Ma'man Allah cemetery of Mamilla is another instance in a series of desecrations of holy [Muslim] places. We recall that only a few days ago, somebody caused damage to the Jamassin Cemetery in Jaffa, and previously to the Ijzim cemetery near Haifa, as well as the cemeteries in Nesher, Eilat, Beer Sheva, Safed, and additional places that I don't want to name here. This phenomenon should be stopped. It is impossible to continue living like this . . . It is impossible to pursue tolerance in the context of a center that will be erected above human remains.[8]

Qadi Natour views the Shari'a Court as the last bastion of Islam in the state of Israel, and he acts to preserve and even to expand the autonomy of the institute that he heads. He does this in two ways. The first way is to accommodate the rulings of the Shari'a Courts to the changing reality of a developing Muslim society in the modern era, a society that is affected by the western cultural environment and norms of Israel. For example, today women can initiate divorce easily, in comparison to many other Muslim states.[9] The second way is by writing a series of legal guidelines (Marsum Qada'i), which Natour issues from time to time and which all qadis have to sign and commit themselves to uphold.[10] These legal guidelines have no authority under Israeli law, and their validity has yet to be subjected to legal examination (to date there have been no appeals to the High Court complaining that anyone's rights were violated by these guidelines). Natour's guidelines to qadis aim to create a unified ruling policy inspired by his personal interpretation of Islamic law and the interpretations of qadis who follow in his footsteps. Interestingly, the Ministry of Justice uploads these guidelines to its official website, stating that "These legal guidelines are a tool to shape shari'a judicial policy and are issued by the president of the Shari'a Court of Appeals in agreement with the qadis with regard to substantive and procedural issues, and they apply to all of the shari'a courts in the state." The Ministry of Justice thus grants legitimacy to these guidelines.[11]

Since Qadi Natour was appointed as president of the Shari'a Court of Appeals, the Islamic Movement in its two factions, the Northern and Southern Faction, has welcomed his authority, and generally they have not challenged the interpretation of the Shari'a Court. There exists some level of collaboration between the shari'a courts and the activists from the two Islamic Movements in Israel, as well as mutual inspiration between the two. For example, qadis make use of Islamist activists in the shari'a court as arbitrators in marital disputes and as experts and witnesses in court procedures.[12] The shari'a courts and the Islamists share some mutual interests. The shari'a court benefits from the broad public support and legitimacy of the Islamic Movements' followers, while the activists receive respect, public legitimacy, and compensation for quasi-legal positions (the parties to a dispute pay the expenses of arbitrators and experts) from the shari'a court qadis.

The mere fact that state authorities and Jewish enterprises used to ask qadis to issue fatwas permitting the sale of old abandoned Muslim cemeteries for development purposes drove Qadi Natour to conclude that determining the holiness of a cemetery or the removal of its sacredness is the exclusive jurisdiction of the shari'a courts. Moreover, in many cases Israeli civil courts validated fatwas of shari'a court qadis by respecting the qadis' opinions regarding Muslim holy places in disputes over the sale or use of waqf properties and holy sites, without questioning the legal authority of the qadis in issuing the fatwas.

The group of academics and civil society organizations' representatives who joined the High Court hearing against the construction of the MoT in Mamilla argued that the question of whether the cemetery is holy or not should be left to the decision of the Shari'a Court, saying, "in the same way that Halachic questions are determined by rabbis and not by researchers of halacha, so the High Court should respect the religious autonomy of the community of Muslim believers in Israel and the adjudications of their religious leaders." They meant that the High Court should respect the position of the president of the Shari'a Court of Appeals, Qadi Ahmad Natour, in the same way that it respects the decisions of rabbis regarding Jewish cemeteries in Israel, rather than using experts on Jewish law. The academics also criticized their faculty colleagues who supported the MoT through expert opinions that emphasized the ambivalent position of shari'a regarding modern development works in ancient Muslim cemeteries. The expert opinion written by Professor Shimon Shamir stressed this point:

> The Muslim citizens of Israel would be especially enflamed if a decision were made to rescind the holiness of a cemetery on the basis of an interpretation by Jewish experts on Islam. From their viewpoint it would be a twofold expropriation: the expropriation of the cemetery itself and the expropriation of their right to determine the ruling in accordance with their religion. Imagine that an Arab court in an Arab state would allow construction on top of an old Jewish cemetery based on the interpretation of Arab experts on Jewish law, as opposed to the opinions of rabbis who prohibit such works. Like Jews, who would never tolerate such a situation, so too Muslims will never accept the uprooting of part of the Mamilla Cemetery on the basis of a ruling by *Jewish sages of Shari'a*.[13]

Shamir added that "from the perspective of the Arab public in general, the ruling of Sheikh Ahmad Natour, the president of the Shari'a Court of Appeals, who prohibited the construction of the Museum of Tolerance on the Mamilla Cemetery, has unquestionable validity."[14] Israeli Middle East Studies faculties were split between those who supported Shamir and those who endorsed construction of the MoT in Mamilla. Moral and ideological positions, on the one hand, and personal relations with the experts who sided with each of the parties to the dispute, on the other hand, formed the basis of this split.

The position taken by Natour and the Shari'a Court created a turning point in the Mamilla affair and submitted the jurisdiction of the Shari'a Court to examination by the High Court.

One month after the Al-Aqsa Corporation petitioned the High Court, another association, Karama, submitted a parallel petition to the Shari'a Court of Jerusalem in the name of three Palestinian dignitaries from Jerusalem. The family names of at least two of these dignitaries are historic and iconic identity symbols of the city under Muslim control. The three dignitaries declared in their affidavit to the court that their ancestors are buried where the museum is being erected, yet none of them could prove that his relative was buried precisely where the Museum construction was to take place. Muhammad Zaki al-Din al-Dajani, born in 1936, claimed that one of his forefathers, Sheikh Ahmad al-Dajani, who had been a city notable, was buried in the Ma'man Allah Cemetery in 1820, and his burial place is visible. Consequently, his grave could not be in the plot planned for the museum, where the graves are beneath ground. Muhammad Zaki Abd al-Rahim Nusseiheh and Muhammad Hamdi Abd Zayn claimed that their relatives told them that their grandfather is buried in this place. This fact weakened their claims of infliction of emotional distress. A man who does not know exactly where his close relative is buried and who never visited the grave in person would find it difficult to convince a court that removal of the grave from its original place will cause severe emotional distress that justifies overriding the general public interest. Nevertheless, knowing that one's relative is buried in a certain cemetery is an indication of emotional attachment. It should be noted that East Jerusalem Palestinians filed their petition with the Israeli West Jerusalem shari'a court because only an Israeli judiciary's verdict could be legally enforced in Jerusalem.

In their petition of February 2006, which was heard by the Israeli Qadi of Jerusalem Muhammad Rashid Zibde, the three dignitaries claimed that the MoT, the State of Israel, and the Jerusalem Municipality illegally took over the cemetery grounds.[15] The plaintiffs therefore requested that the qadi, in his capacity as the supreme overseer of waqfs under his jurisdiction, appoint two mutawallis to the Mamilla Cemetery. Their request stated that the appointed mutawallis should act to prevent damage to the cemetery and should sue the government's Custodian of Absentees' Properties and demand that he cancel any land transaction that could cause damage to the cemetery. They argued that the cemetery is a holy waqf property and that the Custodian's takeover and sale of the land are null and void in legal terms. Waqf, they claimed, is inalienable and unsellable, and the holiness of a cemetery is eternal. They added that the Israeli legislature of 1965 had rescinded the waqf status applicable to family waqfs, not that of the General Waqf, and especially not the waqf status of holy sites such as cemeteries and mosques. The Muslim plaintiffs claimed that Article 52 of the 1922 Palestine Order-in-Council regarding the authority of the Shari'a Court, which had been adopted by the State of Israel, did not grant Qadi Tahir Hammad or the Shari'a Court headed by him the authority to abolish a waqf. The Shari'a Court's Qadi Muhammad Zibde accepted their arguments, issued a provisional decree ordering the cessation of works on the disputed land, and instructed the police to enforce this decree. In addition, he appointed two mutawallis for the cemetery, instructing them to take any action necessary to protect the cemetery.

Given the position of the Shari'a Court, it is clear why the Northern Islamic Movement realized at some stage that appealing to the High Court would not yield the result they sought and hence the Shari'a Court is the proper venue to pursue its goal. Sheikh Raed Salah expressed distrust in the High Court, referring to another case that the High Court heard during the same period (regarding the right of Jews to enter the Al-Haram Al-Sharif/Temple Mount complex on the Jewish holiday of *Tisha B'Av*), when he stated, "The Israeli High Court has no right to rule on any matter regarding the blessed Al-Aqsa Mosque. The High Court's verdict has dangerous implications at present and for the future."[16]

Regarding the High Court's hearing on Mamilla, Sheikh Salah said the following:

> Indeed, we have no expectations from this court because we have not seen Israeli courts rule justly, and I am concerned that the court will reverse the situation, causing the loss of our rights in this cemetery, and will validate the Israeli–American usurpation of this cemetery. Therefore, we try to preempt these events; *we try to preempt the official Israeli [actions] and to impose our rights in this cemetery, and with God's will, we shall succeed.*[17] [Emphasis added.]

Sheik Raed Salah's final sentence was a reference to a campaign for the cleaning and upkeep of the Mamilla Cemetery that his movement had initiated without a permit, claiming that they were acting in accordance with the Shari'a Court's appointment of mutawallis to administer the cemetery and protect the cemetery.[18]

Qadi Zibde wrote that Tahir Hammad's decision of 1964 rescinding the holiness of the cemetery had been issued by the Jaffa Shari'a Court within its particular jurisdiction regarding the founding of waqf and its internal administration. Hence, the Shari'a Court of Jerusalem has the authority to adjudicate regarding that opinion and its outcomes. He added that the legal issue to be heard is a purely religious and legal question dealing with the holiness of a Muslim cemetery, and that these rules are applicable because it is registered as a true and complete waqf (*waqf sahih*). Therefore, a civil court has no authority to hear this case.

The interference of the Shari'a Court in the dispute while it was being heard in the High Court created tension between two tribunals of different jurisdiction and status. The advocates of the Muslim plaintiffs requested that the High Court leave the decision regarding the eternal holiness of the disputed land to the Shari'a Court. Advocate Durgham Sayf argued on behalf of the Muslim plaintiffs that because the museum entrepreneurs relied on Islamic law in the expert opinions they had submitted to the court to defend their positions, it is only proper that the venue to adjudicate the religious legal question be the Shari'a Court. He stated, "The Shari'a Court should be respected and not ignored."[19]

The MoT entrepreneurs and the state authorities involved in the case understood all too well the Islamic Movement's tactics, which were backed by the Shari'a Court, to circumvent the legal procedure in the High Court, and they reacted immediately. When the Shari'a Court issued its decree, the state's advocate requested the Shari'a Court to immediately invalidate the decree, which had been issued in absence of the defendants. In their request to the court, they wrote that the Shari'a Court had no authority to deal with this issue. The state's advocate appealed the Jerusalem qadi's decision, claiming that the Shari'a Court had no jurisdiction to hear this case given the substantive issue (absentees' properties ceased to be waqf following amendment of the Absentees' Properties Law in 1965) and given that a parallel case was being heard in the High Court. Therefore the Shari'a Court should not intervene in the affairs of another judicial authority. The Shari'a Court rejected this last argument, writing that consideration of a fatwa from 1964 has no connection to the procedure underway place at the High Court.[20]

The lower Shari'a Court decided to reject the state's appeal, ruling that it had the authority to consider the matter. The state then appealed this decision to the Shari'a Court of Appeals. The hearing on the appeal was delayed several times while the parties participated in a mediation process facilitated by the former president of the High Court. In the meantime the police refused to implement the decree of the Shari'a Court to halt the digging and the removal of human remains from the disputed plot. The Karama Association then appealed to the High Court, requesting it to order the police to enforce the Shari'a Court decree.[21] The MoT entrepreneurs also petitioned the High Court, requesting that it declare that the Shari'a Court lacks the jurisdiction to consider the dispute. As a result, the High Court issued an intermediate decree prohibiting the Shari'a Court from hearing the dispute.

The intervention of the Shari'a Court generated a state of competition between two tribunals, one of them religious and the other the highest civil state tribunal, regarding the authority to adjudicate this case. At this stage the Karama Association submitted to the High Court a report written by an academic expert, Dr. Issachar Rosen Zvi.[22] His report did not refer to the question of under whose jurisdiction applied, but to the question of whether it was appropriate that the High Court rule in this matter or, alternatively, allow the process to proceed in the Shari'a Court. The report aimed to convince the High Court that it is improper to intervene in issues that come under the jurisdiction of a religious court. Rosen Zvi argued that the High Court itself had established a judicial approach according to which similar cases should be determined by the religious court before they were submitted to the High Court. He analyzed the High Court's doctrine of alternative judicial remedy, which holds that the High Court will not hear a case when another judicial institution has authority over the same matter. According to him, the Shari'a Court had parallel authority to the High Court in this case. Another argument put forward by Dr. Rosen Zvi was that the dispute is of a civil rather than administrative nature, and the High Court of Justice serves as a tribunal for reviewing the administrative actions of state authorities. Hence a purely civil dispute should be left to the decision of the Shari'a Court. The High Court rejected both of Rosen Zvi's arguments.

Justice Ayala Procaccia wrote in her verdict regarding this matter as follows:

> The long delay in submission of the Dajani complaint to the Shari'a Court, the lack of good faith entailed in filing a petition with the Shari'a Court on a matter that is being heard in the High Court, and the resulting damage to the entrepreneurs all constitute exceptional circumstances that justify deviation from the alternative judicial aid doctrine. Moreover, and most importantly, it is impossible to disassociate the questions related to the authority of the Shari'a Court, the secondary issue in these petitions, from the central issues that are being heard in the main case before the High court, which challenge the legitimacy of the construction in the compound where the remains of Muslim graves were found.[23]

The MoT entrepreneurs for their part used another ruling of Justice Procaccia from 2003 regarding the authority of the Rabbinical Court, in which she stated, "A judicial instance should not exceed its recognized boundaries and venture beyond its granted jurisdiction".[24]

The MoT entrepreneurs claimed that the Shari'a Court is like a rabbinical court in which jurisdiction is defined by the state laws. They added that in 1964, when Qadi Tahir Hammad issued the fatwa changing the use of the cemetery, the land was still a waqf. However, the status of this land was ultimately and retroactively changed by the 1965 amendment to the Absentees' Properties Law. They emphasized that a fatwa is a legal opinion issued by a religious sage, and therefore another sage can express a different opinion but cannot rescind the opinion of a sage. They added that in 1964 Qadi Hammad had been requested to provide a legal opinion as a senior religious sage who was a graduate of Al-Azhar (and not as a judge or qadi). Therefore, there was no place for a legal procedure to rescind his opinion. According to them, what Dajani and the other two Palestinian plaintiffs requested of the Shari'a Court was a ruling that Qadi Hammad, "did not hold the opinion that he himself expressed in his fatwa!!!"

It is noteworthy that although the MoT entrepreneurs presented Tahir Hammad's 1964 "*qarar-fatwa*" to the High Court as a fatwa and not as a judicial decision (*qarar*), in responding to criticism directed at the MoT project in 2010, they termed the same document a "judgment" of the highest Muslim religious authority in Israel as well as a final and non-appealable decision.[25]

They argued further that the urgency demonstrated by the Shria'a Court emanated from its drive to preempt the High Court and establish a *fait accompli* before the High Court dealt with the dispute.

The challenge the Shari'a Court created for the High Court forced the latter to address the authority of the Shari'a Court and to intervene in reformulating its jurisdiction. The High Court indicated that the authority of the Shari'a Court emanated from Article 52 of the Palestine Order-in-Council (1922–1947), which states, "Moslem Religious Courts shall have . . . exclusive jurisdiction in cases of the constitution or internal administration of a waqf constituted for the benefit of Moslems before a Moslem Religious Court."

The High Court interpreted the Order-in-Council as granting the Shari'a Court authority only in two limited actions concerning waqf issues: constitution or internal administration of a waqf. They accepted the attorney general's claim that the disputed land was not a waqf endowment approved by a Muslim court. In addition, there was no evidence of an endowment deed. They also concluded that the jurisdiction of the Shari'a Court did not include disputes over the use of land that was under the substantive jurisdiction of civil courts.[26]

As for the first conclusion, indeed the Mamilla Cemetery has no endowment deed because most of the old Muslim cemeteries were spontaneously created in public spaces, rather than on private land that one can endow as waqf or as a result of a specific action of dedication. However, the continuous practice over generations has been that all Muslim cemeteries have waqf status, and thus the Mamilla Cemetery was registered in the land registry of 1938 under the General Waqf Administrator, *Ma'mur al-Awqaf*. The British Mandate government never intervened regarding the status and uses of a cemetery. Even the Jerusalem Municipality, when it planned to alter the status of the cemetery of Mamilla in 1964, approached a Shari'a Court qadi, not a civil court. Therefore, in my opinion, the High Court verdict in this case is incomplete. As for the second conclusion of the High Court, I believe that the court did not understand the true significance of the term "internal administration of waqf." Waqf administration has fallen under the jurisdiction and authority of the Shari'a Courts of the land since the Ottoman period, as evidenced by the court records (*sijillat*), which include cases granting permission for actions in waqf properties such as exchange, sale, development, maintenance, and change of designated use, as well as cases dealing with disputes over what is permitted or prohibited regarding waqf assets. In other words, all the actions that come under the authority of the mutawalli of waqf also fall under the jurisdiction of the Shari'a Court. This jurisdiction therefore applies to the Mamilla Cemetery only if it is waqf property. Put differently, the Shari'a Court is authorized to appoint waqf administrators and to guide them as to how to treat the properties they administer. Yet the High Court ruled that since 1965 the Mamilla Cemetery is no longer a waqf property according to civil law, and hence the Shari'a Court has no substantive authority to deal with a dispute over Mamilla and the MoT.

The High Court's rejection of the authority of the Shari'a Court to deal with the disputed land in Mamilla is anchored in the Absentees' Properties Law. The 1965 amendment to this law stated that General Waqf assets are retroactively owned by the Custodian of Absentees' Properties. Therefore the waqf status of the land was rendered obsolete, and the Shari'a Court had no jurisdiction to deal with it. The effective and legal revocation of the waqf status from the cemetery is based on this 1965 amendment, not on the fatwa issued by Qadi Tahir Hammad in 1964 at the request of the mayor of Jerusalem. That fatwa was primarily intended to grant moral and religious legitimacy for the action in the eyes of the public. It is doubtful whether it holds any legal validity. Using the Absentees' Properties Law, in 1992 the government custodian sold the Mamilla Cemetery to the Development Authority, a government entity, and therefore the Shari'a Court had no jurisdiction over this land. This was the main justification for the High Court verdict, which held that the dispute regarding the construction of the MoT on this particular site did not come under Shari'a Court jurisdiction. Therefore, the Shari'a Court had overstepped its jurisdiction in issuing decrees on this matter. Moreover, the Shari'a Court had no authority to issue decrees for the state institutions (including the police) to take proactive action. This was yet another case of the Shari'a Court overstepping its jurisdiction. In addition, the High Court strongly criticized the Muslim plaintiffs for the long delay in submitting their case to the Shari'a Court and for doing so only after a complaint was submitted to the High Court, hence not acting in good faith. The High Court's remarks were also an indirect criticism of the Shari'a Court for its two instances of intervention in the Mamilla affair.

The High Court dealt another blow to the standing of the shari'a court system through the issue of how to rebury the human remains that had been disinterred. One might expect that the justices would instruct the defendants to rebury the bones in a respectful manner and in accordance with Muslim rules, but the problem is that it is unclear what religious authority would be in charge of such a process. In Jerusalem there is no Muslim burial authority (with the exception of the East Jerusalem Waqf Administration, which has no jurisdiction in West Jerusalem). Given that the Shari'a Court was disqualified from dealing with the case, the question arose as to who is the appropriate Muslim authority to handle the reburial of hundreds of human remains. The High Court justices ruled in the following manner:

The burial arrangements . . . shall be conducted in cooperation with and under the supervision of the Antiquities Authority, as well as the authority responsible for planning and construction in cemeteries within the Ministry of Religious Services. We assume that the authority within the ministry will consult with the leadership of the Muslim community in Israel before taking a decision.

Thus, the High Court instructed the state institutions and the museum entrepreneurs to deal with this question in consultation with the Muslim leadership, without defining who this authority actually is, thereby leaving all possible options open. Unlike Justice Meir Shamgar, who ruled in 1988 that Qadi Tawfiq 'Asalia should decide the dispute regarding a cemetery in Umm al-Fahm (see the next chapter), in the Mamilla affair the High Court refrained from vesting even this purely religious task in the hands of the Shari'a Court. Moreover, for their own reasons the Shari'a Courts tended not to cooperate in the task of reburying human remains. When this issue was raised in a hearing of the Knesset Committee of Internal Affairs and Environment, Qadi Ahmad Natour stated, "I am saying explicitly that the qadis will not cooperate in transferring the bones and they will not negotiate with these people. We think that they are committing a crime. The qadis will not communicate with them as a matter of principle and will not even listen to a corrupt proposal that they put forward."[27]

Since the qadis did not cooperate in the reburial of the unearthed bones, it is unclear which Muslim authority the Prime Minister's Office approached regarding the reburial of the human remains.

In conclusion, the dispute over the compound designated for construction of the MoT in Mamilla played a significant role in reformulating the status, authority, and jurisdiction of the Shari'a Court system in Israel regarding waqf issues and holy places such as cemeteries. The Shari'a Court under President Qadi Ahmad Natour tested the boundaries of its jurisdiction. The qadis (as well as the Muslim plaintiffs) believed that they were the authentic representatives of Islamic law in Israel. They believed that they would be able to convince the High Court justices that only official religious clerics should be authorized to rule on the following questions: whether a certain place is holy; whether holiness can be revoked and through what procedure; whether a cemetery has waqf status; the meaning of this status (eternal or revocable); and the validity of a fatwa issued in a particular case, including the question of whether such legal opinion can be revoked due to changing circumstances. Apparently they believed that the High Court, which generally embraces liberal values in its rulings and refrains as much as possible from intervention in the affairs of religious courts, would likewise refrain in the Mamilla case. They were mistaken, however. Moreover, Qadi Natour apparently expected that his previous rulings on Muslim cemeteries would be accepted by the High Court, as they had been accepted previously by lower civil courts.

The Muslim plaintiffs engaged in a process of "forum shopping" (seeking the most favorable jurisdiction), and the delay in submitting the case to the Shari'a Court suggests that they did not act in good faith. If the major case submitted by the Al-Aqsa Corporation had been submitted to the Shari'a Court rather than the High Court in the first place, I doubt the High Court would have overruled a decision of a qadi. However, filing the case in the Shari'a Court was a clear attempt to circumvent the High Court and to create a *fait accompli.* The High Court justices viewed this action as an attempt to ignore and circumvent the High Court.

The consequences that followed severely undermined the status and authority of the Shari'a Court, which was strongly criticized by the High Court for overstepping its jurisdiction. The High Court ruling on the Mamilla dispute essentially abolished the accepted practice of district and magistrate courts of taking into account the legal opinions of the Shari'a Court of Appeals regarding abandoned Muslim holy places. In addition, the High Court issued a precedential verdict that revokes the Shari'a Court's authority to deal with properties that previously belonged to the General Waqf. Moreover, the High Court verdict also revoked the Shari'a Court's jurisdiction to issue decrees for proactive action to the police in order to enforce Shari'a Court decisions.

Finally, the High Court's dealing with the status of the Muslim shari'a courts in Israel actually serves as a microcosm of the status of the (predominantly Muslim) Arab minority in Israel. The Shari'a Court is a semi-autonomous institution of the Arab minority. Restricting its authority means restricting the rights and status of the Arab minority in Israel. This fact was reflected in the words of Advocate Hussein Abu-Hussein in the High Court: "Why step on 15% of the citizens of Israel? Why spit in our face on a regular basis? . . . The whole issue of the law of human dignity and freedom doesn't touch us? I would expect to be given the feeling that I am part of this system."[28]

These words echoed throughout the High Court hall but were not embraced by the justices.

Notes

1 They are appointed following the recommendation of a committee of nine members: two qadis, two government ministers, three members of Knesset (of whom two must be Muslim) and two advocates (at least one of whom must be Muslim). In other words Muslim members have a majority on the committee responsible for the selection of qadis. Israel's minister of justice (in the past it had been the minister of religious affairs) has the authority to nominate the president of the Shari'a Court of Appeals for a limited time or for a life term. The qadis are sworn in by the president of the State of Israel and commit themselves to remaining loyal to the state and judging people justly.

2 Article 9 of the 1961 Qadis Law (amending a previous law of 1953).

3 For example, they cannot recognize the marriage of minors (according to the definition of minors under state law); they cannot approve polygamous marriage, and if they do, they would be prosecuted under criminal law. On the impact of the Knesset legislation on personal shari'a matters in Israel, see Y. Reiter, "Qadis and the implementation of Islamic Law in present day Israel" in R. Gleave and U.

Kermeli (eds), *Islamic Law in Theory and Practice* London and New York: I. B. Tauris, 1997, pp. 205–231; M. Abou Ramadan and D. Monterescu, "Islamic justice in a 'Jewish and democratic' state: Cooptation and Islamization of the shari'a field," *Mishpat U-Mimshal* 11:2, 2008, 435–73 (Hebrew); A. Layish, "The adaptation of a religious legal system to the modern period in a foreign surrounding: The shari'a in Israel," Proceedings of the Israel Academy (Hebrew Series), vol. IX, no. 2, 2005, pp. 13–51. There are two problems regarding implementation of the Qadis Law and practicing shari'a jurisprudence in Israel. The first problem involves the training of qadis in shari'a. In post-1948 Israel, there were only five graduates of the high-ranking institute for shari'a studies, Al-Azhar University in Cairo, who served as qadis of the Shari'a Court. Yet it was unclear in which track they had trained at Al-Azhar and for how many years. For example, Sheikh Tawfiq Asaliya, who served as president of the Shari'a Court during the 1970s and 1980s and approved the sale of or construction on Muslim cemeteries, is considered a graduate of Al-Azhar.

The professors who submitted expert opinions on behalf of the MoT conveyed that Asaliya was in fact an Al-Azhar graduate. However, in 1947, when Israel's war of independence broke out, Asaliya was only 22 years old. It is unclear how many years he studied at Al-Azhar. In contrast, Qadi Tahir Hammad, who rescinded the sanctity of most of the Mamilla Cemetery, not only graduated from Al-Azhar but also served as a teacher at this institute. The situation is even more severe today. Since those five Al-Azhar graduates (most of whom are now deceased), Israel within the Green Line has no Muslim graduates of an institute of advanced shari'a instruction such as Al-Azhar University in Cairo. On the higher education of qadis, see Y. Reiter, "Qadis and the implementation of Islamic Law in present day Israel," op. cit. The law today states that qadis should "acquire a high religious education of shari'a and Islam to the satisfaction of the Committee of Appointments, or he should be a lawyer and member of the Bar Association who has practiced law for at least five years." The law also states that a candidate for the position of qadi should be examined by another committee headed by the president of the Shari'a Court of Appeals with the participation of one Muslim Knesset member and a former qadi or an advocate nominated by the minister of justice. Qadis can learn *shari'a* informally at Israeli universities in accordance with the western system of critical science and research, but not from a religious outlook. The exposure of a student to Islamic law during an academic track in the departments of Middle East history or in the law schools is limited because the number of courses and subjects in their curriculum is limited. Hence, Israeli qadis have to complete their knowledge of shari'a independently, whether by reading Islamic sources on their own or, alternatively, by following the rulings and phrases of previous qadis. The second problem is the lack of a position of mufti in the state of Israel. A mufti is an expert in Islamic law whose legal opinion is non-binding but contributes to the development of the shari'a, accommodating it to the circumstances of a specific time and place, while qadis are expected not to divert from the existing law unless a fatwa was submitted to them, which they can adopt if they wish as an interpretation of shari'a law. Hence, in the case of Israel, qadis in fact also act as interpreters of the shari'a. See Y. Reiter, "Judge reform: Facilitating divorce by shari'a courts in Israel," *Journal of Islamic Law and Culture,* 11:1, March 2009, 13–38.

4 See E. Nave, "Implementation of shari'a in 20th century civil courts: A compara-

tive study of adjudication in personal status and waqf issues of Muslims in a Muslim country (Egypt) and a non-Muslim country (Israel)," PhD dissertation, Hebrew University, 1997 (Hebrew).

5 Another important change in the status of the shari'a courts occurred in 2002, when the Knesset amended the Qadis Law, transferring authority over the shari'a court system from the minister of religious affairs to the minister of justice. The minister of justice has respected the independence of the shari'a court system more than it was previously respected.

6 Expert Opinion of 5 January 2006 submitted to the High Court (Hebrew).

7 Expert Opinion of 25 April 2007 submitted to the High Court (Hebrew).

8 Minutes 566 from 15 February 2006, available on the Knesset website: www.knesset.gov.il/protocols/data/rtf/pnim/2006-02-15.rtf (Hebrew).

9 See Reiter, "Judge reform," op. cit.

10 See I. Zahalqa, *The Shari'a Courts between Adjudication and Identity*, Jerusalem: Bar Association, 2009 (Hebrew).

11 http://www.justice.gov.il/MOJHeb/BatiDinHashreim/MaagreiMeida/Minsharim (Hebrew). See also I. Shahar,"Legal reform, interpretive communities and the quest for legitimacy: A contextual analysis of a legal circular" in R. Shaham (ed.), *Custom, Shari'a, and Statute in the Muslim World: Studies in Honor of Aharon Layish* (Leiden: Brill, 2007). An example of the accommodation of Israeli shari'a court rulings to universalized western norms based on re-interpretation of Islamic law under the leadership of Qadi Natour is the issue of custodianship over children in cases of divorce. The 1962 Legal Capacity and Custodianship Law requires that custodianship of children in a divorce case be determined by the best interests of the child. This principle differs from the ruling of Muslim jurists who grant preference to the father in accordance with the age and physical condition of the child (fathers are granted custody of boys at age six and of girls at age nine; until then mothers have custody). Today, Israeli shari'a courts, being subject to state laws, use social workers to determine the best interests of the child before making their decisions. Qadi Natour himself uses the tools of state law, but he ordered the qadis not to mention the civil law of the state as a basis or reference in their rulings, only the shari'a. Natour developed an innovative interpretation in this context, arguing that the age-based principle of the *shari'a* in this case was determined by the divine lawgiver in accordance with the principle of the best interests of the child as perceived in the past. Hence, shari'a should not be interpreted according to the literal written text but according to "the legislator's intention." In other words, shari'a also adopts the doctrine of the best interests of the child. In terms of the outcome of such verdicts, the result is the same. However, the qadi's decisions draw legitimacy from shari'a rather than state law. Some would view Qadi Natour's order as a challenge to the legitimacy of the State of Israel; others would consider it a pragmatic approach that allows Israeli qadis to maneuver between their Muslim identity and principal commitment to religious law, on the one hand, and their Israeli citizenship and practicing within the framework of the society and law of the state of Israel, on the other hand.

12 See Reiter, "Judge Reform," op. cit.; A. Natur, "The battle for the Muslim cemeteries in Jerusalem," in M. J. Breger, Y. Reiter, and L. Hammer (eds), *Religion and Politics: Sacred Space in Palestine and Israel*, London and New York: Routledge, 2012, pp. 168–192.

13 Expert Opinion of 25 February 2007 submitted to the High Court (Hebrew).

14 Ibid.
15 Jerusalem Shari'a Court file 254/06 (Arabic).
16 Nazareth local radio station, 4 August 2006, as quoted from the Islamic Movement website: http://www.islamic.aqsa.com/ar/modules.php?name= News & file=print&sid=987; http://www.islamic.aqsa.com/ar/modules.php?name=News&file=print&sid=987 (Arabic) accessed 9 September 2006.
17 http://www.pls48.net/News.php?name quoted in Article 249 of a proclamation submitted to the High Court on 3 January 2007 (Hebrew).
18 Article 250 of a proclamation submitted by the MoT entrepreneurs to the High Court on 3 January 2007 (Hebrew).
19 High Court hearing of 3 October 2006 (Hebrew).
20 Jerusalem Shari'a Court file 254/06.007 (Hebrew).
21 High Court file 1331/06 Muhammad Khayr al-Dajani vs. Israel Police et al. (Hebrew).
22 Expert Opinion of 22 December 2006 submitted to the High Court (Hebrew).
23 Article 81 of HCJ 52/06 (Hebrew).
24 HCJ 8638/03 Simma Amir vs. The Great Rabbinic Court of Jerusalem et al. (Hebrew).
25 R. Israeli, S. Berkovits, J. Neriah, and M. Hier, "The architecture of erasure – fantasy or reality?" *Critical Inquiry* 36:3 (2010) 582.
26 Articles 75–80 of HCJ 52/06 (Hebrew).
27 When this issue was raised in a hearing of the Knesset Committee of Internal Affairs and Environment, Committee Chair Ghaleb Majadla asked IAA Director Yehoshua Dorfman, "who is the Muslim moderate, not a fanatic, a moderate official, formal authority, appointed by the State of Israel, and being paid by the state, that you contacted regarding this question? Not Sheikh Raed Salah, but a person who is on the state payroll, who was appointed formally by the state, who is recognized as representing the Muslims?" Dorfman responded, "I do not know of such an authority, I know only the Prime Minister's Office." The representative of the Ministry of Interior who spoke at the same hearing, Ya'aqub Salama (a Druze in charge of religious services for non-Jewish communities), said, "I would like to say, that we support what has been said here. We are against any desecration of a holy place, particularly graves. The dignity of the dead equals the dignity of the living person, and there is no difference between the two. A holy place is holy to each community. We are definitely against the desecration of graves." Minutes 566 from 15 February 2006, available on the Knesset website: www.knesset.gov.il/protocols/data/rtf/pnim/2006-02-15.rtf (Hebrew).
28 High Court session of 3 October 2006 (Hebrew).

CHAPTER 5

The Sanctity of Cemeteries in Islam: Science, Belief, and Interpretation

Does Islamic law permit the removal of a grave or building over a Muslim cemetery, and if so, under what conditions? The shari'a is not unequivocal in this matter, and as we shall see in this chapter, the answers to the above questions vary, depending on legal interpretation.

We will discuss below the tensions resulting from the confrontation between academic experts on Islamic law and Muslim clerics regarding interpretation of the Mamilla dispute. The MoT entrepreneurs provided the High Court with a series of expert opinions by professors of Islam and Middle East history and holy places, some of whom were Jewish and others Muslim, with one Christian living and teaching abroad. The Al-Aqsa Corporation also provided an expert opinion by a local Muslim professor. In addition to these opinions, qadis issued fatwas, even though they are not experts in *ifta'* (the writing of a legal opinion), because Israel has no official fatwa-issuing institution as other Muslim countries have.

When a strong controversy involving contrasting interpretations erupts, the position that typically prevails is the one belonging to those with greater political power. In the case of Mamilla, the powerful party is the MoT entrepreneurs and the state institutions that have the same position, which has been further buttressed by academic experts.

The mechanism for determining the position of shari'a in a matter such as Mamilla is a petition before a learned sage of shari'a seeking his response in a form of a fatwa.[1] The fatwa institution has been extremely important in the development of Islamic law and in its accommodation to the changing needs of Muslim society. Islamic law differentiates between adjudication and interpretation of the law. Authority for adjudication rests in the hands of the shari'a court qadis, whose task is to resolve disputes in accordance with the law and local custom. It is not the task of the qadis, and usually it is not within their expertise, to provide an interpretation of the law on ambivalent legal issues. The mufti, however, is an expert with broad knowledge of Islamic law and usually with more education than a qadi would have. The mufti provides responses to specific or general questions based on his interpretation of shari'a. The separation between the judicial role and the provision of a legal opinion is expressed in Islamic discourse in the following phrase: *Al-mufti la yaqdi, wal-qadi la yufti*, meaning that the qadi should not issue a fatwa and the mufti is not authorized to judge and adjudicate.[2] This separation between the authorities of the qadi and the mufti emerged in an early stage of the development of Islamic law (during the early days of Islam, religious sages fulfilled a number of legal and religious tasks simultaneously) and was intended to prevent situations in which a qadi issues a legal opinion, as occurred in the case of the Mamilla Cemetery.

What is the ongoing Islamic practice in such cases? When private individuals or public authorities seek to excavate a grave, remove it from its original place, or change the purpose of a burial plot, they petition a mufti (the question is termed *istifta'*). The mufti then studies the specific case details presented in the petition, including the relevant facts specified, and he responds by issuing an opinion supported by legal sources, including previously issued fatwas. The mufti rarely issues an answer that would be unsatisfactory to the petitioner. In this sense, the mufti serves as a "professional legal advisor" (in most cases he is also paid for issuing his opinion). Anyone who is not satisfied with the response provided by the mufti can petition another mufti in the hope of obtaining a different legal opinion suitable to his or her interests. Moreover, two parties to a dispute could petition different muftis and receive opposing responses.[3] Therefore, the fatwa is not a binding legal decision and in practice the reputation and professional authority of the issuing mufti play a decisive role in determining the extent of the fatwa's implementation. It only has the authority of a recommendation. Its role is to grant religious legal legitimacy to an action and to the position of the petitioner and to try to resolve an issue in light of changing circumstances and urgency.

The removal of a grave from its original place or the change of a Muslim cemetery's function and status would reach a qadi for adjudication only if a dispute was submitted for judgment. For example, if somebody purchased land to construct a house and during the course of digging found human remains and decided to remove them in order to rebury elsewhere and continue building his house, then other people who believe that their relatives were buried in this place can file a petition with the shari'a court, demanding cessation of the construction even if the owner had obtained a fatwa supporting his action. The qadi will decide in accordance with his personal outlook and the local custom in answering this question. As noted, the shari'a has more than one answer regarding how to resolve such a debatable issue. Most likely, the land owner will provide the qadi with a fatwa that supports resumption of work and his opponents will present an opposing fatwa. The qadi is not obliged to accept any of the fatwas presented.[4]

The non-binding and voluntary nature of a fatwa opens the door to a legal loophole. The mufti does not see examination of the facts presented to him by the petitioner as part of his duty. Even in dealing with an actual case, the fatwa that he issues is based on how the petitioner presented the facts to him, and he will respond as if the question were theoretical. As a result, in many cases the muftis' responses are unsuitable to the relevant objective facts. A good example is a dispute in which the Israeli Northern Islamic Movement was involved regarding a piece of land adjacent to the Church of Annunciation in Nazareth, which the Nazareth Municipality had designated for the construction of a public plaza. The Islamic Movement sought to have a mosque (the Shihab al-Din Mosque) constructed there instead. The Islamic Movement and the Nazareth Waqf Administrator petitioned the Chief Mufti of Jordan, requesting that he issue a response justifying construction of the mosque, and their petition included "facts" that the Nazareth Municipality rejected as fabricated (for example, a sketch from a nineteenth century travel guide to which a line was added to create the illusion that the entire plot of disputed land belonged to the waqf, and an argument that a school that had existed there was a religious school that served also as a mosque).[5] When the Christian mayor of Nazareth, Ramez Jeraisy, saw the fatwa, he traveled to Jordan with official documents disproving the "facts" as presented to the mufti of Jordan, and the latter issued a new fatwa overturning his previous decision.[6]

All of these ways to manipulate a fatwa are directly relevant to the case of Mamilla. As we will see below, the person who issued the fatwa that permitted works in the cemetery was a qadi, not a mufti. His opinion has no valid legal standing. It is unclear to what extent the qadi investigated the facts that were presented to him by the mayor of Jerusalem or if he ever visited the cemetery before issuing his fatwa.

In the State of Israel another public and legal question arises regarding the authority to approve changing the function of Muslim cemeteries.[7] Although a shari'a court system exists in Israel, there is no institute of *ifta'* authorized to provide fatwas in lacunae of the shari'a.

This gap in the interpretation of Islamic law related to the Mamilla dispute was taken up not only by shari'a court qadis, who are prevented from issuing fatwas under ordinarycircumstances, but also by professors who are experts in Islamic law – Jewish Israelis and Muslim and Christian experts from abroad. The High Court received fatwas issued by qadis, such as Ahmad Natour and Tawfiq Asaliyya, and by muftis and experts on Shari'a from Jordan. In parallel, the court also received reports from professors of Islamic law. The two sides disagreed over interpretation of the shari'a rules pertaining to Muslim graves and cemeteries, an issue that we will discuss in this chapter.

The Al Aqsa Corporation argued that the holiness of a cemetery can only be rescinded by a judicial procedure in the shari'a court, and not by a fatwa as in the 1964 case of Mamilla. Alternatively, they argued that if a fatwa is legitimate in this case, then the High Court should consult the present-day highest Muslim functionary, that is, the president of the Shari'a Court of Appeals, Qadi Ahmad Natour. According to the Al-Aqsa Corporation, an

Israeli court whose source of authority is civil (secular) law has no standing to determine the holiness of a place under Islamic law. The same is applicable to the opinion of academic experts, whose opinion has no validity from a religious point of view. Therefore, they claimed, the Shari'a Court has the sole authority, or at least a parallel authority, to deal with a case involving violation of a Muslim cemetery, and only this Shari'a Court can issue decrees to stop such violation and issue orders to the police to enforce these decrees. Moreover, the Al Aqsa Corporation argued that Qadi Tawfiq Asaliyya, who in the past had issued fatwas allowing change of function of Muslim cemeteries, now reversed his previous opinion by issuing a new fatwa stating that the holiness of a cemetery is eternal. The Al-Aqsa Corporation submitted to the High Court a hand-written fatwa by Asaliyya from 1989 in which he overruled his 1969 opinion (rescinding the holiness of Salama B Cemetery in Kfar Shalem, formerly the Arab village of Salama and today a neighborhood in Tel Aviv). He supported his new opinion by saying that the Shari'a Court of Appeals, which is the highest Islamic institution in Israel, has determined that "the qadi is not authorized to issue a fatwa, just as the mufti is not authorized to issue a verdict." Paradoxically, Asaliyya wrote his new legal opinion overruling his previous opinion under the title "fatwa" yet signed it as Chief Qadi and President of the Shari'a Court of Appeals.

Presumably, a mufti may reverse a previous opinion if new facts that were previously unknown to him are exposed, as the Chief Mufti of Jordan did in the case of the Shihab al-Din Mosque in Nazareth. However, Asaliyya did not overrule his previous fatwas as result of the discovery of new facts. Hence, it is doubtful that a document abolishing a legal opinion in a fatwa issued 32 years previously is valid, considering also that development works had already been initiated in the cemetery, making the situation a *fait acompli.* It should be emphasized that the Al-Aqsa Corporation employed a verbal sleight of hand (on brink of deception) by terming Asaliyya's fatwa a "Judicial Opinion" (in Article 13 of the petition to the High Court) and by so doing, they repeated the deceptive action of Qadi Tahir Hammad in 1964, which the plaintiffs themselves criticized. They indirectly tried to deceive the High Court into accepting a fatwa issued by a qadi as having the standing of an authorized judicial decision.

The Al Aqsa Corporation was guided by the following rationale: if the state and the museum entrepreneurs based their argument on the legal opinion of Qadi Tahir Hammad as a binding document, then they must try to abolish that document within the same legal system that the original opinion was issued, namely the Shari'a Court. However, the strategy of the Muslim plaintiffs and the Shari'a Court was outdated. A year after Qadi Tahir Hammad issued his fatwa rescinding the holiness of most of the Mamilla Cemetery, the Knesset legislated an amendment to the Absentees' Properties Law that revoked the religious status of General Waqf Properties and the jurisdiction of Shari'a Court regarding these properties.

One question that the High Court never discussed, because none of the parties to the dispute referred to it during the court hearing, is whether the ongoing and customary practice in the State of Israel since its establishment according to which changes to the function of Muslim cemeteries require a fatwa from a senior qadi has become a legal procedure that is binding in every similar case.

In any event, the Muslim plaintiffs argued that the legal opinion of Ahmad Natour, his judicial guidelines of 1994, and a special fatwa issued by him in December 2005 for the specific case of Mamilla presented at the High Court in combination overrule the fatwa issued by Qadi Hammad in 1964.

The MoT entrepreneurs claimed that Qadi Natour is not authorized to abolish a past fatwa. They claimed that the fatwa was a legal opinion issued by a sage in response to a petition by the mayor of Jerusalem in 1964 to the qadi, a senior sage and graduate of Al-Azhar. There is no room, so they said, for a legal procedure abolishing the opinion of a sage. According to them, what the Muslim plaintiffs were essentially claiming was that the present qadi should decide that Qadi Hammad was never of the opinion that he expressed in the fatwa. The High Court did not agree with the position of the Al Aqsa Corporation. Moreover, based on the 1964 fatwa of Hammad, many developmental actions had taken place over the past four decades, creating facts on the ground that a legal opinion could not reverse.

The Holiness of the Dead in Islam: Does Shari'a Allow the Removal of Graves?

One can learn about the shari'a standing regarding the holiness of a cemetery, and whether it is permissible to revoke the status of holiness and transfer a grave from its original place, from the various fatwas and academic reports that the plaintiffs submitted to the High Court. The questions that the Mamilla issue raised regarding the position of Islamic law were the following: Is it permissible to remove or to transfer a grave, and if so, under what circumstances? Does the holiness of a cemetery expire after a certain period of time? Who is authorized to determine the holiness or to revoke the holiness of a cemetery and through what procedure? Finally, is a fatwa issued by a senior qadi in Israel rescinding the holiness of a cemetery valid from a shari'a point of view, and what are the implications of such permissibility?

On the question of the scared status of a Muslim cemetery in the State of Israel, the legal position is unclear. In fact, qadis have in the past issued fatwas that permitted revoking the holiness of Muslim cemeteries, which the state authorities accepted and followed. The special case of Mamilla raises some additional questions: Is a fatwa in this case a binding legal procedure or is it a voluntary action that has no legal validity? What is the law if a qadi issued a fatwa authorizing revocation of the holiness of a Muslim cemetery and a few years later he reverts back to his original position? Is a present-day qadi authorized to issue a legal opinion that overturns the fatwa of another qadi from the past? Who is authorized to determine Islamic law's binding rule in Israel? Is it the senior sage in the shari'a court system? Or should the position under shari'a be interpreted in accordance with state law? May the shari'a court president interpret shari'a as he sees fit, including in a selective and purposefully motivated manner, and must the state authorities follow his interpretation? Finally, does the interpretation by academics of Islamic law add weight to the value of the interpretation by the president of the Shari'a Court of Appeals? Who overrules whom? All of these questions – reinforced by tension between the different interpreters of law – surfaced in the case of the Mamilla Cemetery, where the MoI was the point of contention.

Let us first discuss the interpretations of Muslim scholars regarding the question of whether removal of graves and building over a cemetery are permissible according to shari'a. This question was a major issue in the petition that the Islamic Movement submitted to the High Court. Interpreting religious law is as old as the days of religion itself. Every religion is also a legal code. Political splits within Islam were in part an outcome of disagreements regarding the interpretation of the rules and laws of religion. The most famous political divides in this context were the deviation of the Khawarij and the split of the Shi'a from the Sunnah.[8] The development of a number of schools of law within Islam and the multiple sub-sects within each of these schools indicate that shari'a is structurally pluralistic.

The multiplicity of opinions is also reflected in the issue of excavating graves and making functional changes to cemeteries. From the standpoint of the Islamic Movement in Israel and the Shari'a Court, the Mamilla issue was a case study of old Muslim cemeteries in Israel, and therefore the advocates on behalf of the Al-Aqsa Corporation dwelled on the argument that a cemetery is a holy place. [9]

In order to support their argument that the Museum compound is a holy place, the Al-Aqsa Corporation cited a number of legal opinions, to be discussed below, that endorse its approach that the sacredness of a cemetery is eternal and irrevocable.[10]

The Al-Aqsa Corporation presented an expert opinion issued on 8 December 2006 by Professor Hussam al-Din 'Afana, who holds a PhD in Islamic Law from Umm al-Kura University, Saudi Arabia, and currently teaches at Al-Quds University in Jerusalem. Afana cited a *hadith* (a record of the sayings or customs of Muhammad and his companions) emphasizing the holiness of the dead and their graves and quoted a fatwa by the former chief mufti of Saudi Arabia, Sheikh Mohammad ibn-Ibrahim Aal al-Sheikh, according to which cemeteries are holy and should be protected from any violation because a grave is the house of the human person after his death and should not be harmed, just as the house of a living person should not be touched. The Saudi mufti added that the location of old cemeteries within the center of a city does not justify their violation, not even for the pavement of roads or expansion of an existing road because roads can also be routed so as to circumvent the cemetery.[11]

The museum entrepreneurs dealt with the above arguments using three distinct approaches. First they "flooded" the High Court with expert opinions by professors of Islamic law who presented positions opposing those submitted by the Muslim plaintiffs, their expert Dr. 'Afana, and the president of the Shari'a Court. The professors claimed that the shari'a is flexible and includes opinions that support building over an old cemetery that no longer operates as a burial ground and where the human remains have already decomposed and become part of the earth.

The second approach entailed the submission of a long list of examples of Muslim cemeteries in Israel and in Muslim countries that had been transformed with the approval of Muslim sages in order to accommodate Islamic law to the reality of modern urban development. The third approach was to raise the legal question of whether cemeteries are holy places according to law. They claimed that, "the general judicial practice of courts in Israel is that the cemetery is not necessarily a holy place."[12] They claimed that when asserting the holiness of a particular place, a plaintiff must prove this status of holiness to the civil court, and that in the case of Mamilla the Muslim population has not exhibited the respectful attitude required for a holy place.

What follows is a survey of the different approaches of Islamic law to the above questions, organized chronologically according to the arguments and counter-arguments that were presented in documents submitted to the High Court. Therefore, it is not a complete description of what Islamic law says about these questions, but only a survey of the positions presented to the court regarding this specific dispute and the references provided by the parties.

Let us first investigate the justifications provided by Qadi Tahir Hammad, who was the first to revoke the holy nature of most of the Mamilla Cemetery in his 1964 legal opinion, followed by the counter-arguments of the Al-Aqsa Corporation and the current president of the Shari Court of Appeals, Qadi Ahmad Natour. Then we will analyze the legal opinions of academic experts on Islamic law that were presented to the High Court by the MoT entrepreneurs.

The Israel Land Authority and the Jerusalem Municipality did not need a fatwa or Shari'a Court approval in order to designate the disputed land for the establishment of the MoT. Yet the fatwa issued by Qadi Tahir Hammad in 1964 still played an important role. It gave religious legitimacy to the planning process by transforming the function of a cemetery to a public park. The fatwa was needed only in order to complete the planning process by changing the designated purpose of the land, but it also provided added value. The state authorities and the Jerusalem Municipality were then able to proceed with a clear conscience because a senior Muslim personality had granted religious approval to the revocation of the presumed sacredness of this cemetery. This manner of action does not differ from the approach that Muslim countries use when they seek to make use of old and abandoned cemeteries for the purpose of urban development.

In 1964, when he issued the legal opinion rescinding the holiness of most of the Mamilla Cemetery, Sheikh Tahir Hammad was serving as both qadi of Jaffa and president of the Shari'a Court of Appeals. He issued a fatwa, yet in the document itself he wrote that the outcome followed a shari'a session in Jaffa, that is, adjudication in a dispute involving litigants and witnesses. However, this document does not name the litigants or witnesses, which is unusual. Moreover, the only documents before Qadi Hammad were a letter and a few other papers that he said were presented to him by the mayor of Jerusalem. These documents were not filed in the records of the Shari'a Court. Another defect in the permit that he issued was that he titled it "qarar fatwa" in Arabic, giving the impression that his opinion (fatwa) is also a judicial decision (qarar).

Hammad accepted the details presented to him by the mayor regarding the history of the Mamilla Cemetery, without investigating the facts or challenging them.[13] He quoted from the mayor's letter, which stated that according to records contained in the Municipality's archives, the Supreme Muslim Council during the British Mandate had decided to declare the Mamilla Cemetery *mundaris* (obliterated) because a certain period of time had passed since anyone had been buried in this cemetery. Hammad added that according to these documents the Supreme Muslim Council planned to construct houses over the cemetery, including a building for the Arab League (a decision from 1946). As we shall see in the next chapter, no such decision was recorded, and the plans are mentioned only in an exchange of letters reflecting negotiations. During that time the Supreme Muslim Council was subject to the strict control of a British committee.[14] In the 1950s the Israeli Municipality of Jerusalem decided to transform the entire cemetery into a public park, and in 1960 the minister of finance issued a decree expropriating the land and transferring it to the ownership of the state. In his fatwa, Qadi Hammad discussed two legal questions that he framed as following: First, is this cemetery indeed mundaris according to shari'a? Second, what changes are permitted in a mundaris cemetery?

The first shari'a source on which Qadi Hammad based his fatwa was the book by Fakhr al-Din 'Uthman b. Ali al-Zayla'i, a Hanafite[15] jurist from the fourteenth century (d. 1343).[16] Al-Zayla'i stated that the yardstick for determining whether the reopening of a grave is permissible is the extent of decomposition of the body. After the duration of time required for the body to decompose into the earth has passed, it is permissible to open the grave for various purposes: to bury an additional body in it, to plow it, or to build above it. It should be noted that there are different interpretations regarding the time it takes for a human body to decompose, as will be further discussed below. Al-Zayla'i's opinion is the strongest and clearest regarding permission to transform cemeteries for construction purposes. Therefore, Hammad used this source. However, Hammad himself also cited the opposing position, which appears in a Hanifite fatwa collection entitled *Tatarkhaniyya* from the same period (the fourteenth century), issued by Alim b. 'Ala al-Din.[17] This source states that opening a grave for any purpose is an indecent act. Thus we have two important sages from the same century and the same school of law with opposing opinions. In order to decide between the two opinions, Hammad used another important shari'a source from the nineteenth century. He argued that a more recent source is more applicable because opinions change in accordance with the changing times. This argument is based on legal commentary by Ibn-'Abidin,[18] who served as the mufti of Damascus, among other positions. Ibn-'Abidin wrote that the opinion rejecting exploration of graves in the Tatarkhaniyya is a command that the public in our times (nineteenth century) cannot uphold, particularly in large cities, because if it is not permissible to re-open graves in order to rebury the deceased, then cemeteries will occupy vast urban and agricultural spaces, and there will not be enough room for the use of the living. From this statement, Qadi Hammad concluded that *once the buried dead have decomposed and become dust, it is permissible to change the utility of the grave, even if some bones still remain in the grave.*

Qadi Hammad's conclusion is thus that *if the Mamilla Cemetery is mundaris, then it is permissible to change its purpose for any use*. However, there is another question that requires attention: how much time is needed for a body to decompose to the point where it is permissible to open the grave? Here Qadi Hammad used another medieval source, written by the thirteenth century Shafi'ite jurist, Yahya ibn Sharaf al-Din al-Nawawi. In his book, Al-Nawawi discussed the question of the timeframe for determining the decomposition of a human body. He stated that this period differs from one place to another according to the type of earth. Indeed, the science of taphonomy relies on various factors such as temperature, humidity, existence of insects, and so on, all of which affect the time span of a body's decomposition process. In a temperate climate, usually at least ten years must pass before the flesh is decomposed and only the bones remain. Hammad concluded his opinion by saying that unlike mosques, the holiness of cemeteries is not eternal but temporary (until decomposition of the bodies), adding that the Supreme Muslim Council stated that this particular cemetery is already mundaris. Hence, it is permissible to use the land for any action, as with any other regular plot. In his opinion, Hammad therefore issued instructions to transfer the graves that were scattered and visible in the cemetery, adding that he would visit the cemetery in order to supervise this process. Finally, he welcomed the decision of the mayor of Jerusalem to leave intact a small part of the cemetery, approximately one dunam only, as a historic living memory of the cemetery. Interestingly, the mayor of Jerusalem, Mordechai Ish-Shalom, did not seek to obliterate the historical remains of the cemetery completely, as was the case in many other Muslim cemeteries in Israel, and he himself initiated the plan to leave part of the cemetery as a symbol and memorial to the old Ma'man Allah Cemetery.

In 1964, Tahir Hammad did not see any particular problem in permitting the transformation of the majority of the cemetery. From Hammad's point of view, the entire Israeli society would benefit from having a public park replace the Cemetery.

Today however, Qadi Natour has a different interpretation of the shari'a principle of public benefit (*maslaha*). The public good derived should benefit only the Muslim community rather than the Jewish society, which would be the major benefactor from the future utility of the cemetery (the MoT being built atop the cemetery). The High Court did not embrace the opinion of Natour and the Muslim plaintiffs, according to which only the highest Muslim cleric in the shari'a court system of today is authorized to interpret the situation based his understanding of the principle of benefit to the Muslim community. Another issue, which was not emphasized in the arguments presented to the High Court, was that Qadi Hammad had permitted use of the cemetery only for the purposes of a *public park*, as the mayor had specifically requested in his petition. *Qadi Hammad had not been asked about, and therefore did not grant permission for, building over this cemetery.* A public park, parts of which still preserve Muslim graves, does not symbolically obliterate a cemetery but, on the contrary, could contribute to preserving the historical identity of the place. However, construction completely obliterates the original character of the place and damages deep underground graves. Nevertheless, the Jerusalem Municipality approved construction over the cemetery, although Qadi Hammad had only permitted changing the use of the cemetery to a public park.

In the High Court hearing, the legal opinion issued by Qadi Hammad was defined by the Al-Aqsa Corporation as illegal and invalid. The corporation claimed that Qadi Hammad had acted under pressure during a period of martial rule over Israeli Arabs, and that in fact he had no alternative but to agree to the mayor's request (or demand). In addition, they insinuated that Hammad was corrupt because during the same period he had been convicted by the court of "acting in a deceitful manner that can harm the public"[19] and the circumstances surrounding this verdict cast a shadow on Hammad's integrity.[20] Hammad was convicted and his appeal to the High Court rejected. Another argument presented by the Al Aqsa Corporation against Qadi Hammad's legal opinion was that he presented his opinion as a judicial decision although it was not one. They concluded that it is improper to follow this qadi's opinion in general and regarding the Mamilla Cemetery document in particular.

Against Hammad's fatwa they presented an opposing opinion, namely, an announcement by the Shari'a Court dated 28 December 2005, which Qadi Ahmad Natour had written especially for this court case and which stated:

> I have been informed that a corporation whose name I do not know is conducting excavation works in preparation of construction atop Ma'man Allah Cemetery in Jerusalem. The president of the Shari'a Court of Appeals, Qadi Ahmad Natour, strongly condemns these shameful actions that severely offend the sentiments of Muslims and desecrate holy places, and that also contradict Qadi Natour's instruction to prevent completely any harm to cemeteries. Therefore, the

> president of the Shari'a Court of Appeals reemphasizes for the thousandth time his permanent position, according to which Muslim holy places have an eternal holiness, irrevocable until the Day of Judgment, and they are prohibited for any use other than burial. The Shari'a Court of Appeals, its president and members, and all the Shari'a Court qadis condemn the irresponsible actions that deviate from religion, morality, and law, which are known to everybody. The Shari'a Court system in all of its instances and qadis reemphasize clearly what was adjudicated in the past, whether by Legal Decree Number 1 or by the fatwas issued by the president of the Shari'a Court of Appeals, that it is prohibited to dig and build over graves . . . particularly in the Ma'man Allah Cemetery, where righteous people and forefathers are buried. I appealed to the prime minister and speaker of the Knesset, asking them to cease the sabotage of the Mamilla Cemetery immediately. The Shari'a Court of Appeals and the other shari'a courts repeat their demand to take immediate action to punish those who violate the law, and to put an immediate end to their activities.

The Legal Decree Number 1 that he mentioned was an instruction that he had authored as part of his struggle to stop the phenomenon of changing the utility of cemeteries, a practice in which his predecessors in the Shari'a Court had engaged. The Legal Decree (*marsum qada'i*) is an innovation of Natour in the shari'a courts in Israel.

The legal decree that Qadi Natour issued makes clear that he interpreted the legal principle of the "public interest" (*maslaha 'amma*) as the general good of the Muslim community only. In this context the transformation of Muslim cemeteries serves mainly the predominantly Jewish state and Jewish businessmen, and therefore it is prohibited by shari'a. Natour's position on this point is also expressed in other fatwas that he has issued since he was a qadi of the lower Shari'a Court. In November 1987 he wrote a fatwa regarding Jamasin al-Gharbi Cemetery in Tel Aviv (formerly part of the Jaffa District and located in the Tel Aviv neighborhood known today as Bavli). The fatwa opens with a declaration that every qadi has general jurisdiction over waqfs and has to take the initiative of preserving waqf properties and conducting investigations if he is informed that somebody intends to damage waqf property. In such a case the qadi need not wait until a complaint is submitted. Natour stated further that he was informed that a commercial corporation registered a note of warning with the land registry regarding the Jamasin Cemetery, which had apparently been sold to this corporation by the Jaffa–Tel Aviv Waqf Board of Trustees (appointed by the government under the 1965 Amendment to the Absentees' Properties Law). He wrote that he has a different opinion from previous qadis who issued permits for transactions of waqf properties regarding a Muslim cemetery, adding that a certain word in al-Zayla'i's interpretation (mentioned above in the fatwa of Qadi Hammad) was mistakenly understood as "permissible."[21]

He added that al-Zayla'i's interpretation permitting the transformation of a cemetery was perhaps correct at time, but not today. In other words, Natour was stating (according to my understanding) that during the Mamluk period, when the only beneficiaries of the transformation of a cemetery were Muslims, perhaps it was permissible. In present-day Israel, however, when the beneficiaries are mainly Jews, it is not. Qadi Natour's fatwa ends with his instruction to the land registry to change the registration and to replace the warning note regarding the Jamasin cemetery with another note saying, "This is a Holy Waqf, prohibited for sale, long-term rent, mortgage, or exchange".[22]

It seems that at that time Qadi Natour was attempting to test the civil state authorities and see if they would accept his instruction regarding a cemetery as legally binding. However, as one might expect, the land registry ignored Natour's instruction. Natour informed me that in addition to writing the fatwa he announced a boycott of the Waqf Board of Trustees, which had sold the cemetery, and he dismissed the mutawalli Ali-Rashidi. He said that as a result, government officials began to label his actions as "extreme and nationalistic," and that the Ministry of Religious Affairs began harassing him. However, most of the Arab population of Jaffa supported his standing.[23]

Qadi Natour was encouraged by the fact that some of his fatwas were respected by Israeli courts and the Muslim public. In the case of another Muslim cemetery – Nabi Yamin, near the city of Kfar Saba – based on a fatwa issued by Natour, the Magistrate Court of Kfar Saba ruled against digging in the cemetery in order to insert a groundwater pipe.[24] Similarly, the Israel Highway Corporation accepted his opinion and decided to change the highway route near the village Furaydis in order to avoid damaging Muslim graves.[25] Backed by these precedents, Natour believed that the High Court would respect his opinion, as the Magistrate Court had, but he soon realized that his assumption was wrong.

Let us look at another example. In 2004, when Natour was already the president of the Shari'a Court of Appeals, he issued a fatwa regarding the Muslim cemetery of Ijzim, an Arab village destroyed in the 1948 war. This village is located some 20 kilometers south of Haifa and on its ruins Israel established Moshav Kerem Maharal in 1949. The case of Ijzim resembles the Mamilla case in a number of aspects, with one exception: it was not proven that the specific plot where the village planned to build a new neighborhood was part of an old Muslim cemetery. In 2002, the Israel Land Authority sold a piece of land to build a new neighborhood in the Moshav. When works began, a number of old Muslim and Jewish graves were exposed. The Ministry of Religious Affairs determined that it was impossible to transfer the graves and ordered that construction proceed by building columns over the ground, without digging deep into the earth, in order to prevent damage to the graves. The moshav residents claimed that this space was covered by shrubbery and they proved that this land had not been part of the Muslim cemetery during the British Mandate period. Here again the Al-Aqsa Corporation and three of the original inhabitants of Ijzim filed a petition with the High Court opposing construction and claiming that the land is part of the old city cemetery.[26]

In his legal opinion regarding Ijzim, Natour referred to a Yemenite jurist from the last third of the nineteenth century, Muhammad al-Shawkani.[27] Shawkani is considered a modernist who permitted the reopening of graves, but Natour offered a different interpretation. Natour asserted that, given the holiness of the human body, Shawkani had permitted reopening a grave to rebury another body only after *all of the bones* had decomposed. Hence, as long as bones remain in the earth, it is impermissible to open a grave.[28] Natour then quoted the famous sage al-Shafi'i (d. 815) who is considered the founder of the Shafi'i school of Islamic law. Al-Shafi'i wrote that it is preferable to bury a body in a designated cemetery, rather than in open space outside a cemetery, in order to prevent people urinating on the body or searching the grave site. He added that if somebody dedicated a plot of land as waqf for the purpose of a cemetery, and then wished to reverse and return the land to his ownership, according to shari'a, he can use only the part of the land that was not used for burial. Natour emphasized that this is what shari'a says about changing the use of a cemetery by the original owner, and it thus applies all the more so in the case of distant foreigners (Jews). Finally, Qadi Natour sited a hadith transmitted by Aysha, wife of the Prophet Mohammed, saying that, "Breaking a dead person's bones is equivalent to breaking the bones of a living person." Natour concluded that the dead body should remain intact in its grave until the Day of Resurrection.[29]

Al Aqsa Corporation's complaint succeeded in delaying construction in the mosahv for five years, until a final verdict was issued by the High Court. Justice Ayalah Procaccia, the same justice who issued the verdict regarding the Mamilla Cemetery, ruled in June 2009 that the Al-Aqsa Corporation's position was an "extreme and imbalanced position because it rejected the practical solution of adapting the building plans to the findings on the ground."[30]

In the complaint levied by the Al-Aqsa Corporation against the building in Kerem Maharal, the plaintiffs submitted a special fatwa issued by Qadi Natour to support their claim. The same pattern was apparent two years later in the Mamilla dispute. In the first fatwa, Natour attempted to use the same legal sources on which Qadi Tahir Hammad had relied when he permitted the transformation of the cemetery, but he interpreted them in the opposite way. First he stated that there is a general agreement among Muslim sages that a Muslim cemetery has an eternal status of holiness. A survey of the sources that he cited, however, reveals that there is no such consensus. Natour claimed that those who permitted the transformation of a cemetery rely on one sentence in the Book of al-Zayla'i (quoted by Qadi Hammad), adding that al-Zayla'i himself stated that "the body should not be removed from the grave after it has been covered by soil." Qadi Natour went on to quote another sage, Shihab al-Din al-Shalabi (died in the early seventeenth century), whose interpretation was printed in the margin of al-Zayla'i's book.[31]

Shalabi wrote that it is prohibited to open a grave for the sake of removing an article that was accidently dropped into the grave, such as coins or cloth, and that it is prohibited to transfer graves from one place to another. Natour says that Shalabi added that the interpretation of later sages (whose rulings permit building over or transferring graves) should not be followed. Shalabi further stated that the practice of removing a grave is based on the case of the forefather Jacob, who had died in Egypt and whose grave was subsequently transferred to al-Sham (which included Palestine), and that the transfer of Jacob's coffin from Egypt to al-Sham by Musa (Moses) was an ancient precedent, prohibited in our time. Natour posed the question: "What are the Muslim public benefits from the destruction of cemeteries?" He queried further, "If al-Zayla'i were alive during present times, would he permit the same today [in a Jewish State]?" Qadi Ahmad Natour concluded that the rulings of al-Zayla'i, "do not apply to any of the cemeteries in present times. Moreover, al-Zayla'i's opinion was opposed by the sages of the Maliki school of law, and the Tatarkhaniyya [Hanafite] volume."

The second source cited by Qadi Hammad (who had allowed the construction over old Muslim Cemeteries, as noted) was the book by Ibn-'Abidin of the nineteenth century, which Qadi Natour also critically analyzed.[32] Natour believed that the permission Ibn 'Abidin granted to reopen graves was justified by the circumstances of his place and time, considering the lack of land for burial. Hence, in Natour's eyes Ibn-'Abidin permitted reopening graves only for reburial of more bodies in the same grave, and his opinion cannot in any way be used today to legitimize construction of facilities, parks, or buildings over existing Muslim cemeteries.

It is interesting to note that while the High Court was hearing the case of the MoT in Mamilla, the members of the Islamic Movement obtained a fatwa from the chief mufti of Jordan, signed by him and by three other senior Jordanian official adjudicators, each of whom had a PhD in Islamic Law. The four senior muftis copied word for word most of the fatwa that Qadi Natour had issued regarding the Muslim Cemetery of Ijzim, changing only the name of Ijzim to Ma'man-Allah.[33] This action teaches us about the connection between the substance of a response and the petitioners.

The museum entrepreneurs presented to the High Court other Muslim opinions supported by expert opinions of professors of Islamic law. They quoted the opinion of the chief qadi of the Palestinian Authority, Taysir al-Tamimi, who had stated in a previous case that:

> There are shari'a laws that permit it. If a cemetery was flattened and after a long period, which the sages determine is more than sixty years, if there is a benefit for the Muslims and a necessity to build over it based on the decision of a ruler, *then the shari'a qadi may use legal justifications to rule that the human remains can be transferred to another cemetery, so that the former cemetery can be used for the benefit of the Muslims* [and this is the same] in cases of urgency even if there is no legal justification for such an action.[34] [Emphasis added.]

Tamimi's fatwa represents a well-known shari'a ruling that permits the change of a cemetery's use when there is a vital necessity or strong public interest in it.

Let us now discuss a different type of "fatwa": the opinion of professors who are experts in Islamic law. Such expert opinions were submitted to the High Court by the MoT entrepreneurs with the aim of challenging the interpretation of both the Al-Aqsa Corporation's academic expert 'Afana (mentioned above) and Qadi Natour. The first expert opinion was written by Professor Aharon Layish, an internationally renowned authority on Islamic law. Layish wrote that a Muslim cemetery becomes a waqf endowment by definition, meaning that from the point of view of the Hanafite school of law, the ownership of a waqf property is transferred to God, and therefore the waqf property is eternal, irreversible, and inalienable. However, Islamic law has developed and, over the course of time, permitted transformation of cemeteries under certain conditions. Layish mentioned the names of five Israeli qadis, the first generation of qadis after the 1948 war and the establishment of Israel, who permitted development work in Muslim cemeteries and the most prominent of whom was Qadi Tahir Hammad. He quoted a fatwa issued by Hammad in early 1953 in which he stated, basing himself on the above-mentioned sage Ibn-'Abidin, that the shari'a permits the transfer of graves in cases in which the dead that were buried on private land must be moved to serve the interests of a private individual, and all the more so when the case is in the interest of the public. From Hammad's point of view, after 36 years have passed since the last burial in a cemetery, it is considered obsolete and obliterated (mundaris) because the last buried body is considered completely decomposed.[35] It is unclear to me how Hammad determined the period of 36 years.

Layish avoided this important question of time and the challenge that Natour posed in his fatwa regarding the Ijzim cemetery. As mentioned, Natour quoted Al-Shawkani, who permitted reopening a grave only when *all the bones* had decomposed. Layish did not address the question of how to define decomposition in order to declare a cemetery mundaris: decomposition of the flesh only, or the bones as well. As noted, the average period of decomposition for flesh is roughly ten years; bones, however, could remain for thousands of years. In his opinion, Layish employed several contradictory expressions regarding this question: "flesh and bone of the dead," "remains of a bone," "if the bodies of the dead have decomposed . . . then it is permissible to transfer the bones," "if the occupants of the graves have decomposed." As we shall see below, Professor Wael Hallaq, who is also a renowned authority in Islamic law, referred specifically to this question and clearly concluded that it is enough in Islamic law that the flesh be decomposed, adding that the shari'a sources hold that the flesh decomposes one year after the act of burial.[36]

In his opinion, Professor Layish cited a fatwa issued in 1972 by Qadi Tawfiq Asaliya, who permitted the evacuation of Ijlil al-Gharbiya Cemetery (in the area of Herzliya today) on the basis of one primary legal principle: a situation of necessity arising from neglect of the cemetery and fear of disrespecting the dead. Asaliyya ordered the transfer of graves under his inspection to another cemetery in order to allow a road to be paved in its place. Despite this initial ruling, in March of 1991 Asaliyya reversed his previous position because of public pressure, stating:

> Given that in the past, on 1 January 1969, I issued a legal opinion regarding the Salama B Cemetery, by which I rescinded the holiness of that cemetery, and given that I had been told that those who were buried in this cemetery had decomposed, and given that on 19 January 1974, the Shari'a Court of Appeals decided to abrogate all legal opinions issued by qadis on such issues, and given that my role as a qadi is to adjudicate in disputes, not to issue legal opinions, on this basis on 11 September 1989 I issued a legal opinion proving that *the holiness of a cemetery is eternal and irrevocable* because revocation is the right of God only, and this legal opinion applies also to the Salama B Cemetery. Let there be no doubt that this cemetery is one of the holy places of Muslims, and it is prohibited to search or remove bodies from the graves. (Signed by the President of the Shari'a Court of Appeals).[37] [Emphasis added.]

It is interesting that Qadi Asaliyya mentioned a Shari'a Court decision opposing his opinion, which abrogated his 1973 fatwa regarding Tasso Cemetery (Abu-Kabir, Tal al-Rish). At the time, his granting of permission was made public to the press, and the Shari'a Court came under pressure. The acting president of the Shari'a Court of Appeals, Qadi Amin al-Habash, then acted to abrogate that permission, justifying this abrogation by saying that a qadi is authorized only to rule, not to issue fatwas.[38] Apparently Asalyia had to use a decision that had been issued against him in order to defend himself from public criticism by activists of the Islamic Movement in the 1990s.

Layish wrote that Qadi Hammad and Qadi Asaliyya, who had permitted the transformation of cemeteries, were graduates of the Al-Azhar Institute, the highest institute of Islamic law in the world, and that they based their permission on modernist jurists, also Al-Azhar graduates, who used the principle of the benefit of the public as an independent source of law, not bound by the textual sources of Quran and hadith.[39] However, Layish ignored the fact that the benefit of the public refers to the Muslim public only. Layish also described the practice of transferring graves in Islam. According to him, the Ottoman state had allowed the evacuation of cemeteries for the purpose of constructing roads and buildings.[40] To illustrate the flexible practice of Islam, Layish cited the examples of three fatwas. The first was written by a senior lecturer at al-Azhar University, Dr. Misbah Hammad, responding to a petitioner who had bought a plot of land adjacent to an old cemetery that was still in use, and while preparing the land for construction, had discovered four old graves, removed them, and transferred them to another cemetery. The petitioner wanted to know whether he had acted legally according to shari'a and whether he was allowed to resume construction. The mufti ruled positively based on the principle of necessity (*darura*).[41]

The second fatwa was written by the secretary-general of Al-Azhar's Fatwa Committee, Sheikh Ahmad Al-Sharbasi.[42] The mufti wrote that when one intends to build over a cemetery, he has to make sure that there are no remains of bodies or bones because as long as the body has not decomposed, the holiness (of the cemetery) still prevails. Neither the mufti nor Professor Layish refers to the question of the timeframe in which a body is classified as decomposed.

The third example cited by Layish was of a Syrian mufti named Muhammad Nasr-al-Din al-Albani (d. 1999), who also permitted building and planting on a past cemetery if there are no "remains of bone" in that cemetery.[43] This legal opinion does not in any way support the construction of the MoT in Mamilla because in Mamilla hundreds of entire skeletons were excavated.

Dr. Shmuel Berkovits, an expert on Jerusalem and holy places who also submitted an opinion at the initiative of the MoT entrepreneurs, provided additional sources to those mentioned by Layish. He cited Article 33 of the Ottoman Land Law of 1858: "Land possessed privately with a legal document (*kushan*) is not permitted for burial of the dead, neither the possessor nor anybody else; and if it was used for burial there are two possibilities: if the *flesh of the body* has not decomposed, it is removed to another place with the permission of an officer; and if it has decomposed, it is plowed and the soil is flattened."[44] [Emphasis added.]

In other words, Ottoman law permitted transfer of graves when only the flesh of the body had decomposed. Berkovits detailed Israeli verdicts that have permitted the transformation of a Muslim cemetery, such as Al-Istiqlal Cemetery in Haifa (transformed for construction by an initiative of Muslim waqf trustees but never implemented because of public criticism). In that case the qadi of Haifa declared that 30 years are enough time for bodies to be considered decomposed and to have become dust.[45] Berkovits criticized Qadi Natour's opinion that the interpretation of Al-Zayla'i is the only one that permits the opening of graves. He quoted a Syrian sage of the twentieth century, Wahba al-Zuhayli, who presented the permission to build over graves as the opinion of all of the Hanifite school jurists.[46]

The report of Professor Yehoshua Porath reinforces what Professor Layish and Dr. Berkovits had previously implied, namely, that the current president of the Shari'a Court of Appeals is motivated by an extreme political and ideological outlook and therefore claims that Natour makes selective use of shari'a sources in order to reach the conclusion he seeks.

The MoT entrepreneurs submitted two additional expert opinions by professors who live abroad, Dr. Said Bouheraoua of the Islamic University of Malaysia and Professor Wael Hallaq (a Christian who was raised in Nazareth,

Israel) from Columbia University in New York. My impression from reading these two opinions is that the professors had no idea of the purpose their opinions were intended to serve, and the opinions are therefore politically and ideologically impartial. Each professor drafted an expert opinion about the principle of the transfer of graves, without knowing that his opinion would be used in the context of a dispute over a famous, ancient Muslim cemetery in Jerusalem under Israeli control. Apparently they prepared and submitted their opinions through a non-Israeli intermediary. Professor Bouheraoua from Malaysia wrote that his opinion addressed a question posed to him regarding "a Muslim country in the Middle East," and he assumed that the graves were discovered incidentally and that the owner of the land did not know in advance that he would find graves beneath the ground. Bohouraeau clearly did not know that this was a historic cemetery, and he therefore opined that it is permissible to transfer graves aged 50 years or more if they are removed under appropriate religious supervision and transferred to another cemetery where the deceased's relatives can visit. He cited a hadith that Qadi Natour had previously cited, as narrated by Aysha: "Breaking the bone of a Muslim dead is equivalent to breaking the bone of a living person." Yet, he added, there are exceptional cases, and here he quoted from other hadiths conveying that under certain circumstances, the deceased had been transferred from their original graves, including by order of the Prophet himself.[47] Bohouraeau concluded:

> It is permissible to transfer graves in the following cases: to benefit the deceased, to remedy an improper burial, at the request of a first-degree relative, if a landowner discovers graves on his private property because his right to the land supersedes, and in cases where graves were found in land not designated for burial. Today the practice is to permit the transfer of graves if there is a necessity or public benefit.[48]

In other words, there is flexibility in interpretation of the shari'a in order to accommodate the law to changing reality.

The expert opinion of Professor Wael Hallaq of Columbia University[49] was the most decisive in support of works in cemeteries. He wrote that the holiness of graves and land emanates from the holiness of the human body. Therefore, when the remains of that body have decomposed in the soil, there is no more holiness to the soil in which he was buried. Hence the land of graves in which only the core skeleton of the buried remained may be used for other purposes, including agricultural development, real estate, and the like. According to him, al-Shafi'i stated that it is prohibited to dig into a new grave over the period of only one year.[50] Others, however, permitted digging into a new grave, as did jurists from the Hanafi and Hanbali schools of law. [51] He added that the transfer of graves to another location is anchored in the hadith.

Let us now examine contemporary cases that were presented to the High Court and additional cases that I discovered through research. Contemporary practice indeed indicates a more flexible approach among muftis than in the past regarding construction over graves. There are also muftis who have a more conservative approach. An example of a conservative approach is a case that took place in a village named Darma' in Saudi Arabia, where elementary school pupils engaged in tree-planting activities discovered human remains in the earth. The municipality had intended to build another school on this spot, and the students' parents petitioned Mufti Abdallah ibn al-Jabrin, asking him whether it was permissible to build a school over part of a cemetery where nobody had been buried in over 30 years, given that the village was in urgent need of a school, and no other public land was available for construction according to the village engineer. The mufti's response was that even if only a few bodies were buried in the land and even if hundreds of years have passed since the last burial, construction on this land is prohibited because of the holiness of the deceased. The mufti supported his opinion by quoting hadith stating that it is better to sit over burning embers then over a grave. He added that if the graves belong to the deceased of other religions, then it is permissible to dig up the graves and build over them.

There are, however, fatwas that present a pragmatic approach. In a village in Sudan, it was discovered one day that 80% of the houses had been constructed over a cemetery, and it was not known which of the houses cover graves and which do not. Dr. Abd al-Hay Yusuf, a lecturer in Shari'a and Islamic Civilization at Khartoum University, responded to the question of whether it is permissible to reside in these houses by saying that if the cemetery has become mundaris and no longer contains the remains of bones, then there is no problem in building over it and residing in the houses constructed.[52] In another case, a mufti was petitioned about whether it is permissible to widen a road over a graveyard. His answer was that it is prohibited to dig up a grave except for a legal purpose such as necessity, when there is no recourse other than to broaden the road.[53] In other words it is permissible to broaden a road at the expense of the cemetery when there is the justification of urban planning.[54]

Further reinforcement for the opinion that it is permitted to build over a mundaris cemetery was provided by a fatwa in a case that took place in the United Arab Emirates. A cemetery in one village was transferred to the ownership of a development corporation, which intended to build hotels and an amusement park over this land. A petitioner, in his question to the mufti, indicated that the facility could open the door for non-shari'a-based behaviors and actions (indecent actions according to shari'a). With the aim of transferring the graves to another location, the development corporation constructed a wall around this cemetery, and the local residents stopped burying their dead within it. The petitioner wanted to know what to do, and he asked for a fatwa signed by the mufti because this website (Islamweb) has a good reputation among the villagers. The mufti responded that because this cemetery is not mundaris, it is prohibited to change its purpose, and the corporation has to remove itself from this land.[55]

In light of the findings from other Muslim states, the MoT entrepreneurs in their defense before the High Court argued:

> It is strange that while in Muslim countries such as in Jordan, Egypt, Saudi Arabia, and Lebanon, practice allows the transfer of graves for public utilities . . . in the State of Israel, the Al Aqsa Corporation alleges that a different and surprising (perhaps not so surprising . . .) rule applies, ordering the sudden adoption of a strict approach according to which it is prohibited to render a cemetery for public use *forever and under any circumstances*. The only possible conclusion is that this change of opinion was influenced by pressure from extreme elements and in fact does not express the religious standing *but reflects the use of religion for political anti-Israel purposes*.[56] [Emphasis in the original.]

It seems that the assessments of experts made a greater impression on the justices of the High Court than did the opinion of the president of the Shari'a Court of Appeals.

Justice Procaccia summarized the dispute over the position of shari'a regarding this question in the following words:

> I see no room to address the conceptual debate that was conveyed to us in the various expert opinions submitted to the court by clerics and experts regarding the question of how strict Islam is in defending cemeteries and to what extent it permits overriding a holy place for the needs of the living, particularly when considering old burial sites that were hidden underground. There were opinions from each side, and it is not necessary to decide this question at the general level. The constitutional analysis that we are required to deal with is based on general constitutional principles that give relative weight to the religious commandments. However, those commandments, whatever they are, cannot overrule a constitutional question. *In our case it is appropriate to assume only that there is a debate* regarding the question of the extent to which the legal commandments of Islam permit construction and development in land underneath which there are *remains* of old graves, and the extent to which it allows the transfer and removal of graves to alternative places and makes development possible. *We can also say that there is at least one dominant stream of thought in Islam that strives to balance between old and new in this sphere as well*, and the reality is that even in Israel there have been construction and development works over Muslim burial compounds in different regions of the country, which were not conducted against the position of the Muslim Community.[57]

The High Court ignored the opinion of the highest authority on shari'a in Israel today, Qadi Ahmad Natour. It embraced the position of academic experts, whose opinions were widely quoted in the verdict, saying that there are different opinions within shari'a on this matter. Apparently the High Court was impressed by the argument of the defendants (MoT entrepreneurs and state authorities) that Qadi Natour's interpretation emanates from an ideological and political approach.

In conclusion, the dispute over locating the MoT in Mamilla exposed a controversy regarding the question of whether shari'a permits revoking the holy status of a cemetery. The president of the Shari'a Court of Appeals, Qadi Ahmad Natour, and the Islamic Movement argued that according to shari'a a cemetery has an enduring holiness that cannot be revoked. On the other side, the MoT entrepreneurs, assisted by academic experts on Islamic law, claimed that shari'a has diverse opinions on this issue, and contemporary practice is flexible in a way that permits the removal of graves and construction over Muslim cemeteries.

The question of the holiness of graves and cemeteries in Islam has been debated since medieval times, but this debate has increased relevance in the modern era. The adjudication of muftis and sages has always depended on the political context. Muslim tradition and legal interpretation have permitted reopening and transferring graves under certain circumstances, on the condition that the body has decomposed. Opinions vary regarding the questions of when a body is decomposed and whether decomposition applies only to the flesh or also to the bones. Some believe that one year is enough time to render a cemetery mundaris, while others believe that a generation or some other lengthy period of time must pass before the remains are considered completely decomposed. From the point of view of the shari'a court, the shari'a interpretation depends on context and authority. In other words, who interprets the shari'a in order to decide between permission and prohibition? It is impossible to deny Qadi Natour's interpretation that in the Mamilla case the two principal legal justifications for permission (maslaha, the public interest, and darura, necessity) do not exist. On the contrary, the public interest from the shari'a point of view should be the interest of the Muslim community alone, not the interest of Jewish State authorities and a Jewish corporation. In this context it is also impossible to deny the Muslim plaintiffs' claim that the case of Mamilla is different from many other cases where graves were accidentally unearthed. In Mamilla, the case was an attempt by a Muslim community, a minority ruled by Jews, to preserve its heritage. It was an important historic cemetery, known to everybody. The Mamilla plot is not land where only a handful of graves or even dozens of graves exist, but a site where approximately 1,000 graves exist, 400 of which have already been disinterred and removed during the excavation process. The Muslim plaintiffs also claimed that construction of the MoT over the cemetery is not a necessity because there are several appropriate alternative venues for the museum, and finally, that the correct interpretation in our time according to Muslims (as well as the Jewish academics and civil society organizations that objected to locating the museum in Mamilla) can only be articulated by the official authority, the head of the shari'a court system in Israel, Qadi Ahmad Natour, and not by professors of Islamic law.

As mentioned above and discussed below in chapter 8, the High Court decided the matter while ignoring the shari'a position and while engaged in a confrontation with the Shari'a Court and the ideology behind the latter's position. Apparently the High Court justices were impressed by the expert opinions they received that asserted that the president of the Shari'a Court is biased and motivated by an ideological agenda that contradicts the interests of the State of Israel, and hence, they did not consider the claims of those who opposed the location of the MoT in Mamilla.

Notes

1 The mass media revolution has enabled quick and widespread dissemination of the opinions (fatwas) of authorized muftis. Today one can find hundreds of new fatwas published every day in many web sites. Some important muftis have their own web sites, and there are also more general Islamic sites in which muftis issue fatwas in shifts. Some of these sites have a mufti council that issues collective responses on highly important social and political questions. During medieval times a distinction was drawn between official muftis salaried by the ruler and independent muftis. The former were organized hierarchically by provinces and districts headed by a chief mufti. On political issues the official muftis of the state will usually support the government's policy while the independent muftis will challenge this policy. Today, muftis who belong to Islamist organizations issue fatwas that contradict the opinion of the state muftis and in some cases even attack these muftis. The latter are cynically termed "the muftis of the government." Nevertheless, the official muftis are generally more learned; they are graduates of higher educational studies at the Al Azhar Institute in Cairo or an equivalent institution, and they usually also have more legal experience than independent muftis. There are few independent muftis who can compete with the official ones. The status of the state muftis varies one country to another. See J. Skovgaard-Petersen, *Defining Islam for the Egyptian State: Muftis and Fatwas of the Dar Al-Ifta*, Leiden: Brill, 1997.

2 See for example S. Abu Ghosh, *Qararat Shar'iyya min al-Mahkama al-Isti'nafiyya*, Jerusalem: Ministry of Religion, 1992, pp. 203–5 (Arabic).

3 See for example the attempt of the Supreme Muslim Council to take over the administration of the Tamimi family waqf in Hebron. The parties provided the shari'a court with two contradictory fatwas, one from Egypt and the other one from Syria. See M. Bakhit al-Muti'i (former mufti of Egypt), *Surat Fatwa 'an Waqf Tamim al-Dari al-Sahabi wa-A'qabihi*, Cairo: Bulaq: Dar al-Tiba'a al-Fu'adiyya, 7 Rajab 1350 (18 November 1931) (Arabic).

4 In some Muslim states there is a state Mufti who serves as a civil servant of the ministry in charge of the shari'a courts. In such cases the ministry can impose fatwas on the courts.

5 *Sawt al-Haqq wal-Huriyya*, 2 January 1998, p. 19 (Arabic).

6 Y. Reiter, "Manipulating fatwas" (forthcoming).

7 Article 99 of the 1965 Planning and Building Law states, "An instruction in any local or district zoning plan regarding the safeguarding of holy places or cemeteries will be issued in consultation with the minister of religious affairs and in

case of monuments or sites that have historical and archaeological importance, in consultation with the minister of education and culture."

8 The Khawarij is an extreme subversive sect that clashed with the fourth and fifth caliphs and nominated their own caliphs. They objected to arbitration between the caliphs Mu'awiyah and 'Ali, and they had their own interpretation of Islamic law. The Shi'ites view Ali ibn Abu Talib, prophet Muhammad's cousin and husband of the prophet's daughter Fatima, as Mahammed's sole heir. The establishment of the sect and its separation from Sunni Islam are believed to be initiated by the son of 'Ali, Hussein, who was killed with another seventy of his family in Karbala (today's Iraq) by a Sunnite army. The theological differences between Shi'a and Sunna lie in different beliefs regarding the principles of Islam.

9 The Al-Aqsa Corporation claimed that the plot planned for the MoT is part of a Muslim cemetery in which tens of thousands are buried, among them highly important Islamic leaders, and it is a holy place for Muslims. Therefore the works conducted on this land should be regarded as burrowing in graves. When old graves were unearthed in this compound, they claimed that this space is a holy Muslim site and any building or development on it is prohibited. They added that the 1967 Israeli law safeguarding holy places states that any harm to a holy place is completely prohibited and whoever causes damage to a holy place should be prosecuted in accordance with criminal law. They also claimed that dead bodies are holy, their graves are holy, and hence a cemetery is an eternal and irrevocable holy place. The corporation submitted to the court an expert opinion on this matter by Dr. Raid Fathi Jabarin dated 28 December 2006.

10 These included fatwas issued by the president of the Supreme Shari'a Court of the Palestinian Authority dated 9 December 2006, a manifesto written by Dr. Musa al-Bist, dean of the faculty of Islam and Sharia College of Umm al-Fahm in Israel, a fatwa by the Palestinian mufti of Jerusalem, Sheikh Ahmad Hussein, dated 10 December 2006, an opinion by Professor Hussam al-Din ibn Musa 'Aafana of Al-Quds University dated 8 December 2006, and a fatwa by the cheif mufti of Jordan dated 9 February 2007. All of these expressed the opinion that every action except for burial at the Mamilla Cemetery is ultimately prohibited (Appendix 728 to the updated appeal to the court). The plaintiffs submitted an expert opinion by Dr. Ahmad Qa'dan, a lecturer at Al-Qasemi College, who asserted that a cemetery is a holy waqf property that cannot be sold or exchanged.

11 Afana taught in the Islamic College of Umm al-Fahm (affiliated with the Islamic Movement and not recognized by the state institutions) and other academic institutions. His report was dated 8 December 2007.

12 Additional announcement submitted by the MoT entrepreneurs to the High Court, dated 3 January 2007 (cited in Articles 49–50 of HCJ 52/06). They also cited a number of legal rulings supporting their claims.

13 Letter of Mayor Mordechai Ish-Shalom dated 2 June 1964.

14 Y. Reiter, *Islamic Endowments in Jerusalem under British Mandate*, London and Portland, Oregon: Frank Cass, 1996, p. 25.

15 The Hanafite school of shari'a is named after the great Imam Al-Nu'ma ibn Thabit Abu Hanifa, who lived in Kufa (today's Iraq) during 699 -767 A.D. The Hanafite school of law is considered to be more liberal and less rigid and tough than others. This school was adopted by Sunnites of Egypt, the Fertile Crescent, Turkey, the Balkans, and Central and East Asia, and it is the basis of the Turkish Majeleh of 1869, the legal code that organized the tenure laws throughout the Ottoman

Empire. About thirty percent of the current Muslim world adheres to the Hanafite school.

16 He is also the author of a commentary on a book by a jurist who lived four decades before him, Abdallah al-Nasfi, who authored *Kanz al-Daqa'iq*, Cairo: Dar al-Ma'rifa (n.d.).

17 Al-Dahlawi, *Al-Fatawa al-Tatarkhaniyya*, Karachi: Idarat al-Qur'an wal-'Ulum al-Islamiyya, 1990.

18 *Al-Hawashi ala al-Durr al-Mukhtar*, Vol. 1, p. 628 [year, publisher].

19 A. Natour, "The battle for the Muslim cemeteries in Israel," in M. J. Breger, Y. Reiter, and L. Hammer (eds), *Religion and Politics: Sacred Space in Palestine and Israel*, London and New York: Routledge, 2012, pp. 168–92.

20 *Piskey Din*, High Court, part 3 1966, pp. 57–70 (Hebrew).

21 The words in question were: *sahha zar'uhu wal-binaa' 'alaihi*. Moreover, the Tatarhkaniyya fatwa collection does prohibit the digging of graves, even for the burial of another body inside, as Hammad correctly observes.

22 Jaffa Shari'a Court Records file 851/87, pp. 7–10, cited by Natour, op. cit.

23 *Yafa* (local newspaper of Arabs of Jaffa), Issue 5, 21 March 1988, p. 1 and Issue 17, 25 March 1989, cited by Natour, op. cit.

24 Kfar Saba Magistrate Court, 6005/04, unpublished verdict dated 19 September 2004.

25 Letter by Eng. Lev'on to Qadi Natour dated 9 August 2005, filed in the Shari'a Court of Appeals in file titled "Holy Places."

26 High Court file 8497/04, Al-Aqsa Corporation et al vs. Kerem Mararal et al. (Hebrew).

27 See his book *Al-Fath al-Qadir*, Cairo: M. al-Babi al-Halabi, 1349–1351 (1930–1932) (Arabic).

28 Moreover, according to Natour, Muslims continued to bury their dead after the village was abandoned in 1948 and until the 1960s.

29 For a fatwa by Natour regarding the Qishleh Cemetery of Jaffa see: *Alarab*, 20.1.2010.

30 See feature by Meir Hilzernet at www.news.co.il published in June 2009 (Hebrew).

31 Al-Zayla' ī, Fakhr al-Dīn' Uthmān ibn 'Alī. *Tabyīn al-Haqā'iq: Shar' Kanz al-Daqā'iq*. Cairo, Būlāq: al-Matba' ah al-Kubrá al-Amīrīyah, 1313–1315 (1895 or 6-1897 or 8) (Arabic).

32 M. A. Ibn-Abidin, *Radd al-Muhtar*, Vol. 4, p. 396 (Arabic).

33 Signed by Dr. Sa'id 'Abd al-Hafiz Hijawi, Chief Mufti of Jordan, Dr. Muhammad Najib al-Bist, Dr. Muhammad 'Abdallah Abu Sa'aliq and Dr. Tahir Ahmad Khazana.

34 Article 63 of the additional declaration submitted by the MoT entrepreneurs on 3 January 2007.

35 He underlines that in this fatwa Qadi Hammad based his opinion on a fatwa issued by Sheikh al-Azhar and the mufti of Egypt, published in the collection of fatwas *Al-Fatawa al-Mabdiyya fi al-Waqa'i' al-Misriyya*, part 1.

36 Apparently the Al-Aqsa Corporation advocate did not understand this element of shari'a. It seems that the attorney for the Al-Aqsa Corporation Abu Hussein, also missed this principle of shari'a. He argued at the High Court against defining the cemetery as mundaris by asking: "It is a fact that after sixty years the Authority of Antiquities unearthed dozens of graves. How could it be mundaris [a cemetery

that is in such poor condition that no one has been buried there for a period of time]?"

37 Submitted to the High Court by the Al-Aqsa Corporation.

38 See ruling by the Shari'a Court of Appeals 74/22, in Abu Ghosh, op. cit., pp. 203–205.

39 Layish implied a criticism regarding the ruling of Qadi Natour that, unlike qadis of the first generation in Israel, he was not educated at Al-Azhar but was a graduate of the Hebrew University and Tel Aviv University. He is an autodidact in shari'a. Natour also attended courses in Islamic law at the Hebrew University. It seems that Layish did not view this education as adequate training in shari'a although the State of Israel nominated Natour as qadi and vested in his authority the important position of president of the Shari'a Court of Appeals. Layish stated that Natour employs the principle of "public interest" to create impressive reforms in the ruling of the Shari'a Court of Appeals in personal status matters, but is a stubborn conservative in the realms of waqfs and cemeteries. Referring to the legal decrees of President Natour, Layish wrote that there are not in accordance with Israeli law and that they are aimed at reforming Islamic law external to the Knesset by selectively using shari'a literature from different schools of law.

40 S. Ory, "Makbara," in *Encyclopaedia of Islam*, 2nd edn, Leiden: Brill, 1991, IV, p. 125.

41 *Al-Liwa' al-Islami* of 16 September 2004 refers to the book of Muhammad ibn 'Ali al-Shawkani, *Nayl al-Awtar Sharh Muntiaqa al-Akhbar,* Beirut: Dar al Jil, 1973 (Arabic). The author was an eighteenth to nineteenth century jurist who served as the qadi of San'a and an advisor to the Zaiydi Imams of Yemen. He was considered a modernist who rejected *taqlid* (following in the footsteps of the main four orthodox schools of Sunnite Islam).

42 Ahmad al-Sharbasi, *Yas'alunaka fi al-Din wal-Hayah*, Beirut, Dar al-Jil, 1977, p. 444 (Arabic).

43 Citing the renowned Shafi'i jurist, Muhi al-Din Sharaf al-Din al-Nawawi.

44 M. Dukhan, *Land Laws in the State of Israel*, Jerusalem: Achva,1953, p. 469.

45 Haifa Magistrate Court, 2289/81, Al-Madi vs. the mutawallis of Waqf al-Istiqlal in Haifa, who sought to prevent of the removal of human remains, to be reburied in another cemetery, as planned in order to make room for the construction of a housing project over a cemetery, with the permission of a qadi. HCJ verdict 232/76 Shukri vs. the Shari'a Court, cited also the Haifa Shari'a Court decision from 25 January 1976 that permitted construction over the Al-Istiqlal Cemetery.

46 W. Al-Zuhayli, *Usul al-Fiqh wa-Adilatihi*, II, p. 1557 (Arabic).

47 Referring to the grave of 'Abdallah Ibn 'Ubay (*Sahih Al-Bukhari* translated to English by Muhammad Muhsin, published by Al-Maktaba al-Salafiyya) and referring to Aisha bint Talha ibn 'Ubaydallah who narrated that she saw her father in a dream thirty years after he died and that his grave was flooded with contaminated water. She disinterred his remains and reburied him in the courtyard of her house in Basra (Ibn Qutayba, *Kitab al-Ma'arif,* Cairo: Dar al-Kutub, 1960, pp. 228–9 (Arabic)). Ahmad ibn Hanbal narrated that the graves of Aisha and of Talha bin 'Ubaydallah were moved to another location (Ibn Qudama al-Maqdisi, *Al-Mughni*, Beirut: Dar al-Kitab al-Arabi, 1983, vol. 2, p. 390 (Arabic)). According to another tradition, narrated by Anas, the Prophet himself ordered the uprooting of graves of infidels from a plot of land that he designated for the building of a mosque in al-Madina (*Sahih al-Bukhari*, vol. 3, p. 92 (Arabic)).

48 *Fatawa al-Lajna al-Da'ima lil-Buhuth al-'Ilmiyya wal-Ifta'*, Riad: Maktabat al-Ma'arif lil-Nashr wal-Tawzi', 1997, IX, p. 122 (Arabic).

49 Hallaq was a Christian Arab born in Nazareth, Israel, and he graduated from Haifa University in Middle East Studies.

50 M. b. Idris al-Shafi'I, *Al-Umm*, vol. 1, p. 316 (Arabic).

51 Abd al-Razzaq al-San'ani, *Al-Musannaf*, vol. 3, p. 192 (Arabic); Yahya b. Sharaf al-Din al-Nawawi, *Al-Majmu': Sharh al-Muhadhdhab* (mentioned in the 1964 fatwa of Tahir Hammad), vol. 5, p. 273 (Arabic); M. b. Habib al-Mawardi, *Al-Ahkam al-Sultaniyya wal-Wilayat al-Diniyya* (Arabic); Ibn Qudama al-Maqdisi, *Al-Mughni*, Beirut: Dar al-Kitab al-Arabi, 1983, vol. 2, p. 194 (Arabic).

52 http://www.meshkat.net/index.php/meshkat/index/10/101213/content (Arabic).

53 http://www.islamweb.net/ver2/fatwa/PrintFatwa.php?lang=A&Id=10802 (Arabic).

54 http://www.islamweb.net/ver2/fatwa/PrintFatwa.php?lang=A&Id=10802 (Arabic).

55 http://www.islamweb.net/ver2/fatwa/PrintFatwa.php?lang=A&Id=109834 (Arabic).

56 Article 84 of the additional declaration submitted by the MoT entrepreneurs to the High Court dated 3 January 2007 (cited in Articles 49–50 of HCJ 52/06) (Hebrew).

57 Article 245 of HCJ 52/06 (Hebrew).

CHAPTER

6

The Palace Hotel and Other Precedents of Construction over Muslim Cemeteries

Every legal or judicial system has internal dialectics between legal theory and practice. The practice nourishes and influences theory and shapes the law. The same could be said about the development of the rule of Islamic law regarding the question of whether an old and inactive cemetery could be rendered for new uses. This chapter focuses on examples of actual changes to Muslim cemeteries that were introduced by Muslim authorities in Israel and in Muslim countries. The most prominent example is the construction of the Palace Hotel in Mamilla by the grand mufti of Jerusalem in Palestine, Haj Amin al-Husayni, in the 1920s. No wonder, therefore, that the MoT entrepreneurs and the state authorities focused specifically on this precedent. They claimed that this building was constructed over another part of the same historical cemetery of Mamilla at the initiative and with the authorization of the highest Palestinian-Muslim religious authority during the British Mandate. Was the Palace Hotel indeed built over the Mamilla Cemetery? This issue was debated among the experts who submitted professional opinions to the High Court.

The MoT entrepreneurs focused on this precedent in order to defuse the moral question, namely, the possibility of offending Muslims and desecrating a holy place. According to them, not only does the shari'a permit changing the utility of a cemetery, as discussed in chapter 5, but the highest Muslim authority of the Palestinians during the 1920s and 1930s, Grand Mufti Amin Al-Husayni, was the one who had initiated and was responsible for construction of the Palace Hotel. The Muslim plaintiffs as well as the Jewish academics who opposed construction of the MoT in Mamilla viewed this argument as a serious challenge, which required a response. The group of academics and civil organizations submitted an expert opinion by Professor Yehoshua Ben-Arieh claiming that, according to the city's zoning plan, at the time of its construction, the Palace Hotel already stood on land that was not part of the cemetery. This argument triggered a separate debate, not unrelated to the interests of the parties regarding the dispute over the location of the MoT. This chapter explores the complexity of this issue by discussing various positions and actions regarding construction of the Palace Hotel on an old Muslim cemetery.

I will begin by describing the construction of the Palace Hotel. I will then discuss the expert opinions that were submitted by the parties to the Mamilla conflict and the High Court decision regarding these opinions. Following that I will analyze documents from the years 1927 -1931 that shed some light on this issue, and I will conclude with my own analysis. Finally, I will present other precedents from both Israel and the Muslim world. Some of these were mentioned in the expert opinions submitted to the court, and others are newly researched and mentioned here for the first time.

Was the Palace Hotel Constructed over a Cemetery?

In 1925, Haj Amin al-Husayni, president of the Supreme Muslim Council and grand mufti of Jerusalem and Palestine, initiated construction of a hotel on a plot of land belonging to the waqf south of the Mamilla water reservoir pool. Haj Amin headed the Muslim institutions in British Mandate Palestine and, as such, was in charge of all waqf properties including cemeteries. The mufti viewed the construction of a hotel in Jerusalem on land belonging to the waqf as an investment that would benefit the institute he headed. According to the calculations of the Supreme Muslim Council, within 10 years the hotel was supposed to return the entire investment, which was estimated at 56,000 Palestinian pounds at the time the contract was signed with a British construction company in December 1927. The Muslim Council was unlucky, however, because construction expenses reached 73,500 Palestinian pounds, and while the building was completed in 1929, they calculated that the investment could at the soonest be returned within 15 years. They then discovered that the King David Hotel had been completed just before the Palace Hotel, and it overshadowed the Palace Hotel. Moreover, the world economic crisis of the 1930s placed the economic enterprise of the Palace Hotel against the backdrop of difficult times and an international economic recession. In the end, the Palace Hotel building never served as a hotel. Instead it was adapted to serve as the offices of the Supreme Muslim Council and a number of British government offices.[1]

Another construction project, which the Supreme Muslim Council initiated over a different Muslim cemetery in Jerusalem, was more successful. During the period that the Palace Hotel was under construction, the Jerusalem Municipality paved Saladin Road, beginning at the Al-Sahira Gate of the Old City, continuing northward through the Bab al-Sahira cemetery, and touching the Sa'd wa-Sa'id saints tombs. The Supreme Muslim Council used this opportunity to build houses and stores on this new main street. They demolished the cemetery's wall and moved a number of graves to the west of the street in order to make room for these new buildings.[2] Today this street is one of the busiest areas of East Jerusalem near the Old City.

For our purposes, the relevant question regarding the Palace Hotel is whether it was constructed over part of the Mamilla Cemetery. Professor Joseph Ginat discussed the Palace Hotel case extensively on behalf of the MoT entrepreneurs (as did Professor Aharon Layish and Dr. Shmuel Berkovits in their expert opinions before the High Court). Ginat wrote that the cemetery included land south of the present-day Agron Street, known at that time as the Al-Qalandariyya section of the cemetery, on which a number of buildings were constructed, including what today serves as the American Consulate of West Jerusalem as well as the Palace Hotel. He quoted the contractor Baruch Katinka, who wrote in his memoires as follows:

> The plot that was designated for the hotel is located *directly opposite* the old Muslim cemetery. When we dug three meters down, we found old graves with human remains. I was afraid that the Arab workers would tell the mufti that we desecrated graves; therefore, I came to the mufti and told him about the whole issue. To my surprise, he instructed me not to publicize this affair, and to keep it as a secret between the two of us. He said that he will make sure that the Arab workers keep quiet about it. He asked me to collect all of the bones and at the end of the excavation work, to relocate them secretly to another grave. [Emphasis added.]

These words teach us three things, two of which contradict Ginat's opinion. The first is that the land designated for the Palace Hotel was "directly opposite the cemetery." Therefore, from an official zoning and planning perspective, the land was not part of the cemetery. The second point is that unearthing a few graves was not grounds for abandoning the construction project. Third, building over graves is not a publicly acceptable norm. Therefore, the mufti, who feared public criticism, ordered that the human remains be hidden. Indeed, the mufti's opponents strongly criticized the entire initiative of construction over parts of old cemeteries, as I will discuss below.

As previously noted, the group of academics who opposed construction of the MoT in Mamilla submitted an expert opinion by Professor Yehoshua Ben-Arieh, a leading historical geographer of Palestine/Eretz Israel and the Middle East. Ben-Arieh wrote that already in the nineteenth century, the Mamilla Cemetery was re-delineated by means of a stone wall in order to make it possible to build around the cemetery.[3] This wall is indicated on British and other maps and also appears in aerial photos from that period. According to him, the Palace Hotel was constructed outside the wall of the cemetery to the south (where other buildings were also constructed, such as the house of the Christian Missionary Wester, which serves today as the house of the American Consulate; this area also served as the site of the lepers' hospital and the Jewish neighborhood of Makhane Yisrael). In his opinion, the discovery of a number of graves within land designated for the Palace Hotel does not indicate that this land was part of the cemetery because in the past, before the cemetery was officially re-delineated, Jerusalemites used to bury their dead wherever they could beyond the Old City walls. Before the State of Israel was established, however, no damage had been inflicted on the officially re-zoned area of the cemetery within the walls. At the same time, paths had been paved within the cemetery grounds, and according to Ben-Arieh various public affairs would take place therein (implying that the cemetery was used for other purposes), but there were no buildings within the demarcated boundaries of the cemetery.

Drawing on archival documents, Ben-Arieh related that in 1958, when Israel was celebrating its ten-year anniversary, the municipality sought to establish an outdoor entertainment arena in the cemetery grounds. When this idea was announced in the press, it encountered opposition on the part of Israeli Muslims. The secretary of the Muslim Advisory Community of Haifa (a committee established by the minster of religious affairs), Suhayl Shukri (mentioned in chapter 2), approached the mayor of Jerusalem at the time, Gershon Agron (d. 1959) and asked him not to locate the anniversary entertainment arena within the cemetery. Agron agreed to Shukri's request "out of special consideration and in order not to offend public sentiments," and he ordered that the entertainment arena be transferred to the municipal park on King George Street. Ironically, after his death, a public services building was constructed on another part of the cemetery and named in his honor – Beit Agron (the Agron House), which served as the headquarters of the journalists' association in Jerusalem – and it is located opposite Hillel Street, where the MoT is now being constructed. In addition, the eastern part of Gaza Road, which borders the Mamilla Cemetery, is also named after him: Agron Street.

The events recounted above demonstrate that Israeli Muslims were sensitive to possible damage to the Mamilla Cemetery, even though most of them could not reach Jerusalem under the martial regime imposed on their towns and villages. In order to visit Jerusalem, Muslim citizens of Israel from the Galilee, the Triangle (Wadi Ara area), and the Negev had to obtain a permit to leave their town or village from the military governor. Only Arabs who lived in mixed cities, such as Haifa and Jaffa, could freely travel to Jerusalem.

Archival documents can at times be misleading, as described in chapter 2 above. Suhayl Shukri himself was responsible for damage to Muslim cemeteries under his administration in Haifa. He sold the major cemetery of Haifa, a possession of the waqf for which he was the trustee (Istiqlal), to the Ministry of Housing for the construction of housing units for Muslims and for the benefit of the waqf that he controlled.[4] In addition, he sold many waqf assets and another cemetery in Haifa, located at the Neve Sha'anan neighborhood. According to press reports, in the early 1980s Shukri emigrated abroad and disappeared along with the funds that he had received from facilitating such projects.[5]

Professor Ben-Arieh added that "the fate of the Mamilla Cemetery did not improve" after the State of Israel came into being. The municipality expanded a city park at the expense of the cemetery in order to create "Independence Park." In the 1960s, state authorities caused further damage the Mamilla Cemetery. A road was paved in order to connect the streets of Hillel and Ben-Sira, and the Agron House was constructed, as were an elementary school and later a parking lot (where the government intends to build *Hekhal Ha-Mishpat*, the Judicial Compound for Jerusalem).[6]

The MoT entrepreneurs responded to Ben-Arieh's expert opinion with an expert opinion prepared for them by another leading geographer, Professor Gideon Biger from Tel Aviv University. In his submission, Biger distinguished between the formal boundaries of the Mamilla Cemetery as delineated at the beginning of the British Mandate and shaped by the network of roads surrounding the cemetery, on the one hand, and the substantive area of the cemetery, which according to him included the compound where the Palace Hotel was constructed, on the other hand. The High Court justices cited from Biger's expert opinion, which suggests that they were more inclined toward his opinion.[7] They also noted the claims of the IAA that they have "maps from the 1860s and aerial photos from 1927 that, although partially unclear, indicate that the Palace Hotel's land was very likely indeed part of the Mamilla Cemetery."[8]

Biger argued that the wall of the cemetery had been constructed only around those areas where gravestones were still visible. The land where the Palace Hotel was later built was possessed by the waqf and registered as a cemetery, and therefore no construction took place there until the Palace Hotel was initiated. Yet the area around it had been designated for construction of housing (and already had some houses built on it). He added that in 1925 British Mandate map (the year that the Palace Hotel was planned), the cemetery was not yet walled.[9] Here again, the expert opinion enabled different interpretations. On the one hand, Biger demonstrated that the Palace Hotel was constructed over an area that in the past had served as a cemetery, while on the other hand, he also demonstrated that the continuous encroachment upon this cemetery was a natural process, and hence the land designated for the Palace Hotel on the other side of the Gaza Road was perceived as a development zone.

Legal and Historical Documents Regarding the Palace Hotel Precedent

Historical documentation sheds light on the status of the Mamilla Cemetery, showing that in the eyes of Muslim dignitaries during the British Mandate, as well as in the eyes of representatives of the Supreme Muslim Council, the spot where the Palace Hotel was constructed was indeed considered part of the historical Mamilla Cemetery. Shortly after al-Husayni signed the contract to build the Palace Hotel in 1927, an opponent of the mufti named Yusuf ibn

Abd al-Razzaq al-'Alami filed a petition with the Shari'a Court of Jerusalem against the president of the Supreme Muslim Council (Al-Husayni) and the director of the Waqf in Jerusalem, the two authorities who had approved the construction over two Muslim cemeteries in Jerusalem, Mamilla and Bab al-Sahira. He claimed that prior to construction of the houses by the waqf, human remains had been removed from the graves and relocated to another site. It should be underlined that the Shari'a Court at that time was subject to the Supreme Muslim Council, and as we will see below, this affected the court's decision. Nonetheless, the court hearing and the response of the waqf expose new important facts regarding this matter.

The qadi who handled the petition asked Mustafa Yunis, the advocate representing the president of the Muslim Council, to provide him with factual evidence on the matter. He wanted to know, so wrote Yunis to Al-Husayni, the detailed decisions of the Council, the grounds for the public benefit (*maslaha*) of the construction project, and whether there was a legal justification of duress (*darura*) for this action (the two justifications in shari'a for approving transactions involving waqf properties), as well as whether the land that was removed from graves contained old structures and whether graves were relocated. The qadi's decision conveys an interesting factual picture, as reflected in the following verdict, taken directly from the Shari'a Court record and translated from the Arabic:

> In the noble Shari'a session that took place at the Shari'a Court of Jerusalem the following people appeared [in front of me] Advocate Ibrahim Effendi [Effendi is a title of honor] Ali, representing Yusuf Effendi ibn Sheikh Abd al-Razzaq Effendi al-'Alami [the plaintiff] by power of attorney dated 21 March 1927, together with Sheikh Ziad Effendi Qassab and Hasan Effendi al-Budayri, jointly and severally, in the claim submitted against the President of the Supreme Muslim Council and against Ma'mur al-Awqaf [Director of Waqf] requesting that the character of the two cemeteries Bab al-Sahira and Ma'man Allah [Mamilla] not be changed, that construction in these places be declared illegal, that they be left intact in their present condition (before building), etc., as the claim was read in front of us by Advocate Ibrahim Effendi Ali, and is filed in this case folder. In addition, two attorneys (for the defendant) appeared; one is Raghib Effendi Abu al-Sa'ud al Dajani and Sheikh Mustafa Effendi Yunis al-Husayni, representing Haj Amin Effendi [Al-Husayni], the President of the Supreme Muslim Council, and the second is Badr Effendi Yunis al-Husayni, representing Ma'mur al-Awqaf by general power of attorney signed by the court registrar dated 9 April 1927, numbered 639/214 and signed by the one who sent him to represent him, which was presented to the two parties. Ibrahim Effendi, the plaintiffs' advocate, complained to us that the two defendants, Haj Amin Effendi in his capacity as the President of the Supreme Muslim Council and Badr Effendi in his capacity as Director

of Awqaf of Noble Jerusalem, took out part of the Bab al-Sahira cemetery located outside the Old City walls east of the public road known in its boundaries where warriors and righteous sages as well as Muslim laymen are buried. Over this land they constructed shops in order to make revenues for the General Waqf, but their construction has yet to be completed. The boundaries and space of this cemetery are known to the public and therefore there is no need to describe it. *They also took part of the land of Turbat Ma'man Allah (Mamilla Cemetery), the eastern part of which is also known as "Turbat al Jabaliyya," located on the public road whose boundaries are also known to the public, where warriors, righteous sages, and Muslim laymen are also buried. They unearthed bones of the dead from their graves and relocated them to other places in order to build on this land shops, large housing units, or hotels that will bring revenues to the General Waqf.* In light of this and because it is prohibited to take part of the above mentioned graveyards or even of one of the two graveyards in order to construct houses, stores, or something else for the purpose of profit (usufruct), and because it is prohibited to use them for utilities other than the original purpose of the land that was dedicated as waqf, even if the graves have decomposed and no evidence of the dead remained, then it is prohibited take land from them according to the texts of the Shari'a.

Given that the two above-mentioned cemeteries have been dedicated to burial of the dead since ancient times, and given that no one challenges the fact that they are an endowment, and given that this waqf dedication is mentioned in historical volumes . . . [two unclear words in the document] . . . and given that every Muslim is permitted to file a claim regarding charitable institutions benefiting the general public such as cemeteries, as enumerated in the Shari'a texts and the Majala (Ottoman Code of Law), I demand in the name of my representative Haj Muhammad-Yusuf Effendi al-'Alami, under his title as individual of the Muslim public, to decree a prohibition on the changing of the character of the two above-mentioned cemeteries because of the illegality of constructing the buildings that they seek to build there, and to leave the two cemeteries in their present condition and then to impose upon the defendants the court fees and attorney fees.

Then Sheikh Ahmad Raghib Effendi [representing al-Husayni] said the following: The plaintiff submitted a claim against the President of the Supreme Muslim Council and against Ma'mur al-Awqaf. In such claims involving the Waqf Administration, the official party should be the Director of Waqf, namely today's Ma'mur al-Awqaf of Jerusalem. According to the guidelines of the [Ottoman] Ministry of Justice, as stated in page 88 of the procedural rules, and given that the President of the Supreme Muslim Council is not party to such a claim, I ask the Court to dismiss him as a defendant. Now referring to the waqf affairs, *my response is the following: briefly, there is a debate among Shari'a*

> *jurists regarding the question of whether cemeteries can be rendered for construction and graves permitted to be excavated or not. Some jurists prohibit it completely, while others ultimately permit it.* [This is indicated in the]following texts: page 21 of the book titled 'Qashf al-Ghima' by Sheikh 'Abd al-Wahab Sha'rani, in the chapter entitled Bab al-Jana'iz (burial issues); page 274 in the volume entitled Waqf al-Bahr volume 5; the decision by the Majala Council, from 26 of the Month of Muharam 1306 A.H., appearing on page 165 of al-Muqararat al-'Ilmiyya; and in the book of Al-Zayla'i and the book of Ibn Abidin. Then Advocate Ahmad Raghib Effendi stated that the construction at Bab al-Sahira was already completed and according to the plaintiff himself, the buildings were already rendered for use. If the plaintiff were a legal party to the claim and if the Court were to hear his claim, then it should be rejected because claims regarding waqf issues should be submitted in a procedure of accounting (*hisbah*), and the plaintiff submitted his claim after a delay of five days, therefore it should be rejected according to Shari'a [a few unclear words] . . . he grounded his claim on a fatwa that was presented to the Shari'a Court.
>
> Then Advocate Muhammed Adib Effendi Ramadan, representing the defendant by general power of attorney, which includes this claim, issued by [a few unclear words] . . . in Jerusalem, dated 28 March of 1927, numbers 1422/1021, . . . regarding the prohibition on unearthing graves and building over cemeteries, basing himself on the book entitled Tartib al-Sunuf fi Ahkam al-Wukuf by Ali Haidar Effendi, who was the head of the Fatwa Department of the (Ottoman) Sheikh al-Islam Office, claiming that in matters of cemeteries and waqf affairs, a claim can only be submitted by the Waqf Administrator (mutawalli) or a person who was granted a permit to be a party to such claims.
>
> Decision: because the plaintiff meets none of the above-mentioned requirements, I decide to reject this claim in light of lack of authority to be a party to the claim. This decision can be appealed. Issued today, 8 of the Month of Muharam 1348 Hijra, equivalent to 26 of June 1928.[10] [Emphases added.]

The qadi's decision not to recognize the plaintiff as a legitimate party seems odd because in issues pertaining to the General Waqf for the public good, every Muslim who is a potential beneficiary of the endowment has the right to submit a claim against the waqf administrator. Apparently, the qadi, who was appointed by the Supreme Muslim Council and was subject to it, could not rule against a plaintiff from the opposition. He preferred to relinquish his right to submit a claim than to hear the case.

This verdict teaches us two important lessons. First, the advocate for the director of waqf properties did not deny that the construction had taken place over the land of a cemetery. In the case of Bab al-Sahira cemetery, he argued that the construction was already completed, and therefore the claim was redundant. Moreover, regarding the Mamilla Cemetery, the qadi stated that the construction is over the eastern part of Ma'man Allah Cemetery, named Turbat al Jabaliyya. Second, the attorney representing the Waqf defended his client by arguing that the *shari'a is ambiguous regarding construction over a cemetery* and, in order to justify this position, he referred to Muslim jurists who supported construction over and development of cemeteries.

This document, as well as other Shari'a Court records, makes clear why the construction of the Palace Hotel was used by the entrepreneurs of the MoT. The facts relevant to this Shari'a Court hearing of 1927, when preparatory work to build the Palace Hotel had just started, could undermine Muslim claims that their sentiments were offended or that the sanctity of the cemetery was violated by construction on the same cemetery. Yet the 1927 petition was only the first action taken by the Palestinian opposition to Haj Amin Husayni, as we shall see below. The major action against the Palace Hotel took the form of a booklet printed by three opposition members and distributed among the participants of the All-Islamic Congress held in Jerusalem in 1931. The Islamic Congress decided, among other things, to protest to the British Mandate government over its decision to allow Jews free access to pray at the Western Wall.[11] Additional documentation that reinforces the interpretation that construction of the Palace Hotel took place on the Mamilla Cemetery is presented below.

In December 1931 Amin Husayni convened the All-Islamic Congress in Jerusalem with the participation of 145 senior Muslim religious leaders from around the world to discuss, among other things, Jewish desecration of holy places in Jerusalem. (Among the resolutions of the congress was one protesting the British government's granting of permission to Jews visit the Western Wall.) At the congress the mufti's Palestinian opponents disseminated a manifesto that attacked the mufti, among other reasons, for building over cemeteries. It was written by three oppositionists who were senior and respected figures. As opponents to Al-Husayni, they were biased. However, the facts that they presented to the leaders of the Muslim world were documented with pictures that spoke for themselves. The oppositionists were Gharib al-Khalidi, former District Court justice in Jerusalem, Arif Hikmat al-Nashashibi, former General Waqf director, and Hasan al-Budayri, a renowned lawyer. The Muslim Council had to defend itself against their claims by publishing a response in its organ newspaper, *Al-Jami'a al-Arabiyya*. When, despite their expectations, the issue failed to capture the attention of the participants of the Muslim Congress or the local public opinion, the three oppositionists decided to print and publish their manifesto in a booklet. Also printed in this booklet was the response of the Supreme Muslim Council alongside their comments on this response, as well as pictures of the holy places that they claimed were damaged by the Muslim Council.

The following are relevant sections from this booklet that shed light on the public debate. (Articles 5–6 in the booklet refer to the Mamilla Cemetery):[12]

> [5] The Ma'man Allah Cemetery is one of the most important Muslim Cemeteries, in which 70,000 slain Muslims of the army of Salah al-Din (Saladin) al-Ayubi, as well as the bones of sages, are buried, and their graves were destroyed and their character was changed . . . [14 names of senior religious personalities . . .] all of the above graves were excavated and their use was changed, and part of the cemetery became a stone quarry that still operates today. The quarry operator is Ibrahim al-Husayni, the cousin of the President of the [Supreme Muslim] Council.
>
> [6] The Palace Hotel, built by the Muslim Council, part whose construction was funded by donations to the Council and where delegations of the Muslim world are now convening was constructed over the skulls of warriors in the well-known Al-Qalandariyya cemetery, which is part of the Ma'man Allah Cemetery [pages 6–7 in the booklet]

The response of the Supreme Muslim Council, published in *Al-Jami'a al-Islamiyya*, issue number 738 of 21 of the Sha'ban, 1350 AH (1 December 1931), included the following:

> [5] At the remote edge of the Ma'man Allah Cemetery, there is a stony section that is far from the graves and could not be used for the purpose of burial. The Waqf Administration rented it for the long term for the purpose of removing the stones from this section in order to level the earth and prepare it for burial. During this work, no single grave was excavated, and in particular, none of graves of the slain who are buried there. What was claimed in this regard is a baseless propaganda.
>
> [6] The Waqf hotel constructed by the Supreme Muslim Council was erected on a spot that the Jerusalemite Muslims have known for more than 70 years [that served during the Ottoman Caliphate as a station for horses carrying tourists]. This was also a playground for circus animals and a football yard. Therefore it is not a graveyard. The building was erected only after legal petitions to the Shari'a Courts were submitted based on Muslim sages' fatwas, some of which claimed that it is a cemetery. This plot was transacted by a bid for an annual rent of 7,300 Palestine pounds, which were used for the expenses of the waqf of the Al-Aqsa Mosque . . . [Signed by the Secretary of the Supreme Muslim Councils, Sa'd al-Din al-Khatib, dated 20 Sha'ban 1350 (30 November 1931), pages 10–11 in the booklet].

The response of the three oppositionists was as follows:

> [5] Ma'man Allah Cemetery
> The Council claims in its response that our petition refers to "the

remote edge of the Ma'man Allah Cemetery, [where] there is a stony section that is far from the graves and could not be used for the purpose of burial [and that the] Waqf Administration rented it for the long term for the purpose of removing the stones from this section in order to level the earth and prepare it for burial. During this work, no single grave was excavated, and in particular, none of graves of the slain who are buried there." The truth is that the entire western section [of the cemetery] from south to north, encompassing at least 40,000 graves, is located at the heart of the cemetery between the pool and the Slain Cave. The Council permits Ibrahim al-Husayni to use this holy and historical cemetery as a stone quarry (see picture #7) where he used dynamite and explosives that broke the gravestones. In addition, they created rubble through this action; they excavated and damaged dozens and perhaps even hundreds of graves. All of them belong to important slain people and sages and whoever is interested can witness it in the field. This Cemetery has now become uneven (see picture #8). They bring beasts of burden into this place to carry the masonry machinery as well as iron tools. The Council's response fails to address this. There is also a brick factory owned by Ibrahim al Husayni and his Jewish partner. All the graves that we mentioned in our manifest were destroyed and the gravestones were sold. It is a shame that during the convention of the Islamic Congress, works in this cemetery quarry were ceased, along with the use of dynamite. In addition, the entrance that was specially opened in the cemetery's wall to bring in beasts of burden and cars was sealed so that nobody would see what goes on (see picture #9). What is more despicable is that the Supreme Muslim Council permitted laying down the Palace Hotel sewage at Al-Qalandariyya cemetery through three big holes among the graves. The sewage is pumped to these septic tanks through metal pipes and through the use of pumps. Plans for the sewage were prepared by the engineering department of the Waqf Administration. Whoever wants can go and see the septic tanks and how the sewage spews from among the graves in the Ma'man Allah Cemetery.

[6] The Palace Hotel
The Council's response claims that the hotel was built on a spot that was used as a station for horses carrying tourists and grounds for animals. The truth is that the volume entitled Al-Quds al Khalil [the history of Jerusalem and Hebron], written by Mujir al-Din al-Hanbali (d. 1522), narrates that Sheikh Muhammad ibn Abi Jawz, who died after the year 800 AH [1397], was buried in Ma'man Allah, south of the pool, close to the gate of Al-Qalandariyya. The description of the location of this grave accords completely with the place where the hotel was constructed. The Al-Qalandariyya section is part of the Ma'man Allah Cemetery. In the period when Umar Effendi Abd al-Salam al-Husayni

> [d. 1882/3] served as the mayor of Jerusalem, the road that today separates between the two cemeteries, and in the past was behind the Al-Qalandariyya Cemetery, was paved. When the owners of neighboring plots began to trespass into the cemetery from all sides, the Jerusalemites whose family members are buried in this place, such as the dignitary families of Al-Dajani, Al-Khalidi, Nashashibi, Nusseibeh, Al-Ansari, Al-Duzdar, Al-Asaliya, Al-Namarri, Al-Julani, and more, raised money and walled the cemetery in with what we see today as the stone wall. During the [First World] War more than 1,500 warriors were buried in Al-Qalandariyya. Regarding the claim that this land was used for animals and beasts of burden, this is a baseless lie. The truth is that the Muslim Council rented this land in 1924 for two weeks to serve as grounda for an animal circus that arrived in Jerusalem. The Supreme Muslim Council was the party that used this land as grounds for beasts, and not the Ottoman state . . . [pages 17–19]

What can we learn from the above sources? The factual picture teaches us that a large area west of the Old City was known as Mamilla and served for the burial of Muslims. The entire area had different sections, known by at least three different names: Ma'man Allah, Jabaliya, and Qalandariyya. In the 19th Century, with the westward development of Jerusalem, urban development led to a process of encroachment upon the old burial places. Initially a road was paved within the cemetery. known in the past as Gaza Road and today as Agron Street, it encroached upon the cemetery from its southern side, where later the Palace Hotel was constructed. The graves, however, remained buried deep within the earth.[13]

Recently the Palace Hotel has been extensively renovated by the Waldorf Astoria hotel chain. During these renovations at least three new graves were excavated.

Since the nineteenth century, Jerusalem's development has led to a reduction in the area of the Mamilla Cemetery. Even the Supreme Muslim Council apparently had plans to build over this cemetery in the 1940s. In 1931 the All-Muslim Congress convening in Jerusalem decided to establish a university named Al-Aqsa, and planners began to pursue a design that would locate this university on the land of the Mamilla Cemetery. David Kroyanker, a leading researcher on the architecture of Jerusalem, found photographic evidence of a sketch prepared by an Egyptian architect, placing the Islamic University on the Mamilla Cemetery.[14]

From an exchange of letters we learn that a new construction initiative took place in the 1940s, after the Supreme Muslim Council was placed under direct control of the British government. Correspondence from 1946 submitted to the High Court by the IAA was incorporated within the justices' conclusion that "the issue of construction over the cemetery was already decided positively and what remained for discussion was a debate on the value of the land and the preservation of the old pool in that compound." Indeed,

Desecration of the Mamilla Cemetery According to Mufti's Opposition Pamphlet

correspondence from 27 September 1946 between the British governor of Jerusalem and the local planning and construction committee, as well as the head of the Mandate's antiquities department, reveals that the Supreme Muslim Council, headed by Amin Abd al-Hadi, was interested in developing and building on this cemetery. The municipality was interested in such development in order to increase its income while the Muslim Council demanded higher construction density (per dunam) and even wanted to build above the historical pool, which is considered an antiquity site, but the British Government insisted on preserving the Mamilla pool as a site of antiquities and was prepared to invest in its preservation and in planting a public garden to surround it.[15] The Muslim Council hinted that it would agree to collective relocation of the graves of the Saladin warriors who are buried around the pool, in order to maximize construction density. A general sketch of the building plan was published in 1948 by the planner Henry Kendall.[16]

Plan to Develop the Mamilla Cemetery

In 1946 the Supreme Muslim Council was under the strict supervision and control of the British government, and it is likely that the Mandatory Government was the initiator of the construction plans. Yet during the period when Haj Amin al-Husayni was president of the Supreme Muslim Council and until 1937, the Council itself, together with the Jerusalem Municipality under Muslim mayors, made use of parts of the Mamilla Cemetery for building and development purposes. The fact is that the Supreme Muslim Council itself initiated development works over Muslim cemeteries, including the relocation of graves, and this weakened the Muslim plaintiffs' claims that building over a Muslim cemetery is a desecration of a holy place and is deeply offensive to the Muslim community when there are no visible graves on the surface.

It should be underlined that the formal aspect is less important than the public one. Formally, during the Mandate period the Palace Hotel was built on a plot that was not officially designated as a cemetery according to the municipal zoning master plan. Otherwise, a building permit could not have been issued. However, in terms of public opinion, the above-mentioned documents imply a norm to which the president of the Supreme Muslim Council ascribed, that is, a norm of gradual encroachment on old Muslim cemeteries, including the Mamilla Cemetery, for the sake of modern development. This norm appears in other contemporary Muslim societies. The following section highlights some of the many examples.

Building over Muslim Cemeteries Permitted by Religious Authorities

Many examples were cited in reports submitted to the High Court indicating the practice of building over Muslim cemeteries initiated by Muslims and approved by religious Muslim authorities. In particular, one such case can be found in the home town of the head of the Northern Islamic Movement in Israel, Sheikh Raed Salah, who was the Mayor of Umm al-Fahm. The spontaneous pattern of construction and the residential density in Umm al-Fahm drove both the residents and the municipality to encroach upon the cemeteries of the various family clans. In 1988 the Umm al-Fahm Municipality, headed by Hashem Mahamid from the Democratic Front for Peace and Equality (DFPE) party, paved a local road and walled off a Muslim Cemetery of the Aghbariyya clan. This project, on the eve of the elections to the Knesset, had political significance because the roadworks were conducted by volunteers in a camp organized by the mayor's party, when the Islamic Movement was in the opposition (Sheikh Raed Salah was elected mayor the following year). The imam for the nearby Jabarin Mosque opposed construction of the road because it was planned to traverse a graveyard. At this time, the Islamic Movement joined his opposition and filed a petition to the High Court, claiming that there were human bodies buried beneath the planned road and that shari'a law prohibits the pavement of a road in a cemetery. Interestingly, in this case the Islamic Movement did not claim that a cemetery is eternally holy, as they claimed in the case of Mamilla. They only asserted that according to Islamic law there is a "designated period" during which works over graves cannot be conducted. It should also be noted that the Islamic Movement chose, as in the Mamilla case, to petition the High Court rather than the Shari'a Court. In its response to the High Court, the Umm al-Fahm Municipality claimed that this specific land had not served burial purposes for many years, more years than the shari'a requires for mundaris. They added that the municipality is the only party responsible for the administration of cemeteries and burials, and that the Islamic Movement has no standing over such activity.

The then-president of the High Court of Justice, Meir Shamgar (together with Justices Levin and Goldberg), who heard the case, succeeded in bringing the parties to a peaceful compromise. The court recommended to the litigants that the case be decided by a religious authority. The litigants then agreed that the case be adjudicated by Qadi Tawfiq Asaliya, who at that time was the president of the Shari'a Court of Appeals. Asaliya was also a resident of Umm al-Fahm, and as mentioned above, issued many fatwas permitting the sale of Muslim cemeteries for development purposes (he retracted from these permits only in 1989). Shamgar ruled:

> The process of dealing with this matter should be twofold: first, it is necessary to present evidence to the honorable qadi that there are indeed graves that were freshly excavated during a designated period. The second step is to seek the judicial opinion of the qadi regarding what is permitted and what is prohibited regarding the construction of a wall and the paving of a road. Because we [the High Court] have no authority to order the honorable qadi to hear this case, we recommend that when the litigants approach him on this matter, he deal with the issue in above-mentioned spirit.[17]

It appears that although the High Court of Justice referred the disputed parties to Qadi Asaliya, the qadi refrained from hearing the case. Asalyia was in an awkward position because he himself had in the past permitted the sale of and construction over Muslim cemeteries. The Islamic Movement pressured him and caused him to rescind previously issued permits, as mentioned in chapter 5. His retractions had no practical effect, however, because those cemeteries were already rendered for other uses. After Asaliya continued to refrain from making a decision, the road at the edge of the cemetery became a fact. What I found most interesting is that when Sheikh Raed Salah, representing the Islamic Movement, was elected to the position of mayor the following year, in 1989, the municipality under his leadership continued to encroach upon the same cemetery. During a visit in January 2010, I saw that a new road had been paved in the eastern part of the cemetery, traversing the cemetery from north to south. I also saw that the cemetery has been neglected and that much garbage has accumulated in its margins (see pictures). It seems that the Islamic Movement is quick to complain about damage to Muslim cemeteries in Jewish areas but neglects Muslim cemeteries in its own backyard.

Garbage at Muslim Cemetery of Umm al-Fahm

Returning to the Mamilla dispute, the High Court quoted from expert opinions submitted by the Museum entrepreneurs, particularly from those submitted by Dr. Shmuel Berkowitz and Professor Aharon Layish, highlighting additional examples of Muslim cemeteries that had undergone a process of relocation of graves. The following examples were mentioned: Bab al-Sahira Cemetery, where a waqf building and another building were constructed over the cemetery and a sewage pipe was laid down, followed by construction of shops and an auditorium built over this same cemetery; the Kufr Qasem Cemetery, parts of which were claimed in order to build a soccer field; the Iqsal village cemetery, part of which served as a road; the Juljuliya cemetery, where a road was built in addition to a pavilion and truck parking lot; the Pardisia cemetery in Tybeh, part of which was expropriated by the Tybeh Municipality for residential purposes in 1998; and Al-Istiqlal Cemetery in Haifa,[18] where Shari'a Court Qadi Muhammad Hubeishi permitted waqf administrators to transfer five dunams for a period of 99 years in order to erect residential buildings for the Muslim community, as part of a solution to the housing problems of Arabs in Haifa.[19] The waqf could get seventeen out of seventy housing units from this deal, in addition to four shops, a club, and a kindergarten. Although the benefit to the Muslim community from this transaction was evident, it triggered a public outcry. Finally, the Shari'a Court Qadi had to overrule this decision, but the administrator, Suhayl Shukri, mentioned above, appealed to the High Court and won his case against the Shari'a Court (and due to Muslim public outcry the project was halted).[20]

Road Paved Inside Umm al-Fahm Cemetery under Sheikh Salah's Mayorship

Another precedent reported to the High Court took place in Jordan. The Museum entrepreneurs submitted research from a Jordanian lawyer named Sa'id Karaja, who apparently did not know that he was writing for a court case in Israel.[21] Karaja wrote that the law in Jordan classifies three types of cemeteries: open cemeteries, meaning those that are still active and used for burial; closed cemeteries, with no more room for burial, that no longer serve this purpose; and ruined (i.e., extinct or mundaris) cemeteries, where the most recent deceased were buried at least forty years previously.[22] The two latter types are considered waqf and are administered by the Ministry of Awqaf. Karaja wrote that construction over a cemetery and relocation of its graves are permitted only in cemeteries of the third type. However, even in cemeteries of the first two types, some works can be conducted for the benefit of the public. As an example, he mentioned a road that was paved across the middle of Al-Sahab Cemetery south of Amman. An example of the third type was the case of Ras al ʻAyn Cemetery in the middle of Amman. The Amman metropolitan municipality requested that the Ministry of Al-Qaf hand over part of this cemetery some ten years ago to build the great Amman Municipality, in return for substitute land. Previously, the Ministry of Al-Qaf itself had built an amusement park over this cemetery.

Similar cases took place recently in Egypt. In 2001, fatwas were issued in Egypt to remove with bulldozers over 1,000 Muslim graves in order to construct a road surrounding Cairo and to pave a new road in the Jamaliyya neighborhood.[23] It is also well known that the poor of Cairo have settled in the great Mamluk cemetery, Al-Sitt Zaynab, and they have turned grave tombs into residential facilities, installed TV antennas above them, and used some of them as chicken coops and stores.[24]

In conclusion, present-day reality shows that Muslim societies in Israel and abroad employ a change in the designated use of old cemeteries for the purpose of paving roads and pursuing other forms of urban development, such as buildings and public parks. The Palace Hotel initiated by the Mufti Haj Amin al Husayni at the end of the 1920s is one such example. The hotel was built on a plot that was part of a large Muslim cemetery but was excised from this cemetery in the process of planning and development. Urban development included paving a road and building a wall that designated the active part of the cemetery at the northern end of the Gaza Road (today's Agron Street) and enabled the designation of the land south of that road for building purposes.

It is not surprising that the MoT entrepreneurs used the Palace Hotel precedent to convince the High Court that Muslim religious adjudicators have a flexible interpretation of the shariʻa, according to which practical needs result in permits to build over cemeteries when the public interest justifies it. Senior muftis as well as religious establishment officials in Muslim countries have also approved development projects involving the use of cemetery land for the benefit of the community. The position of Qadi Ahmad Natour in Israel and the Islamic Movement was that the Mamilla case is different because the MoT designated to be built at the expense of the cemetery is a project that benefits the Jewish state rather than the Muslim community.

The High Court verdict regarding the Mamilla dispute used a number of precedents, including the case of Umm al-Fahm, which the same Court under previous president, Justice Meir Shamgar, had handled. However, unlike Shamgar, who left the decision in the hands of the authorized religious authority, that is, the president of the Shariʻa Court of Appeals, in the Mamilla case Justices Ayalah Pocaccia, Edna Arbel, and David Chesim completely rejected the authority of the current president of the Shari'a Court, Qadi Ahmad Natour. Their position is presumably shaped by the views of Qadi Natour, which are identical to those of the Islamic Movement in matters related to waqf properties. The movement is perceived as acting against Zionist interests and the interests of the State of Israel.

Notes

1 U. M. Kupferschmidt, *The Supreme Muslim Council, Islam under the British Mandate for Palestine*, Leiden, New York, Copenhagen, and Köln: E.J. Brill, 1987, p. 136; Y. Reiter. *Islamic Endowment in Jerusalem under British Mandate*, London and Portland, Oregon: Frank Cass, 1996, p. 195.

2 Reiter, ibid.

3 Professor Yehoshua Ben Arieh was the rector of the Hebrew University and a laureate of Israel Prize in Geography.

4 Magistrate Court of Haifa 2289/81 Al-Madi vs. the Mutawallis of Istiqlal Waqf of Haifa; HCJ 232/76 Shukri vs. the Shari'a Court, Piskey Din 31(1) 413 (1976).

5 Yitzhak Reiter, "Waqf in Israel since 1965: The case of Acre reconsidered" in M. J. Breger, Y. Reiter, and L. Hammer, *Holy Places in the Israeli–Palestinian Conflict: Confrontation and Co-existence*, London and New York: Routledge, 2009, pp. 104–127.

6 Expert opinion submitted to the High Court by Ben Arieh dated 20 March 2007.

7 Article 62 of HCJ 52/06 verdict. Biger's report is dated 6 May 2007.

8 Article 60 of HCJ 52/06 verdict.

9 Biger's expert opinion to the HCJ dated 6 May 2007.

10 Al-Quds Shari'a Court, *Sijill Ahkam* 444, Page 19, Document #95 (Arabic).

11 M. Kramer, *Islam Assembled: The Advent of the Muslim Congresses*, New York: Columbia University Press, 1986, p. 123.

12 R. al-Khalidim 'Arif Hikmat al-Nashashibi and H. al-Budayri, *Bayan ila al-'Alam al-Islami 'Ammatan 'An al-Amakin al-Muqaddasa al-Islamiyya fi Filastin*, Jerusaalem: Matba'at Bayt al-Maqdis, 7 February 1933, pp. 6–7 (Arabic). The response of the Supreme Muslim Council to the opposition leaflet of 1931 was published in its organ *Al-Jami'a al-Islamiyya*, issue 738 dated 21 Sha'ban 1350 h. (1 December 1931) (Arabic).

13 It is interesting to note that as these words are being drafted, the Palace Hotel is being reconstructed as a new Waldorf Astoria Hotel in Jerusalem, and when deep excavation took place underneath, a number of Muslim graves were excavated. The director of the Jewish Haredi organization that acts to preserve Jewish graves Atra Kadisha (Aramaic name for holy place) arrived to the site thinking that the graves were of Jewish origin. When he discovered that the skeletons were buried with their head facing southward towards Mecca, in a way that Muslims buried their dead, he did not object to the resumption of works.

14 David Kroyanker, "Museum is Prohibited and a University is Permitted?" *Haaretz*, 10 January 2006 (Hebrew); Idem, *Halom behakitz: Yerushalayim ha-lo-bnuya*, Jerusalem: Migdal David – The Museum for Jerusalem's History, 1993 (Hebrew); On the decision to establish a university regardless of its location, see Kupferschmidt, op. cit., pp. 206–18.

15 Letter from R.W. Hamilton, Director of Antiquities Department to the governor of Jerusalem and another letter from the Head the Local Planning Committee to

the Governor of Jerusalem dated 12 September 1946; Letter from Webster, the Head the Local Planning Committee from March 1946.

16 Henry Kendall, *Jerusalem, the city plan: preservation and development during the British mandate, 1918–1948*, London: H.M. Stationery Office Press and Admiralty Chart Establishment, 1948, p. 53, illustration 181.

17 HCJ 593/86 Islamic Association vs. Umm al-Fahm Municipality (unpublished verdict of 14 February 1988) (Hebrew).

18 Magistrate Court of Haifa 2289/81 Al-Madi vs. the Mutawallis of Istiqlal Waqf of Haifa; H.C. 232/76 Shukri vs. the Shari'a Court, Piskey Din 31(1) 413 (1976) (Hebrew).

19 Haifa Shari'a Court, *Sijill* 76/6 file 95/76 dated 25 January 1976 (Hebrew).

20 Magistrate Court of Haifa 2289/81 Al-Madi vs. the Mutawallis of Istiqlal Waqf of Haifa (Hebrew); HCJ 232/76 Shukri vs. the Shari'a Court, Piskey Din 31(1) 413 (1976) (Hebrew). For other cases see the expert opinion of archaeologist Meir Ben-Dov dated 13 February 2006 and the expert report of Dr. Jaques Neria dated 3 December 2006.

21 His expert opinion was submitted to an American lawyer who commissioned it from him.

22 Jordanian bylaw no. 22 of 1970 regarding cemeteries according to the Public Health Law no. 12 of 1970.

23 Expert opinion by Dr. Shmuel Berkovitz citing the dissertation of Yehiel Shabi "Land and Islamic Religious Land as a Tool in the Israeli–Palestinian National Struggle," Bar Ilan University, 2005, pp. 40–1.

24 Ibid.

CHAPTER 7

"What Is Abhorrent to You, Do Not Do to Your Friend" – Comparative Legal Perspective

"The whole Torah stands on one principle: what you do not want somebody to do to you, do not do to the other." Advocate Saleh Abu Husayn presented this quote from the Talmud on behalf of the Muslim plaintiffs at the High Court hearing of April 29, 2007. The popular interpretation of the Talmudic saying meaning "what is abhorrent to you, do not do to your friend"[1] is attributed to Hillel, the president of the Sanhedrim (the Supreme Jewish Judicial Assembly) during the first century BC. Hillel was known to be tolerant in his behavior as well as his opinions, unlike his opponent Shammai, who was very strict in his outlook. Hillel made the above statement when he converted a person whom Shammai had refused to convert; he presented the above words as the core of the entire Torah.

Hillel's saying represents an important value of Jewish tradition regarding treatment of the other, whether a Jew or non-Jew. Advocate Abu Husayn attempted to convince the High Court justices to follow Hillel's path in their decision regarding construction of the MoT in Mamilla. In fact, with this argument he was trying to present the justices with a mirror image of anti-Semitic activities against Jewish cemeteries in Europe and elsewhere. His strategy was to encourage empathy from the court through an analogy between the Mamilla case and Jewish cemeteries abroad. As we shall see below, the High Court justices preferred a picture that differed from his intended reflection.

From a comparative perspective the halacha holds that excavating human remains from a grave is prohibited. Some views permit the transfer of a grave in certain exceptional cases, however, such as when the location of the grave causes damage to the public. The Jerusalem Talmud states: "It is prohibited to transfer a dead body and bones from an honorable grave to another honorable grave, from a despised to another despised grave, and from a non-despised to an honorable grave, let alone from an honorable to a despised grave."[2] Interpreters of the Talmud explain that there are two reasons behind this rule: The first is based on the decomposition of the dead, that is, it dishonorable towards the deceased to view them in a state of decomposition or as a skeleton and bones.[3] The second is a mystical reason: the transfer of human remains agitates the souls of the dead, who await the Day of Judgment in a state of fear.[4] The Talmud views the opening of graves in severe terms for both the living and the dead.[5]

There are three specific cases mentioned in the book of Jewish law, *Shulchan Aruch*, regarding a grave. First, a grave found in a private field, where the act of burial was conducted without the permission of the owner, was buried illegally and therefore relocation of the grave is permitted. Second, it is prohibited to relocate a grave that was dug with the approval of the owner. Third, a grave that harms the public, such as a grave bordering a public road, where pedestrians could be defiled by the dead, may be transferred in order to prevent harm to the public.[6]

The case of graves causing harm to the public has developed into a legal precedent, which present-day religious adjudicators use to permit the transfer of graves in situations involving a public project, such as paving a road for the benefit of the public. Adjudicators have found halachic and practical solutions to prevent direct contact between the living, particularly *cohanim* (priests), and the contaminated body, for example through creation of open spaces, bridges, and tunnels above or around the graves, thereby allowing the impurity of the grave to remain in the soil and preventing it from touching live people. Graves can then remain in their original location while a road or a building is built above them. Such practical solutions significantly affect the cost of the project, and in the past adjudicators have also addressed the question of whether the high cost should be regarded as harm to the public.[7]

Halacha thus differs from shari‘a regarding the relocation of a grave. In Judaism the starting point is the fear of direct contact between the priests and the impure dead, while in Islam graves are honored because of the holiness attributed to the dead. Yet the High Court applied to the MoT in Mamilla the Jewish rule by ordering the creation of an empty level between the "purple section" and the MoT building. However, the religious laws of both communities are similar with respect to adaptation of the law to present-day reality, namely, the need for urban development and construction. The two legal systems provide different justifications for building over graves. In other words, the issue is entirely a matter of interpretation, which in turn is dependent upon the circumstances of time and location as well as political considerations.

Since the 1950s, a Jewish Haredi group in Israel has struggled to prevent damage to Jewish graves by archeological excavations or by building and development projects. In the late 1950s, an organization named *Atra Kadisha* ("holy place" in Aramaic) was founded by a Haredi group that aims to prevent damage to graves where Jews are believed to be buried. From time to time this organization brings together members of the Haredi community to demonstrate at excavation sites and development projects where graves have been unearthed. Some of these demonstrations escalate into violence. In most cases the protest ends through practical settlement, using the above-mentioned halachic solution of separating graves from the aboveground site in question through open space or a thick concrete divider, by paving a road to circumvent the graves, or by drilling "contamination pipelines" in order to create a hole from the grave to an open area, thereby preventing human contamination.

A 2010 case involving the Barzilai Medical Center of Ashkelon focused on the construction of a new emergency room built for protection from missile attacks. This case sparked a public dispute between a Haredi group and the rest of the Jewish population in Israel, as well as a debate between Haredi and non-Haredi rabbis over the correct legal interpretation. The dispute broke out when digging began in preparation for building the emergency room and six old graves were discovered. The Haredi group members were concerned that these graves belonged to ancient Jewish individuals. It was not known whether these graves had been dug before the emergence of Judaism, or if at the time of burial Jews were already living in the region. If the graves preceded Judaism, then the dead were pagans. According to the Haredi interpretation, this uncertainty is enough to permit leaving a grave intact and treating it as a Jewish grave. Deputy Minister of Health Yaakov Litzman of the Haredi party Yahadut HaTorah, after consultation with the most prominent sage of his group Rabbi Elyashiv, ordered that the location of the emergency room be moved to a spot hundreds of meters away from the hospital, far from the originally planned location, at an additional cost of 130 million New Israeli Shekels (NIS). Initially the Israeli government, which included two Haredi parties, decided to freeze works for a period of one month until it was determined whether the graves belong to pagans or Jews. Public pressure was exerted by the Hospital Doctors Association and general public opinion, compelling Israel's Prime Minister Benjamin Netanyahu to reverse the government decision and enforce construction of the emergency room at the originally planned location after relocating the graves.[8] Non-Haredi rabbis in addition to one Haredi rabbi from the Shas party ruled that it was permitted to remove the graves and build the emergency room on this spot in accordance with the halachic principle of "saving a life" or under the rule of "a grave that damages the public."[9]

This dispute highlighted the gap between the pragmatic approach, prioritizing the needs of the living population, and the conservative approach of honoring the dead, and it has some relevance for the case of Mamilla. In Ashkelon, even though the case involved ancient graves incidentally excavated, rather than a historical cemetery, the Israeli government initially decided to relocate the emergency room at great cost. In Mamilla, the disputed site is part of a historical cemetery where hundreds of graves have been found. Although the case does not entail a life-saving project or matter of strong necessity, the governmental authorities nonetheless took a different position. In the Ashkelon dispute, Prime Minister Netanyahu eventually decided, based on public pressure, to remove the ancient graves and to build the emergency room in its originally planned location.

The Ashkelon case is important for understanding the Mamilla dispute because the radical Ultra-Orthodox group that opposed building the emergency room above the graves' location used the same argument as the advocate Abu Hussein, cited above. For example, Menachem Geshaid, a senior advisor to the deputy minister of health, referring to the Ashkelon dispute in a TV interview, said, "If they remove [Jewish graves] in Israel, why should they [Europeans] not removed them [in Europe]? Lest you forget, [in Europe], there are the graves of my grandfather and your grandfather . . . "[10]

In the case of Mamilla, the principle established by Hillel echoed in the High Court hearing and resonated throughout the dispute over construction of the MoT in two primary aspects, one of which is moral and comparative. Specifically, those who objected to the construction of the MoT in Mamilla underlined in their discourse and arguments before the court that Jews should not do to Muslims what anti-Semites do to Jews when they damage Jewish cemeteries in Europe and elsewhere. In addition, the opponents sought to forewarn the High Court justices that allowing the construction of the museum would be interpreted as discriminatory, with different policies towards Jewish cemeteries in Israel and abroad, where the Jewish public supports their preservation, as opposed to Muslim cemeteries, which it devalues because of the indifference of the Jewish public and Jewish authorities to non-Jewish graves. The second aspect of Hillel's principle entails the possible outcome, namely, that constructing the museum over Muslim graves could in the future be used by anti-Jewish elements in Europe and Arab countries to seeking to justify damage to Jewish cemeteries.

The above argument was a major motivation for the group of academics (mostly Jewish-Israelis) and civil organizations who opposed construction of the MoT in Mamilla. Their position as presented to the High Court reflected an intra-Jewish debate. In their demand to the High Court, they underlined that they work toward the values of "tolerance, pluralism, acceptance of the other, and human dignity." They believed that the three narratives of Judaism, Christianity, and Islam can coexist in harmony without anyone feeling he must struggle to protect his religious identity and sentiments or to protect his holy sites from desecration.

Although the academics and the civil organizations involved in the Mamilla case are not politically or ideologically homogenous, they presented a singular position regarding the value of tolerance, the future character of Jerusalem, and the attitude towards the Arab Muslim community within Israel and abroad. They wrote to the High Court that, "it is important that people in Israel and in the entire world, as well as in this honorable Court, know that the debate regarding construction in Mamilla is not conducted between Muslims and Jews, but is also debated within general Israeli discourse." They emphasized that because the land designated for the project belongs to the government, demonstrating respect for the law has added importance. They also stressed that the Mamilla Cemetery is a historical and cultural asset belonging to the heritage of Jerusalem, and one should distinguish between graves incidentally discovered, and between the desecration of a designated cemetery, such as Mamilla, that has historical value for all of the residents of the city and religious value for the Muslim community. They acknowledged that damage had been caused to the cemetery in the past, but they asserted that the time has come to put an end to this phenomenon. According to them, improper past activities do not justify repeating such activities in the present; e expanding the scope of damage in the present is not reasonable.

Thus the Mamilla affair sparked a public – albeit limited – debate in Israel. For reasons to be discussed in the concluding chapter, most of the Jewish (and Arab-Muslim) public remained indifferent to the entire affair. Nevertheless, the moral debate and conflict of principles exposed by the Mamilla dispute deserve discussion.

The value of tolerance is a subject of dispute in a city as mixed as Jerusalem. The debate is not purely a political question. Most Israeli Jews (not excluding academics and civil organizations apparently) who oppose the location of the MoT in Mamilla believe that Jerusalem should remain a unified, open city in the future, as well as the capital of the State of Israel. The debate is moral (multiculturalism versus hegemonic culture) and strategic (considering the ramifications for Jewish–Arab relations in Israel and abroad). Those who rejected the location of the MoT in Mamilla expressed four major arguments.

The first argument was that a museum aimed at promoting tolerance was, paradoxically, being built on Muslim graves and as such is extremely unreasonable. In their view, tolerance is not merely a theoretical matter that the museum is intended to promote, but a value that should be implemented in practice. The argument is manifested in a series of rhetorical questions that Professor Yehoshua Ben-Arieh raised at the end of his expert opinion:

> Why add to the city an additional locus of religious dispute, are there not many other locations in Jerusalem where the proposed museum could be erected? Isn't it very strange if not delusional to construct a "museum of tolerance" in Jerusalem above a medieval holy Muslim cemetery . . . Doesn't this express only an unnecessary and provocative action?

In the petition to the High Court, joining as *amicus curiae*, Professor Ben-Arieh, Professor Shimon Shamir, and their colleagues stated:

> The establishment of the museum [in this location] will severely damage the two purposes for which the museum is being erected, tolerance and human dignity. The irrationality is so extreme that the state authorities and not only the MoT would be ridiculed and mocked by people both in Israel and throughout the world.[11]

The same opinion was expressed by some Jewish and Muslim Knesset members who also suggested changing the location of the museum. One example was given by Ghaleb Majadla,[12] a moderate Muslim member of the Labor party, who is far from the ideology of the Islamic Movement. When he was the chair of the Knesset Committee of Interior and Environment he initiated a special meeting on the subject. At the beginning of this session he said the following:

> As a high school student I studied Torah, and I completed the examinations on the Bible. I know that the dead are honored not only in Islam, but also in Judaism, which has special honor for the dead. So, [what about] establishing a museum of tolerance over a cemetery? Tolerance and desecration of a cemetery contradict each other. I am happy that some good people have contributed to this cause [opposing the location]. I hope very much that we stop this shame and cooperate in a way that will make all of us feel better.[13]

Another example is found in the words of Knesset Speaker Reuven Rivlin:

> Why the hell should a house of tolerance be erected on a cemetery? . . . As an Israeli Jewish citizen I do not understand why a house of tolerance should be erected over a cemetery. From viewpoint of intellectual honesty, there is an inherent contradiction between the two . . . We paved the road of Emek HaMatzleva [over graves], for example, because Jerusalem would have been 'choked' [by traffic] without this road. We paved road Number6, because the State of Israel could not live without it if you were to look twenty years into the future. However, a house of tolerance? You need only a grain of tolerance to understand that if this [MoT] were to be erected over a cemetery, it would cause difficulty. My mother was buried on the Mount of Olives a year ago and my father some twenty years ago. If somebody digs up these graves in order to glorify tolerance, I would be very angry. I would ask, what do you want from my mother and father that your tolerance is being built upon their heads? At least, if you were to tell me that I had to relocate my mom and dad, who were Jerusalemites and loved Jerusalem, in order to develop Jerusalem [that would be one thing] but why should a house of tolerance sit on a cemetery for God's sake. I want the development and prosperity of the Jewish and democratic state that we live in it together. You can agree or disagree, but I am saying that we were destined to live together, what the hell are we doing here? The house of tolerance could be constructed on Mount Scopus or alternately in Beit Zayit [a moshav bordering Jerusalem], why over a cemetery? At a minimum [the construction could take place] if we did not know about a cemetery there.[14]

A similar opinion was expressed in the same meeting by a Jewish religious member of Knesset from the Shas party, David Azoulay,[15] who responded to the statement by director of IAA, Yehoshua Dorfman, that everywhere in the world, buildings are constructed over Muslim cemeteries:

> You know indeed that we protest against and cry about every desecrated cemetery, everywhere in the world. In my opinion, we in the State of Israel should be a model and a good example to all humankind, of how not to damage graves. Unfortunately, we have not yet reached this level.[16]

The second argument expressed by the group of academics and civil organizations was that approving construction of the museum in Mamilla would foster a strong negative impression of discriminatory state policy. They wrote in their petition to the High Court as follows:

> In the same way that Halachic questions are adjudicated by rabbis, rather than academic experts of Halacha, so we have to respect the religious autonomy of the community of Muslim believers in Israel and the decisions of their religious leaders. We have to regret that science is being exploited to undermine these basic liberties.

Their point was that the court should respect the position of the president of the Shari'a Court of Appeals, Qadi Ahmad Natour, just as the court does make decisions, by itself or through halachic experts, regarding the holiness of Jewish cemeteries in Israel. They also criticized their colleagues who submitted an expert opinion at the initiative of the museum entrepreneurs arguing that shari'a is ambivalent about modern development works over old cemeteries. This position was especially highlighted in the report of Professor Shimon Shamir who added that "from the point of view of the general Arab public, there is indisputable validity in the adjudication of Sheikh Ahmad Natour, President of the Shari'a Court of Appeals, who prohibited the building of the Museum of Tolerance on the Mamilla Cemetery."

The civil society organizations also made use of Jewish tradition. They asserted that the commandment to respect cemeteries of non-Jews is deeply rooted in the values of Jewish tradition. They offered the following tangible example:

> On 22 February 2007, the former chief rabbi of Israel, who is today the chief rabbi of Tel Aviv–Yaffo, Rabbi Yisrael Meir Lau, visited abandoned Muslim cemeteries in Yaffo. When he arrived at the cemetery of the Ajami neighborhood, he said that one should respect Muslim cemeteries, as we expect other states to respect abandoned Jewish cemeteries. Lau said that a human being was created in God's image and in this respect Judaism does not differentiate among human beings according

> to national or religious denomination. We have to respect the dead of all.[17]

One of the civil society organizations that rejected the location of the Museum in Mamilla was an organization of rabbis for human rights known as *Shomrei Misphat* (Guardians of Law), a recipient of the Knesset Speaker's prize for quality of life, in recognition of their contribution to promoting the rule of law and democratic values, as well as human rights, tolerance, mutual respect, and good neighborliness. This organization comprises some 100 rabbis and students of rabbinical study of all Jewish religious streams. In addition, a group of Orthodox and Conservative rabbis in the United States also expressed their opposition to building the museum in Mamilla. The Central Conference of American Rabbis (CCAR, reform congregations) resolved in its annual convention of February 2008 to object strongly to construction of the MoT on an old a Muslim cemetery. The conference announced that "Judaism views cemeteries as holy places, and we should resist building on cemeteries of others in the same way we resist building over a Jewish cemetery, be the purpose of construction important as it may." The press release mentioned that Jewish cemeteries in Europe were frequently damaged during medieval times and modernity, as were Jewish cemeteries under Jordanian rule in East Jerusalem.[18]

Apparently some Israeli rabbis who support protection of Muslim cemeteries nevertheless suspect political motivations and therefore hesitated to support it. In March of 2006, three months after the complaint against building the Museum in Mamilla was filed before the High Court, the Second World Congress of 220 Imams and Rabbis for Peace, from 43 countries, was convened in Seville, Spain.[19] The rabbis who participated in that congress agreed with a Palestinian Sheikh 'Imad Faluji to call for "respecting the attachment and the symbols of all religions as well as their holy places and cemeteries in the Holy Land." Qadi Ahmad Natour, who participated in this convention, approached the most senior of the Israeli rabbis at the congress, Rabbi of Haifa She'ar Yashuv Hacohen, and asked if – in light of this resolution – he and his fellow rabbis would sign a petition against the plan to build the MoT over the Mamilla Cemetery. Indeed the rabbis signed this petition, but when Rabbi Hacohen returned to Israel he sent Qadi Natour a letter rescinding his signature from the petition. He implied that Qadi Natour had not presented all the facts to him regarding this issue, particularly that the case was the subject of a High Court hearing, and he wrote that if he and his fellow rabbis would have known this fact, they would not have expressed their opinion on a matter that is pending court decision, or *sub judice*. He added that when he returned to Israel he was informed that the plot over which the Museum is being constructed is not part of the cemetery but was subtracted by the Jerusalem municipality to serve as a parking lot and that "the Museum of Tolerance will better respect the memory of the buried dead there." Hacohen also added that the process of reducing the area of the cemetery was started by Haj Amin al-Husayni when he erected the Palace Hotel. He concluded his letter by stating that he rescinds his signature and is fairly certain that the fellow rabbis who signed the petition after him will request that their names not be used in this petition and that their signatures be removed.[20]

One of the important comparative aspects regarding the fear of discriminatory policy touched on the double standard of the State of Israel and of many Jewish citizens regarding Jewish and Muslim cemeteries. The group of 70 academics addressed this issue as follows: "Israel and the Jewish people who protested many times against damaging Jewish cemeteries should not behave in a double standard. If any institution in a European country were to erect a building over a Jewish Cemetery, there would undoubtedly be a bitter outcry."

In their joint petition to the High Court they said the following:

> The desecration of tens of thousands of graves in the Mount of Olives between 1948 and 1967 [under Jordanian Rule in East Jerusalem] was deeply engraved in the memory of Jerusalem Jews and in the awareness of Jews worldwide. The anger, insult, and fear of desecration affected not only religious believers, and rightly so. Allowing construction over a Muslim cemetery will generate strong feelings of a double standard, discrimination, and hypocrisy. Desecrating cemeteries is major ammunition in the arsenal of anti-Semites in both the Christian and Muslim worlds. Non-recognition of the holiness of the Mamilla Cemetery will undermine the moral foundation of the right to battle anti-Semitism . . . It will play into the hands of the anti-Semites, to the extent of actual infliction of damage on Jewish cemeteries in Europe, in the Muslim world, and in North and South America.[21]

The American historian of Palestinian descent Rashid Khalidi also referred to this issue, writing that the Israeli government failed to deal with the matter morally given that it had protested desecration of old Jewish cemeteries in East Jerusalem during 1948–1967 (under Jordanian rule).[22]

Here I would note that the desecration of "tens of thousands of graves" on the Mount of Olives under Jordanian rule is an exaggeration. During the early 1960s Jordan expropriated the waqf land of Abd al-Razzaq al-'Aalmi in order to construct a hotel [Seven Arches] overlooking the Old City (250,000 Jordanian dinars were deposited in the bank account of the waqf in exchange).[23] When a road was paved to access this hotel, some Jewish gravestones and graves were damaged. Yet, the "tens of thousands of graves" remained undisturbed. Israeli historian Ze'ev Vilnai wrote that the Jordanians used the gravestones as material in the infrastructure of the road and this assertion created the above mentioned story.[24] Perhaps dozens or a few hundred gravestones were damaged during the works. However, the fact that the cemetery as a whole was preserved to this very day indicates that the damage was apparently marginal and most of the graves remained intact.[25]

It should be noted that under Jordanian rule, East Jerusalem was only six square kilometers and even though this part of the city was short on land for development, most of the Jewish cemetery of Har HaZaytim was not disturbed.

A comparison was also drawn between the Mamilla case and the Jewish Cemetery on the Mount of Olives during the special session of the Knesset Committee for Interior and Environment, where Speaker Reuven Rivlin said, "I remember our outcry when after the Six Day War, we returned to our forefather's graves at the Mount of Olives and saw the destruction there. We let out a bitter outcry that every believer who has a heart can understand."[26]

To these words the Knesset Member Abd al-Malik Dahamsha, a Muslim and member of the Southern Faction of the Islamic Movement, said, "You mention the Mount of Olives. What happened on the Mount of Olives? Some grave stones were broken, and the Cemetery was not properly protected, but did anybody excavate even one grave there, did you see bones of Jews strewn around the cemetery, did you see graves that had been uprooted with authorization and permission granted by law?"[27]

Another comparison between the cemeteries of Mamilla and the Mount of Olives was drawn by advocate Hussein Abu Hussein on behalf of the Muslim plaintiffs before the High Court: "Mamilla should be declared a site of heritage in the same way that today the Mount of Olives Cemetery was designated a Jewish Heritage Site."[28]

Let us now turn to the question of discriminatory policy. The Al-Aqsa Corporation in its arguments underlined the principle of equal rights, writing that, "In the same way that the utmost protection is given to Jewish cemeteries in Israel and abroad, so too should a Muslim cemetery not be desecrated." They submitted to the High Court an expert opinion by Dr. Hasan San'allah who surveyed the widespread protection provided to Jewish cemeteries in Muslim states as well as the overall protection afforded to religious sites under international law.[29]

The preservation of Jewish cemeteries across the world is a sensitive issue because of the Holocaust and trauma of the Jews in Europe as well as several countries in the Middle East. In Europe, a Jewish London-based organization named the Committee for Preserving Jewish Cemeteries in Europe was recently involved in protesting against construction over cemeteries in Vilnius and Prague, the respective capitals of Lithuania and the Czech Republic.[30] In Vilnius, Jewish organizations protested against the construction of a housing project named King Mindaugas on a plot of land bordering a cemetery. The above-mentioned Committee for Preserving Jewish Cemeteries in Europe and some 100 rabbis from Europe organized a protest prayer service in front of the European Parliament of Brussels.[31]

The ancient Jewish Cemetery in Prague is an interesting comparative case. In the year 2000, during preparatory work for the construction of a large insurance company building in the business center of Prague, outside the Jewish Quarter, an ancient Jewish cemetery of the thirteenth century was unearthed. This land had been sold by the Jewish community in the fifteenth century to a local dignitary. The Jewish community leaders of Prague were prepared to compromise, while a group of Jewish Haredi rabbis from the US and Europe demanded that construction be stopped at any cost. The government of Prague promised the Jewish community that the cemetery would be preserved as an historical and archeological site and as part of the building project. The archeologists' salvation excavations yielded 143 skeletons, which were placed in coffins and transferred to the official Jewish cemetery in Prague. However, the issue was posed as a question to the chief rabbi of Israel, Rabbi Yisrael Lau, who responded that the skeletons should be reburied in their original site. This uncompromising approach was rejected by the local Jewish leaders of Prague. Rabbi Karol Efraim Sidon, Chief Rabbi of the city of Prague and the Czech Republic, said that past construction works had resulted in the unearthing of bones, which were then relocated to another cemetery. In July of the same year, the insurance company and the local government did not implement the agreement to preserve the cemetery. The Committee for Preserving Jewish Cemeteries in Europe responded by organizing a campaign against this project. Chair of the Knesset Committee of Immigration and Absorption Noami Blumenthall also joined this campaign. A demonstration of Haredi Jews from Israel, England, the US, and Belgium resulted in the detention of a number of activists and imposition of a monetary fine. Following these events, the parties to the dispute agreed to a compromise, according to which the Czech government decided to compensate the insurance company: the ancient cemetery in the street of Ladislabova would be fenced and integrated into the construction of the building complex. The government also declared this place a cultural heritage site that should not be damaged in the future. According to Rabbi Gluck of the American Committee for Preserving Jewish Heritage, the compromise agreement determined that no building would be constructed over the graves. It further stated that the company would cover over the land where the graves are located with concrete and that a memorial plaque would be displayed in the middle of the building project.[32] The insurance company violated the agreement, however, by building directly over the graves.[33]

This case is an example of how Ultra-Orthodox Jews who act to preserve Jewish cemeteries for religious purposes and non-religious Jews who act based on national motivations to preserve Jewish cemeteries in Europe and worldwide have overlapping interests. It also highlights the intra-Jewish debate regarding the solution. The local community was satisfied with a practical solution, using a concrete divider to separate the graves from the building or relocating the graves and preserving the memory of the cemetery through a memorial plaque, but foreign committees of Ultra-Orthodox Jews in Europe and the US demanded the preservation of the cemetery without construction over it. The position of the Haredi rabbis in this case is reminiscent of the principled position of the Islamic Movement regarding Mamilla, except that the

Haredi rabbis eventually accepted a compromise, which included a halachic solution. Memorialization of the cemetery through a plaque as part of the compromise was a means of preserving the community's heritage. In the Mamilla case, however, the Islamic Movement has rejected every compromise of this sort, as noted in the Introduction.

Concern that European Jewish cemeteries would be targeted was voiced in a Knesset session organized by Member of Knesset Ghaleb Majadla in mid-February 2006, some six weeks after the Mamilla dispute erupted. Sheikh Kamel Rayyan, an activist of the Southern Islamic Movement who also serves as the head of the Municipal Council of Kafar Bara and as Deputy Chair of the Center for Local Government in Israel, stated in a meeting of the Knesset Committee of Interior and Environment:

> . . . I am cautioning, not threatening. In Europe, Islam and Muslims have always been targeted, but when they humiliated our Prophet Mohammad, you saw the reaction. Damaging Mamilla is no different because important and prestigious Muslims are buried there. I do not say that it is legitimate to target other places, but the Mamilla Cemetery has some importance and has a special standing among other cemeteries. Mr. Speaker, I have dealt with this issue for some twenty years, I have in my hands a volume containing pictures and maps, mapping the holy places around Jerusalem, the Triangle, and Ashkelon. It contains almost 200 holy places. The establishment not only murders [violates] the sentiments of the living, but also murders the dead. It is not easy to murder a living person, and it is even more difficult to murder a dead person. I request the cessation of this war against Muslim cemeteries and the mosques of the Muslims. Over the past 10 years, I have had dozens of exchanges of correspondence with the Ministry of Religious Affairs, correspondence that illustrates this phenomenon. Mamilla is a symptom, part of the tragedy we have undergone for decades. This book documents dozens of holy places that were damaged, with systematic map of each of these places: 18 mosques were rendered for use as synagogues; 41 mosques were desecrated and destroyed; 16 mosques were rendered for purposes in conflict with Islamic law, such as restaurants and pubs.[34]

More concrete examples were presented in the same session by Qadi Ahmad Natour:

> When there was a plan to pave a road in Egypt and an ancient Jewish Cemetery was excavated, I remember that Arieh Der'i [then Shas party leader] traveled to Egypt and he spoke with the President, and then a bridge was constructed to bypass the Jewish Cemetery. I defy you to find even one Jewish grave that was damaged in Morocco, Tunisia, or Algeria. Today Jewish Israelis travel on pilgrimage to these countries to

> visit tombs of Jews who passed away decades ago. I ask you not to create the impression that Muslims are damaging Jewish Cemeteries."[35]

To this the Knesset speaker, Reuven Rivlin, responded, "Go to Bratislava and see what was done to the tomb of the Chatam Sofer."[36]

Similar words were expressed in the same meeting by Mayor of Nazareth Razem Jiraisy, a Christian of the Hadash Party:

> I want to ask, did any of you think that this action (in Mamilla), backed by the state authorities, could be used to legitimize damage to Jewish cemeteries around the world? Did you consider this argument before you made this decision? And let me clarify my point with one more question, which might sound rhetorical: In the center of Shifa'amer (an Arab town) there is a Jewish cemetery. I would expect each of you to ask himself if the Shifa'amer municipality were to initiate the establishment of any kind of Museum over this cemetery, even a museum of Holocaust, wouldn't the entire world cry out that a Jewish cemetery is being targeted? . . . Think of the public reaction if the Shifa'amer municipality were to initiate a plan to change the use of a Jewish cemetery in Shifa'amer.[37]

The response of the MoT entrepreneurs to the charge of discriminatory policy was that, unlike Jewish cemeteries that are still designated as cemeteries, Mamilla is not a declared cemetery today, as was in the past; rather, it is a case in which individual graves were unearthed during the course of work in the field. They added that this plot had served in the past as a parking lot, and nobody had protested then. As we saw above, this assertion is not accurate: according to Dr. Shmuel Berkowitz, writing on behalf of the entrepreneurs, the Jordanians and the waqf had complained to UNESCO regarding graves that were found when the parking ramp was initially constructed.

The MoT entrepreneurs submitted an expert opinion by Dr. Jaqcues Neria regarding the principle of equity between Jewish and Muslim cemeteries.[38] Neria listed cases in Israel and abroad in which authorities as well as rabbis had reached practical compromises that permitted construction over or relocation of graves. In Hamburg in the late 1980s, for example, graves were excavated during works to erect a shopping center, and – following demonstrations by Jewish organizations – the local rabbis and the authorities reached a compromise abolishing the underground parking lot and relocating it to the top of the building. The graves were covered with a one-meter layer of concrete, access to the burial area was enabled, and a memorial plaque was displayed. This practical halachic solution was authorized by the former chief rabbi of Jerusalem and a member of the Rabbinical Court of Appeals. In his response, Rabbi Yitzhak Kolitz noted the entrepreneurs' argument – that when they purchased the land they had not known that it contained a Jewish cemetery – and responded that he permits building over the cemetery without digging underneath it, and that construction would take place under his strict supervision. He added that his decision was made "with a heavy heart and considering the special circumstances, the entrepreneurs having invested significant capital in purchasing the land. Yet it is clearly disrespectful to a cemetery to have buildings stand above."[39]

Interestingly, High Court Justice David Cheshin, who quoted from this opinion in order to justify resumption of the MoT works, ignored the final sentence, which held that construction over a cemetery is clearly disrespectful. This holding is all the more applicable to a building that is intended to represent the value of tolerance among religious denominations and among people in general.

Neria mentioned also the solution of the problem of the Jewish cemetery in Prague. He offered other examples of cases in Israel that ended in compromise: In Tiberias an ancient Jewish cemetery was discovered during the construction of a hotel originally named Ganei Hamat and today the Holiday Inn. A practical solution was found to allow this project. In this case Chief Sephardic Rabbi Mordechai Eliyahu permitted building the hotel based on his proposed arrangement enabling even cohanim to use the hotel, through the construction of "contamination tunnels." Compromise enabled the resumption and completion of works in many other cases, such as the Wolfson Towers, a massive housing project in Jerusalem that was erected over a burial cave, or construction of a clinic in a religious kibbutz, Sha'alabim,. Neria also cited the case of Road 1 in the French Hill, East Jerusalem, paved in 1995 over an area where Second Temple period remains of graves were found. Here, Rabbi Yoseph Shalom Elyashiv (b. 1910), the most senior Haredi Ashkenazi adjudicator, ruled that one can drill diagonally into the grave to construct "contamination tunnels" underneath the burial area, and that the human remains should be placed at the bottom of the hole. Because the tunnel releases the contamination of the dead to the open air in a way that does not touch the living, the impure dead will not defile living people. It should be mentioned that the same Rabbi ruled against a compromise in the case of the emergency room in Ashkelon mentioned above.

The third argument presented by the group of academics who opposed construction of the MoT in Mamilla was the likelihood of the negative impact on relations between Jews and Muslims in Israel and between Israeli-Jews and Arabs and Muslims worldwide, as well as the possibility of the outbreak of violence. This argument does not refer directly to the moral aspect of building over non-Jewish cemeteries, but rather to the consequences of an action that Muslims and non-Jewish groups might perceive as immoral and to the political ramifications of such action. In this context one might also compare the effect of pressure exerted by Haredi groups in Israel, which ends in success, to the pressure exerted by the Islamic movement. The Ultra-Orthodox organization Atra Kadisha has a strong standing because the government reports to this organization every case of exposure of old graves.[40] In many cases, this organization intervenes and successfully influences development projects towards adoption of a halachic solution at significant cost to the entrepreneur or by relocation of the project from the originally planned location.

Aghbariyya, advocate for the Muslim plaintiffs before the High Court, went too far in describing the Mamilla dispute as one of such supreme sensitivity that the entire Islamic Nation awaits the decisions of the High Court.[41] Professor Shimon Shamir, who headed the group of Israeli academics, wrote in his expert opinion before the court:

> We should prevent unnecessary offense to Muslim sentiments. These actions create explosive situations that could deteriorate to disruption of public order and could exacerbate tensions between Jews and Arabs. If a claim is far from being reasonable, it should be rejected, but it is very difficult to regard the demand for preservation of the historical cemetery of Mamilla – at least those parts of this cemetery that still could be preserved – as beyond the boundaries of reason.

Shamir predicted that construction of the MoT in Mamilla would "create a golden opportunity for leaders and political activists in Muslim countries to riot, and then the museum will become a monumental symbol, permanently representing the Jewish–Muslim confrontation.

Amir Cheshin, who served for ten years (1984–94) as advisor on Arab affairs to Jerusalem's Mayor Teddy Kollek also referred to this issue by writing that "this is one of the most delicate and explosive issues of East Jerusalem, which will spread to the Arabs of Israel and the entire Muslim world as well as the international community. It will cause relations with the government of Jordan to deteriorate.[42]

It should be noted that none of the above predictions came to fruition. Perhaps the reason is that, as the museum entrepreneurs asserted, the Mamilla Cemetery is not so important to the Muslim community after all. Muslims will fight to defend the Al-Aqsa Mosque or the Cave of the Patriarchs in Hebron, but it appears they will not mobilize to defend a secondary site like Mamilla. Nevertheless, as we shall see below, the emergence of a new campaign on the international arena means that we have not seen the last of this dispute.

The museum entrepreneurs presented opposing expert opinions arguing that establishing the museum will actually contribute to positive relations between Jews and Arabs because it will encourage moderates and discourage extremists such as the Islamic Movement. They organized a group of 182 personalities to counter the claims of the 70 academics. The list included academics, military generals, journalists, and renowned writers and was headed by Shabtai Shavit, former head of the Mossad. Shavit wrote as follows to the High Court:

> It is time to end once and for all the ceaseless undermining by the Islamic Movement, under leadership of Raed Salah, of anything Jewish, Israeli, and *Eretz Yisareli* [relating to the Land of Israel in Jewish history]. The Israeli court system should not allow anyone to deliberately undermine the foundations of the State of Israel and exploit its democratic values in order to impose an anti-democratic theocratic regime and prevent the establishment of the Museum of Tolerance.[43]

Professor Joseph Ginat wrote in his opinion to the court that, "in light of the history of construction in the Mamilla Cemetery and Muslim neglect of cemeteries in the world, and given the low level of interest expressed by the Israeli Muslim public in this particular cemetery, there is no real likelihood of outbreak of violence."[44]

The MoT entrepreneurs also presented a moderate Arab expert opinion by Hani al-Farr, Director of the Jewish–Arab Center in Haifa Beit Hagefen, an institute striving since its establishment in 1963 to promote coexistence between Arabs and Jews. Al-Farr wrote the following:

> In recent years there has been an emergence and reinforcement of extremist elements that openly aim to undermine everything that could be viewed as integration into the state, recognition of its institutions, collaboration, or coexistence; throughout the same years, there has emerged a flourishing Arab society that is progressive and sober and strives to promote education, equal rights, women's rights, and the values of Arab culture and sports. The latter actually represent the central and major stream of the Arab public today . . . Although its voice is not amplified to the same extent as that of the extremists . . . The establishment of the Museum of Tolerance will be a benchmark on the road to promoting the values of tolerance and partnership between Arabs and Jews in Israel, and it will definitely be welcomed by the Arab population of the state and will promote the real social aspirations of this minority.[45]

In his report Al-Farr also stated that the general Muslim-Arab public is indifferent to the planned location of the MoT, a place that has served for several decades as a public parking lot and to which the Arab public does not attribute special historical holiness. Therefore, he did not expect any outbreak of violence. He added, "If this issue were indeed important to the Arab public, then it would find a way to protest legitimately, such as by writing op-eds, holding demonstrations, etc., almost none of which has occurred in this case."[46]

An additional argument that the MoT entrepreneurs presented was that one should not surrender to the threats issued or the pressure applied by Islamic groups. They backed this assertion with an expert opinion on security by Professor Uzi Arad, who was appointed in 2010 to head the National

Security Council of Israel, and Dr. Shmuel Bar, both former senior Mossad officers, who wrote in support of the defendants:

> It is unlikely that construction of the museum will have negative consequences among Israeli-Arabs or within the Muslim world. On the contrary, if construction of the museum were accompanied by an appropriate information campaign, emphasizing the concessions that the museum entrepreneurs made during the process in order to decrease potential damage to human remains, it would prevent violence. Moreover, we think that actually surrendering to threats and violence will only encourage more violence in the future.

These two experts based their opinion on the riots that erupted in Europe following the 2006 affair of a cartoon mocking Prophet Mohammed in the Danish Newspaper *Jyllands-Posten*. In their view, appeasement efforts by European governments actually encouraged extremist groups and resulted in the spread of riots. According to the two experts, a similar phenomenon led to the revocation of citizenship and deportation of the Dutch-Somali deputy of Parliament, Ayaan Hirsi Ali, the forced escape to safety of French journalist Robert Redeker, who had published a critical article against Islam, and the cancellation of the opera *In Dominio* by Mozart following threats of terrorist action against the Dutch Opera of Berlin because of a scene that is "disrespectful" of the Prophet Mohammad. The two security experts concluded that:

> The common denominator in all of the above-mentioned events was the readiness of the government to surrender to threats of violence. In contrast, [one may] recall Pope Benedict XVI's *Regensburg* speech, following which extremist groups attempted to incite riots but were very quickly subdued. The position of the Vatican, which also explained that the Pope had not intended to insult Muslims, was firm and unyielding. Senior Muslim religious figures in the west and in the Arab world understood that they would not benefit from a confrontation with the Vatican, and they took measures to calm the atmosphere. [Thus,] in Israel and abroad, decisive policy results in the Arab and Muslim public understanding that violent actions are only self-destructive, and this understanding obviously diminishes the risk of the outbreak of violence.[47]

The fourth argument presented by civil society organizations refers to the number of graves and human remains that were found in the construction site and to the position of the IAA on this matter. An expert opinion by Dr. Raphael Greenberg, a senior lecturer in the Department of Archeology and Ancient Eastern Cultures at Tel Aviv University, holds that the situation in Israel is not akin to the legal situation in the United States, where in 1990 a federal law was passed – the Native American Graves Protection and Reparation Act (NAGPRA) – aimed at protecting the cemeteries of Native Americans by compelling archeologists and development bodies to respect the culture of the dead and their living descendants, in particular by consulting with them, not necessarily by ceasing the work. Israel is unusual in that human remains are excluded from the legal definition of "antiquity," but graves and accompanying articles are protected under the Law of Antiquities. An ancient cemetery requires a systematic archeological survey, but such research is restricted by considerations of culture. Greenberg wrote that granting approval for works on sites that had only been partially excavated is not standard IAA practice in Jerusalem. It is reasonable to assume that a thorough excavation was necessary.

Greenberg was preparing his opinion at a time when only 20% of the graves had been excavated. According to the estimate of IAA archeologist Gideon Sulimani, at this point 200 graves had been excavated, and 250 skeletons out of about 1,000 had been removed from the site. Greenberg wrote that the documents submitted by the IAA to the High Court omitted the excavator's estimate regarding the work still to be completed (exposure and removal of 800 graves) as well as his unequivocal recommendation not to authorize resumption of work on this plot. Sulimani's report concluded, "The plot should not be released for construction before conclusion of the excavation." In an early 2009 press interview, Sulimani claimed that the IAA had misled the High Court by omitting his recommendation from the final report and terminating the excavation.[48] The IAA responded to this accusation during the court hearing by stating that Sulimani's report represented only preliminary information and that his estimate represented only his individual assessment.

Greenberg also addressed the position of the IAA, which had argued before the court that "5000 years of ongoing civilization in the country necessitates that construction be permitted on sites where occasionally graves are discovered. Without the transfer of graves and occasional damage to antiquities, construction and development in our country would be impossible." In Greenberg's opinion it is not the responsibility of the authority to safeguard the development of the country, particularly if such development only benefits private entrepreneurs. He noted that the IAA sided with the museum entrepreneurs.

In a video clip produced by the Ir Amim association,[49] Sulimani compared the damage inflicted on the cemetery of Mamilla (under Israeli rule) to that inflicted on the Mount of Olives cemetery (under Jordanian rule):

> The whole story of Mamilla is in fact, how shall I put it? . . . the un-ending Nakba (Palestinian "catastrophe" of being defeated in the 1948 war and its consequences) . What happened in 1948 – the expulsion, the destruction, the physical erasing . . . and erasure of names – continues today. These same motives have driven prime ministers and

> governments to obliterate the name of every place with a Muslim history where today Jews live . . . There was an interesting story during the British Mandate rule: Jews seeking to disturb Muslims used to inflict damage on Muslim cemeteries, and the Arabs, the Palestinians, used to inflict damage on the Jewish cemetery at Mount of Olives, intending to offend, to insult. To an archaeologist this behavior is not surprising because it has been a very familiar pattern of behavior since antiquity. Since ancient times, when a conqueror arrives . . . and takes over a territory and controls a people . . . then one of the salient expressions of . . . his will to prove that he is the most powerful is desecrating graves. The Jewish cemetery on Mount of Olives had already been under Jordanian rule for 11 years when the Jordanians, for transportation needs, constructed a road over graves . . . It was said [in Israel] that 'the Jordanians desecrated the Jewish cemetery of Mount of Olives and built a road over it.' However, what we did to the Muslim cemetery goes way beyond the pathetic road that the Jordanians paved in the (Jewish) cemetery. Generally speaking, the Mount of Olives cemetery, which is a huge and impressive one, was preserved. Very little was damaged. Yet the Muslim Mamilla Cemetery is in the process of disappearing.

The argument presented by the civil society organizations that opposed construction of the MoT in Mamilla – that Jewish graves abroad could also be damaged if the museum is constructed in its presently planned location – compelled the High Court to consider international law and the national law of other democratic countries. The question that demanded attention was whether building over graves is a uniquely Israeli norm or customary practice in the West.

The arguments asserting a discriminatory policy disturbed the High Court justices, as one can surmise from the text of the final verdict. Justice David Cheshin sought to address the challenge that the plaintiffs posed to the High Court when he stated, "the core of the arguments of the plaintiffs in this regard is that just as Jewish cemeteries in Israel and abroad enjoy the utmost protection from desecration, so too Muslim cemeteries should be protected and not desecrated, and there should be no discrimination between one grave and another.[50]

In his contribution to the verdict, Cheshin expressed the High Court position on three matters. First, the halacha permits development works when graves are inadvertently exposed; second, the legal system of western countries permits construction over cemeteries; and third, the practice both in Europe and in Israel reflects much flexibility and, therefore, there is no discrimination in construction over "discovered graves."

In the case of halacha, Cheshin distinguished between basic halacha and practical interpretation. According to basic halacha as articulated in the *Shulchan Aruch*, which was compiled by Rabbi Yosef Caro during the first part of the sixteenth century, transfer of a dead body from its grave is prohibited, with two exceptions that halacha considers to be for the benefit of the dead: if someone was buried in a temporary grave outside Eretz Yisrael and there is an interest in reburying him in this land; and if there is a fear that the grave could be damaged by pagans or by flood, etc. In addition prohibiting removal of the dead and their bones from their original grave, the halacha prohibits benefitting from the grave, the tombstone, and the building.[51] However, the same *Shulchan Aruch* volume mentions a rule that allows the relocation of a grave that harms the public, such as a grave adjacent to a road.[52] Cheshin quoted from an article by Rabbi Yisrael Rozen, the head of the Zomet Institute for Halacha Matters and Technology, according to which this rule was used by prominent adjudicators to permit the evacuation of Jewish cemeteries for the benefit of the public. The rule is particularly applicable "if after digging started it was discovered that this is a burial compound and if the cost of changing the route of a road or the location of building is extremely high or unreasonable in terms of engineering."[53]

Justice Cheshin adopted this position and applied it to the case of Mamilla: "In our case as well, the fact that the plot served as a cemetery was discovered only after the digging started and relocation of the building for public purposes is not only extremely expensive but even impossible from a professional architectural point of view . . . "

Justice Cheshin cited precedents from Israel and other countries (the same cases mentioned in the expert opinion by Dr. Jacques Neria) concerning construction over Jewish graves. His survey dovetails the comparative legal analysis of Justice Ayala Procaccia, who emphasized that construction over graves excavated during the course of such work is a universal norm. Regarding the issue of relocating graves, US law holds that the sacred nature of a burial place prohibits the transfer of graves unless there is a special need for such transfer, or in cases of necessary and laudable purposes. For example, US courts will generally permit reburial in a family burial section that was purchased after the initial burial, particularly upon request by the relatives of the deceased. In addition, permission for reburial may be granted when repair of a cemetery is required or when a burial place has been abandoned or become run down and unattractive. However, economic profit alone is not sufficient reason to permit relocation of a grave. The court will not allow relocation of a body if the demands of the parties can be reasonably satisfied without relocating the deceased.[54]

Justice Procaccia wrote that US law distinguishes between the extent of protection afforded to old graves and that afforded to active cemeteries serving current needs. The passage of time affects the extent of protection that is provided for a burial compound. She cited the example of a New Jersey court case in which a burial compound had not been used for burial during the preceding seventy years and had been neglected over time. In this case the court permitted the church to transfer the bones of the buried to the edges of the graveyard, thus prioritizing the public interest in developing this area and giving preference to the needs of the living over respect for the dead. The court stated, "Respect for the dead does not require that land once used as a burial ground shall forever be hallowed and set aside as a final resting place. If that were so, the dead would in time crowd the living off the face of the earth."[55]

In New York State, the courts have permitted the removal of graves and re-designation of abandoned cemeteries that have not been used for burial in 20 years, in order to use the land for other purposes.

Justice Procaccia further surveyed the laws of various US states that allow the transfer of unmarked graves only if an authorized body approves it. She summarized:

> Unlike marked cemeteries, those that are unmarked do not enjoy complete protection and their grounds may be used for construction, subject to restrictions and permits as required by law. The question of what area is considered a cemetery, or when a cemetery is considered unmarked, is determined, among other factors, by artifacts indicating the existence of graves and by identifying which part of the compound was used for burial.[56]

Justice Procaccia added that in the United States there are federal laws that provide protection for native burial sites. The most important of these is the Native American Grave Protection and Reparation Act, which regulates certain aspects related to graves located on federal or tribal land. The law recognizes an interest in preserving such sites as well as the rights of the tribesmen to receive the human remains and cultural artifacts excavated from these lands.[57]

In the past, English law prohibited construction in burial compounds owned by a church or any other religious community. In 1981, however, a law was passed permitting construction in compounds that had been owned by a religious community in the past, on the condition that no burial had taken place there within the preceding 50 years or, alternatively, that no one related or connected to someone buried there within the previous 50 years expresses opposition to such construction. English courts have also permitted construction over burial grounds for the public benefit. One such case involved paving a road across a church cemetery. The court determined in this case that the public benefit gained by improving the transportation system overrides the general interest and even the individual interest of relatives of the deceased in preserving the graves in their original locations. However, the court ordered the transfer of the graves to a respectful and more attractive area within the burial compound.[58]

Australia has also passed legislation that permits changing the designated use of cemeteries for the public interest, such as for public parks and road construction. Justice Procaccia emphasized that in its search for a balance among competing interests, Australian law prioritizes the needs of the living: "Generally, human remains will not be disinterred unless construction, or some other procedure, is going to disturb them anyway, but the existence of the legislation itself suggests a tacit acceptance of the primacy of the living over the dead, and a willingness to disturb human remains if it appears necessary."[59]

Justice Procachia summarized the comparative law section of the verdict in the following words:

> In most of the countries surveyed, the public interest in promoting the welfare of the living overrides other interests, even if it involves the relocation of graves. In general, construction over old or unmarked burial compounds is permitted, subject to restrictions designed to protect the honor of the dead and to respect tradition and sentiment. The balancing point differs from one state to another in accordance with its values and heritage.[60]

Justice Procaccia, who headed the court plenum and drafted the verdict, summarized the comparative dimension in the following words:

> It appears that in spite of the sweeping acknowledgement of the importance of preserving the honor of the dead, which is common to the law of many countries, the granting of a constitutional dimension to this value is quite rare. However, the tension between the need to preserve the honor of the dead and respect burial compounds, on the one hand, and the public interest in construction, development of the land, and promotion of the welfare of the inhabitants, on the other hand, is not unique to Israel.[61]

In conclusion, the High Court verdict contained a long section on comparative law, which presumably resulted from a concern that a decision permitting resumed construction of the MoT would be seen as discriminatory and might be used to legitimize damage to Jewish cemeteries around the world – a classic example of Zionist apologetics. However, the fear that ruling for the resumption of the MoT construction in Mamilla could be interpreted as a discriminatory policy and be used to legitimize damaging Jewish cemeteries around the world is a serious and genuine concern. Justice Cheshin attempted to downplay the charge of discrimination by surveying foreign legislation and legal practice allowing development above cemeteries. Yet three factors distinguish the case of Mamilla from other cases.

First, in all other cases, the works involved urban development infrastructure, landscape improvement, and the like. The case of Mamilla, however, involves a project centered on the principle of tolerance, in which the very legal dispute and its evolution seriously challenge the intended purpose of the project.

The second factor is the nature of the cemetery in question. None of the examples cited for the sake of comparison involved a large and historically important cemetery that is located in a city holy to the three major monotheistic religions.

The third factor is the massive number of graves located in the construction compound. According to the estimate of the archeologist who excavated the site, it contained the human remains of about 1,000 deceased, including 400 skeletons that have been removed and packed in cardboard boxes to await relocation.

At the same time, the Mamilla case is also exceptional in several aspects that serve the interests of the MoT entrepreneurs. First, there was long-term neglect by the Muslim community, which did not maintain the cemetery (although political circumstances did not make maintenance an easy task).[62]

Second, the Mamilla dispute entails an identity-based and ideological struggle between a religious and ethnic minority and the state in which it lives, which is subject to the majority rule of a different religious and ethnic group. An ideological challenge posed by one side invites an ideological reaction from the other side.

Third, senior Muslim religious clerics actually contributed to the deterioration of the Mamilla Cemetery, beginning with the Supreme Muslim Council and culminating with the president of the Shari'a Court of Appeals in the 1960s, Qadi Tahir Hammad.

Fourth, the MoT project is not the first initiative that changed the designated use of the cemetery. Before the museum was planned the same plot had served for at least 20 years as a parking lot. In addition, the museum building itself would replace another building that has been there since 1986 and never sparked protest, save for a complaint of the waqf to UNESCO.

Notes

1 *Babylonian Talmud*, Shabbat, 31:1 (Hebrew).
2 *Jerusalem Talmud*, Moed Katan 2:4 (Hebrew).
3 *Babylonian Talmud*, Babba Batra, 154:2 (Hebrew).
4 *Shulhan Aruch*, Beit Yosef, Yoreh De'a, 361 (Hebrew).
5 *Babylonian Talmud*, Yebamot, 63:2 (Hebrew).
6 *Shulhan Aruch*, Yoreh De'a, 363:1; 364:2,5 (Hebrew).
7 Y. Rozen, "Pinuy kvarim letzorkhey tzibur" [Removal of Graves for Public Purposes], *Tehumin* 18, 1998, pp. 254–73 (Hebrew).
8 *Haaretz*, Editorial, 22 March 2010 (Hebrew).
9 *Ynet* news website, 21 March 2010 (Hebrew).
10 Channel 2 Morning News (Israel television), 17 May 2010 (Hebrew).
11 From the request to join the High Court hearing.
12 He later served as a minister in the cabinet of Prime Minister Ehud Olmert during 2006–2009.
13 Protocol 566 of the Knesset Committee of Interior and Environment meeting of 15 February 2006, available at: www.knesset.gov.il/protocols/data/rtf/pnim/2006-02-15.rtf (Hebrew).
14 Ibid.
15 Resident of Acre (a mixed city) and formerly head of a municipal council of Arab villages in Wadi Ara.

16 Protocol 566 of the Knesset Committee of Interior and Environment meeting of 15 February 2006, available at: www.knesset.gov.il/protocols/data/rtf/pnim/2006-02-15.rtf (Hebrew).
17 From the request to join the High Court hearing.
18 http://www.mamillacampaign.org/photos/pdfs/Appendix6.pdf.
19 http://www.imamsrabbis.org/en/congresses/detail/1/10/7.
20 Letter dated 2 April 2006.
21 Manifesto signed by Israeli faculty experts in Middle East studies (Hebrew).
22 For a debate between Khalidi and others see Rashid Khalidi "Tolerance of Whom?", *The Daily Beast*, 10.4.2012; Response by Avra Shapiro, Director of Public Relations of the SWC's MoT related to the cemetery as "adjacent to our property" that served for 50 years as a parking lot; Gil Troy, "How to Model Tolerance", *The Daily Beast*, 17.4.2012. contending that the site "was a graveyard that was no longer in use, no longer considered sacred and oft-violated already by Muslims, not just Jews"; and Khalidi's response to both: *The Daily Beast*, 20.4.2012: arguing that "The SWC new full well that the site was part of the cemetery before they began any construction, having been informed of this fact by the IAA".
23 Y. Reiter, *Islamic Awqaf in Jerusalem 1948–1990*, Jerusalem: The Jerusalem Institute for Israel Studies, 1991 (Hebrew).
24 Z. Vilnai, *Holy Graves in Eretz Yisrael*, Jerusalem: Akhiever, 1996, II, p. 329 (Hebrew).
25 Archaeologist Gideon Sulimani in a short video film produced by Radwan Douha entitled "BeHezkat Yisrael" that appears on a disc entitled "Jerusalem Moments" produced in 2009 by Ir Amim (Hebrew).
26 Protocol 566 of the Knesset Committee of Interior and Environment meeting of 15 February 2006, available at: www.knesset.gov.il/protocols/data/rtf/pnim/2006-02-15.rtf (Hebrew).
27 Ibid.
28 High Court hearing of 3 October 2006.
29 Expert Report submitted to the High Court (Appendix 20 to the amended petition).
30 On the Prague affair, see http://www.jewishgen.org/AustriaCzech/cemetery.htm.
31 See JTA News, Dinah A. Spritzer.
http://jta.org/news/article/2007/07/31/ 103299/Vilniuscemetery
http://www.vosizneias.com/12283/2007/10/18/london-uk-protetse-around-globe-to/.
32 http://www.tip.co.il/news.asp?which=world&id=213 (Hebrew).
33 Another case of harm to Jewish graves in Europe occurred in August 2010, when swastika graffiti appeared on more than one hundred gravestones in a Jewish cemetery in Riga. The president of Lithuania and the Riga City Council published a condemnation of this action. See *Haaretz*, 2 August 2010 (Hebrew).
34 Protocol 566 of the Knesset Committee of Interior and Environment meeting of 15 February 2006, available at: www.knesset.gov.il/protocols/data/rtf/pnim/2006-02-15.rtf (Hebrew).
35 Ibid. For a list of Jewish cemeteries in Egypt see http://www.sephardicgen.com/egypt_sites.htm.
36 Moses Schreiber, or Moshe Sofer (1762–1839) was a leading Orthodox rabbi and jurist. The cemetery containing some 6,000 graves gradually deteriorated over

time. In 1942 human remains were excavated and collected to make room for a road and a tunnel. Following a struggle by the local Jewish community, the grave of Chatam Sofer and 23 nearby graves were rescued and preserved as a modern Jewish memorial, situated below Bratislava Castle on the left bank of the Danube. Another 64 gravestones were also moved to this site, which was turned into a mausoleum that UNESCO declared a World Heritage Site in 2002. The nearby tram station is named after Sofer. In 2005 the mausoleum was vandalized and the gravestone of Sofer was broken. The Slovakian government funded the repair of the damages.

37 Protocol 566 of the Knesset Committee of Interior and Environment meeting of 15 February 2006, available at: www.knesset.gov.il/protocols/data/rtf/pnim/2006-02-15.rtf (Hebrew).

38 Former Israeli IDF intelligence senior officer, who also served as IDF attaché to France, Belgium, and Luxemburg and, after his retirement, as Prime Minister Yitzhak Rabin's political advisor during 1992–1994.

39 Quoted from Justice Cheshin's Article 12 of his part of the verdict, H.C. 52/06 (Hebrew).

40 http://www.haaretz.co.il/hasite/pages/ShArt.jhtml?itemNo=988954 (Hebrew).

41 H.C. hearing of 3 October 2006 (Hebrew).

42 Expert opinion submitted by Amir Cheshin to the High Court, dated 22 March 2007. In response, the Jerusalem Municipality and its Local Planning Committee submitted an expert opinion by Shalom Goldstein, political advisor on East Jerusalem to the mayor of Jerusalem during 1995–2004, who wrote that the "outcry voiced in the petition to the High Court is in fact a political action by Sheikh Raed Salah, who intends to restitute the entire plot of the cemetery to the Muslim Waqf through political-ideological measures." See his report to the High Court, dated 25 April 2007, and Article 65 of the verdict (Hebrew).

43 Letter from Shabtai Shavit to Advocate Ori Stendel dated 22 March 2007, H.C. 52/06 (Hebrew).

44 Expert opinion dated 5 May 2007, H.C. 52/06 (Hebrew).

45 Expert opinion dated 23 April 2007, H.C. 52/06 (Hebrew).

46 Ibid.

47 Expert opinion dated 3 May 2007, H.C. 52/06 (Hebrew).

48 See his affidavit at mamillacampain.com (Hebrew).

49 In a short video film produced by Radwan Douha entitled "BeHezkat Yisrael" that appears on a disc entitled "Jerusalem Moments" produced in 2009 by Ir Amim (Hebrew).

50 See Articles 1–15 of his part of the verdict, H.C. 52/06, especially Article 2.

51 *Shulchan Aruch*, Yod 368/1 (Hebrew).

52 Ibid. 364.

53 Based on Yisrael Rozen, "Removal of Graves for Public Purposes" *Tehumin*, 18 (1998), 254. Rabbi Rozen argued in this article that it is permissible to evacuate a grave for "the need of the public" such as expanding a synagogue. He cited a rabbi who permitted such removal for landscape development for a park or if the government has already created facts on the ground by paving a road or constructing a building if it is impossible to pay reparation, but it is unclear if by "government" the rabbi also meant a Jewish government (Hebrew).

54 Art. 197 of H.C. 52/06 verdict (Hebrew).

55 Quoted from *The Trustees of the First Presbyterian Church in Newark V. David Alling*, 54 N.J. Super. 141, 148 A. 2d 510 1959.
56 Art. 204 of H.C. 52/06 verdict (Hebrew).
57 Art. 205 of H.C. 52/06 verdict (Hebrew).
58 *Morley Borough Council v. St. Mary the Virgin* (1969) 3 All ER 952, cited in Art. 206 of H.C. 52/06 verdict.
59 Prue Vines, *Law and Justice in Australia: foundations of the legal system 2nd ed*, Oxford University Press, 2009], p 11 quoted in the H.C. 52/06 verdict.
60 Art. 209 of H.C. 52/06 verdict (Hebrew).
61 Ibid.
62 On the neglect of the Mamilla Cemetery, see Zippi Molchov, "From a Cemetery to an Urban Garbage Site," *Ynet Jerusalem* 25 July 2010 (Hebrew).

CHAPTER

8

"Hidden from Sight": The High Court Verdict

In *The Judge*, a television documentary about former High Court president Aharon Barak, Barak stated, "As a judge I do not represent a particular outlook," adding that "to be a judge is a profession."[1] In other words, a judge should have the professional tools to balance clashing interests and values. Barak also wrote in one of his verdicts that in interpreting the language of legislation, "there are a number of possibilities among which a reasonable justice may choose. Two reasonable justices might arrive at different conclusions."[2]

In the course of its judicial work, a court approaches normative issues by "balancing interests" while examining all relevant considerations and giving proper weight to each. When a judge is required to choose between or among conflicting values or interests, he does so in accordance with the nature and relative – that is, weighted – importance of each.[3]

Courts distinguish between two types of balance: "vertical balance" and "horizontal balance".[4] A vertical balance is invoked when judges believe that one interest overrides the other. For example, maintaining public order overrides the freedom of speech if there is a high likelihood that public order would be disrupted by the speech in question. In such a case priority should be given to the stronger interest, which is determined through a "likelihood test," unless a competing interest is severely threatened. A horizontal balance, in contrast, is used to prioritize between competing interests of equal weight such as freedom of movement and the right to hold a protest rally. The balancing equation will determine the conditions of time, place, and extent that will allow implementation of both rights. Even if the particular conditions set by the judges are not completely accurate, in any case of tension between two interests, the court decision ultimately inclines towards the interest with the greater relative weight as assigned by the judges for the specific circumstances of that case.

Segev and Kremnitzer discussed the difficulty of applying the balancing equation when unified criteria for ranking considerations are lacking.[5] The terms "proportion" and "balance" are taken from the exact sciences.

Nonetheless, as Aharon Barak noted in the quote cited above, two judges will not necessarily arrive at the same result, particularly when deciding on a matter in which one of the parties to the dispute belongs to a different culture. In the Mamilla dispute, the Muslim plaintiffs represent not only a competing interest but also a national ethos that challenges the national affiliation of the judges and the national ethos of the State of Israel as well as its Jewish majority, all within the framework of the "politics of identity." This problem emerges clearly from the analysis in chapter 2 of the High Court verdict of 29 October 2008 regarding construction of the MoT in Mamilla.

In matters of social and cultural dispute, the role of the court is to issue a ruling in accordance with the social norms of the society. This role is especially important in a society as diverse as Israel, which is known for its socio-cultural and ideological rifts. The High Court of Israel is frequently asked to decide between conflicting norms. The laws passed by the Knesset do not always provide a remedy for the tensions within society because at times the Knesset cannot or opts not to make the necessary political decision. As a result, a series of High Court verdicts have shaped and reshaped important legal and social norms, simultaneously cultivating the liberal concept of political rights, human rights, and minority rights at the expense of the collectivist concept that characterized Israel during its first two decades.[6] The judicial activism that had characterized the High Court, particularly since the 1990s under President Aharon Barak, has drawn significant criticism. The High Court has been accused of making decisions based upon political considerations rather than judicial values.[7] In this context, much criticism has been leveled at the High Court justices in recent years. Claims have been made that these justices, who are appointed on the basis of their professional skills, represent the secular and liberal elite rather than the multifaceted character of Israeli society. One argument holds that if the High Court is involved in the ideological sphere, then perhaps the justices should be appointed based on their social and political outlook, not only their judicial skills, as in the US.[8]

This chapter addresses the dilemmas inherent in the High Court's adjudication of the Mamilla dispute. In reaching its decision, the High Court justices highlighted the complexity of this dispute, which involves different values and considerations that require an appropriate balancing process:

> The questions . . . are both complex and delicate in legal, public, and humanitarian terms. Conflicting values are at stake. They bring together the world of the living and the world of the dead, as well as the world of the past and the needs of the present and future. The interests of the individual compete with the sentiments of the community; the values of tradition confront the public values of development and progress. Resolving these questions requires finding an appropriate balance among different values.[9]

The justices believed that this dispute was an important precedent, which could influence similar cases in the future. Therefore, they felt it necessary to strike the proper balance among the competing values, as Justice Procaccia emphasized in concluding her verdict:

> This process raises a general question of principle that is constitutional in nature and has public ramifications beyond the particular issue of direct relevance to the litigants. This issue necessitates striking a constitutional balance among the importance of implementing the museum plan, the obligation to respect human remains found in the construction compound, and respect for the dignity of the deceased. The issue has implications for the entire population regarding general matters of principle; it is not restricted solely to the circumstances of this particular case.[10]

The way in which the High Court framed the different values to be balanced is highly important. The High Court justices defined the clashing narratives to be balanced as follows:

> A constitutional balancing mechanism is needed in order to balance the historical and religious value of the site with the property rights acquired by private entrepreneurs, against the background of approved building plans and the clear public interest in developing the area for an important public purpose that has a local, national, and international character.[11]

The High Court placed on one side of the scale the "historical and religious value of the site," which usually has a high priority in this court when it comes to protecting human dignity. On the other side of the scale, the High Court placed three values: the property rights of private entrepreneurs, the approved building plans (reflecting the importance of maintaining consistent construction processes), and the development of the area for a public purpose.

The third value was expressed by the High Court in a way that grants priority to a particular view: "an important public purpose that has a local, national, and international character."

The High Court did not clarify who the relevant "public" is whose interest should be respected in a politically sensitive city such as Jerusalem. In other words, the "public interest' according to the court appears to be the interest of the Jewish public. In fact, *the above wording of the High Court makes it is clear that it overlooked the right of a minority group to preserve its own heritage, including the cemeteries that form part of its historical and cultural legacy.*

As noted in the previous chapter, Justice Ayala Procaccia quoted laws from the US and other countries that grant special protection to the cemeteries of native groups. The Israeli High Court in the case of Mamilla, however, did not consider such special protection to be one of the values that must be balanced with the others. Moreover, in contrast to the laws cited in the verdict, which require authorities to consult with representatives of native groups in such cases, the Israeli High Court ignored the opinion of the senior religious Muslim cleric in Israel, namely, the president of the Shari'a Court of Appeals. The reason for this approach by the High Court might be that it regarded the position of the Shari'a Court as lacking in objectivity and as having an identical position to that of the Northern Islamic Movement, which struggles against the Zionist interests of the state. If such is the case, then the High Court justices could not remain indifferent.

The High Court did not see the disputed land as part of a historical cemetery, nor did it see itself as symbolically representing the identity of a religious and national community that was demanding protection for the remains of its religious and ethno-national heritage.

Although the justices noted at the outset that the historical and religious nature of the site grants it significant value, they neglected the historical value of the site for the Arab Muslim minority as one of its identity symbols. This court made this oversight even though the significance of the Mamilla Cemetery to the Muslim community had been explained not only by the Muslim plaintiffs but also by the Jewish academics and civil society organizations. The expert opinions submitted to the High Court on behalf of the plaintiffs had emphasized that the cemetery dates at least as far back as the twelfth century, and that many important Islamic figures were buried there. Yet the High Court referred to the disputed plot as if it were detached from the greater cemetery, despite its close proximity to visible and fully preserved graves along the southern border of the plot designated for the museum's construction.

Durgham Sayf, advocate for the Muslim plaintiffs during one of the High Court hearings, argued that even if the Mamilla Cemetery were declared Absentee Property, the change to its legal status would not overturn its character as a cemetery. He asked rhetorically, "Are the bones there? . . . Were there skeletons there?"[12]

The way in which the High Court justices framed the dispute actually determined the outcome, especially the way in which they defined the plot designated for construction. The central question in this case is the following: Is the disputed compound part of a well-known historical cemetery where one should have expected to unearth many human remains during the course of preparatory excavation, or alternatively, were the graves hidden from view and exposed incidentally during the course of excavation? The latter case is similar to many other cases in Israel and elsewhere where a small number of graves were unearthed incidentally, and it differs from the case of an important historical cemetery where the area designated for construction contains 1,000 skeletons (according to the estimate of an IAA archeologist), 400 of which have already been removed.

The High Court described the process as an incidental discovery of graves that were "hidden from view" and did not form part of a known historical cemetery. By framing the dispute in this way, the court predetermined its own opinion regarding the major issue and secondary questions:

> The central issue in this case relates to the question of what is permitted and what is prohibited during the development and construction of compounds where, upon initiation of the work and after completion of all planning processes, *the remains of graves and human bones were discovered beneath the ground*. Secondary questions arising from this issue are the following: How much weight should be attributed to the timing of the complaint submitted to the court by those who oppose resumption of the construction, long after the planning processes had been completed and approved? What jurisdictional authority does the Shari'a Court have in this matter?[13] [Emphasis added.]

The following quotations from the High Court verdict indicate that the justices did not see the disputed land where the museum was planned as an old cemetery, but as *a plot that borders a cemetery*, where hidden graves were incidentally unearthed during the works:

> The dilemma in our case does not relate to construction within a known cemetery designated as such in the municipal master plan. It arises in regard to a compound that was classified as an open public space for nearly 50 years and was later designated for construction of a parking lot and a road. It arises only after all of the planning processes, which took decades, had been conducted and completed on the basis of the assumption that this area is open for development and construction without any restrictions requiring preservation. The same applied to the final plan for construction of the museum, all of whose planning processes had concluded and received final authorization *with no awareness of the existence of remains of graves underneath* . . . [14]

> The space of the upper parking ramp *borders* a fenced area, which is an old Muslim cemetery named Ma'man Allah, also known as the Mamilla Cemetery . . . [15]

> The planning processes for the museum compound began in the 1960s and indicate that for nearly 50 years this compound *was not part of the cemetery* in either the normative or practical sense, nor was it utilized for various public purposes.[16] [Emphasis added in all the above excerpts.]

The conclusion of the High Court justices also highlighted the depiction of the disputed land as located outside the Mamilla Cemetery, not within it, as exemplified in the following excerpts:

> This case involves the remains of old graves dating back about 300–400 years ago, which were found under the ground, as indicated in the professional opinion of the Authority of Antiquities. Throughout the years this site was *hidden from view, buried underground, not known to the public or community members, and therefore not a source of individual or collective sentimental attachment.*
>
> [. . .] There is a substantive difference between the visible and the hidden; between a situation in which the location of graves that must not be damaged is known from the outset, and a situation in which the graves are hidden, the land is designated for various uses, and the graves are discovered after the planning process was concluded, during preparatory work for implementation of the plans.
>
> [. . .] The various uses of it, for public parking and a road, are evidence of the way in which the public, including the Muslim community, regarded this compound.
>
> [. . .] For decades this space was not viewed as part of the cemetery, and throughout all of the planning processes for the compound over the course of decades, nobody objected to this situation. Not only was this compound not identified as an area of religious holiness or as a focal point of any sentimental attachment, but on the contrary, it was the subject of planning for various purposes over the course of the past decades, without any objections based on the holiness of the site.
>
> [. . .] The identities of those buried in the graves are unknown, and the plaintiffs as well as *the community had no attachment to this site* or to the particular graves within it *throughout all of the years that passed.* Under these circumstances, the extent of damage by the plan [for the MoT] is limited and does not undermine the 'essential core' of the right [of the plaintiffs], but only impinges upon the external aspects, which are less substantive.
>
> [. . .] These are remains of graves found under the ground *whose existence was not known to the public.*[17] [Emphasis added in all the above excerpts.]

The High Court's depiction of the disputed plot of land – which was indeed part of a historical cemetery, as described above – grants priority to the facts as presented and interpreted by the MoT experts over the expert opinions and supporting evidence submitted by the group of academics and civil society organizations. The latter material included a 1958 letter from the secretary of the Haifa Muslim Committee, Suhayl Shukri, to the mayor of Jerusalem (submitted by Professor Yehoshua Ben Arieh), objecting to the Jerusalem

Municipality's plans to use the cemetery as an entertainment stage, as well as the fact that the mayor honored Shukri's request to relocate the stage outside of the cemetery. Evidence that this plot was part of a cemetery also appeared in complaints by the Supreme Muslim Authority opposing the installation of infrastructure in the cemetery during the 1980s. These facts were presented in the expert opinion of Amir Cheshin. Even the expert opinion of Shalom Goldstein on behalf of the MoT entrepreneurs noted that during his ten-year tenure as the mayor's advisor, the municipality had received two or three complaints from the Muslim public. In addition, the complaint of the waqf to UNESCO in 1986, when the municipal parking lot was built, further contradicts the High Court justices' conclusion.

The High Court explained why it ascribed little weight to the importance and holiness of the Mamilla Cemetery in this case:

> The extent of holiness attributed to a cemetery varies across communities, across religions, and across cultures. This complexity is compounded when considering a country with a history of thousands of years, where many ancient burial sites can be found throughout the land, most of which are hidden from view and concealed deep beneath the ground. Such unknown sites are naturally not a focal point for a contemporary community, and in most cases members of the community are not even aware of the existence of the remains of graves hidden in that area. When a graveyard ceases to serve as a point of reference for the individual or the community, when it has been abandoned, neglected, and hidden from view, and over the generations it has been covered by earth, then gradually the power of the constitutional principle of honoring the dead at this site diminishes. The more a cemetery is covered by earth and disappears from view and the less it is visited or its existence is known with the passage of generations, the lower the expectation is that the site be preserved. This is especially true if over the years the area has been used for various purposes that have no connection to the remains of graves under the ground. A visible cemetery that constitutes a point of reference for the individual and community differs from hidden graves that were used for burial in the remote past, are hidden deep under the ground, and are not known to the surrounding community. The passage of time has weight when assessing the impact of the constitutional right to honor the dead if it conflicts with other known interests. The lower the impact of this right, the more weight one should ascribe to the needs of the living.[18]

This High Court verdict effectively granted retroactive legitimacy to many earlier construction projects that had taken place over Muslim graveyards in Israel in the past, when the Muslim community was under the authority of a military regime and too weak to organize protests as it does these days. It is questionable whether during the 1960s the Muslim population of Israel in fact knew that most of the area of the Mamilla Cemetery was rendered for use as a public park (Independence Park), given that in 1964 almost no Muslims resided in West Jerusalem and that only after 1967, when Israel annexed East Jerusalem, did the Muslim Council of East Jerusalem begin protesting construction or development projects at the Mamilla Cemetery, such as laying a sewage pipeline or building a parking lot. The High Court justices weighed the extent of harm to the dignity of the dead against the benefit to the public from the construction project by analyzing five values: the dignity of the dead, the offense to people's sentiments, the delay in filing the complaint, the purpose of the construction project, and the maintenance of consistent planning and construction processes. What follows is a summary of each of these five interests as presented in the court's verdict.

The Dignity of the Dead

The High Court held that the dignity of the dead is a constitutional value that must be protected and that sometimes overrides other values: "The dignity of the dead is a constitutional principle derived from the dignity of the living human being and his right of personal autonomy. The two cannot be separated from each other."[19]

The verdict added:

> Desecration or destruction of a grave not only dishonors the memory of the deceased and offends the sentiments of his relatives. Such acts also offend the sentiments of many others who visit the cemetery and for whom the respectful appearance of the site is important as part of the private and public expression of protection of the dignity of the dead as well as the dignity of the living who honor the dead . . . Protecting the dignity of the dead has a general public aspect reflecting the continuation of respect that society affords a person during his life and after his death.[20]

Offense to People's Sentiments

After considering the dignity of the dead, the verdict discussed the extent of offense to people's sentiments, whether it is severe and real or weak and vague:

> Causing damage to a known cemetery not only dishonors the dignity of the deceased and their families and offends family sentiments but might also offend the sentiments of the public and the community to which the deceased belonged during their lives. The offense might relate to religious belief, community identity, or affiliation. Protection from offense to public sentiments is a public interest deserving protection in

> itself . . . However, not every offense to sentiments, deep as it may be, will tip the scale against a strong competing interest or basic right. In order for an offense to the sentiments of a person or the public to negate or restrict the implementation of competing rights or interests, the offense must cross a "threshold of tolerance." This threshold is not fixed but changes in accordance with the nature of the offense and the content of the competing rights. For example, the protection afforded religious sentiments is not absolute; it must be balanced with competing public interests. The extent of protection from offense to sentiments reflects the relative weight to be attributed to the conflicting interests. In the framework of the above-mentioned balance, there is a "level of tolerance" of offense to sentiments that the public in a democratic society can bear. This level of tolerance is not uniform. It varies from one right to another and from one offense to another. *The threshold of tolerance of an offense to sentiments is influenced by the strength of the competing basic right or public interest . . . An offense to the sentiments of the public that involves damaging a cemetery through construction or development deserves attention and requires assigning the proper weight to the nature of this offense alongside the competing rights and interests.*[21] [Emphasis added.]

The relevant question is how much weight the High Court assigned to each of the above-mentioned values. The court's characterization of the possible offense to sentiments – "the offense might relate to religious belief, community identity, or affiliation" – overlooked another source of potential offense, namely, that *the site is a collective identity symbol of Arab-Muslim historical, cultural, and national heritage.*

As observed, the High Court did not accept the opinion of the group of academics and civil society organizations regarding the importance of the Mamilla Cemetery to the Muslim community. It was apparently more impressed by the experts who submitted opinions on behalf of the MoT entrepreneurs. These expert opinions emphasized that Israeli Muslims do not demonstrate much interest in the cemetery which they have neglected for many years.

Delay

The fact that the Muslim plaintiffs had not previously expressed any objection to the new intended use of this and nearby plots of the cemetery, and that they had not filed a complaint regarding the construction plans while it was under review in the planning committees, was an obstacle in the eyes of the High Court justices, who ascribed some weight to this delay. The delay had the effect of reducing the relative weight attributed to the offense to sentiments resulting from the re-designated use of this plot because such delay suggests that this site was not especially important to Muslims. Given the public importance of the dispute, however, the court decided not to dismiss the case solely on the basis of this delay. Nonetheless, the delay had a significant effect on the final verdict of the High Court.[22] The following is what the High Court justices had to say on the matter:

> The question that we must resolve in this case is whether implementing a municipal construction plan, which received final approval, to build the Museum of Tolerance in the designated plot meets the conditions of the restrictive clause of the law, taking into account that graves, remains of old graves, and human bones *that were hidden from sight were discovered in a relatively small part of this compound*. Does the infringement upon the basic right of the dignity of the dead in this case, alongside values relating to protection of holy places and public sentiments, meet the necessary criteria to establish the constitutionality of the offense? *The long delay in submitting this complaint has an impact on the question of the strength and weight that we should attribute to the alleged offense caused by implementing the plan and exposing the remains of the graves*.[23]
>
> Indeed, the exposure of remains of graves and human bones in the compound occurred only a number of months before the complaint was submitted, but this does not affect the claim of delay in light of the fundamental position of the plaintiff, which is based on the long-standing holiness of this compound. *The claim that the museum was planned to be built in a compound that is an integral part of the Muslim cemetery of Mamilla should have been asserted at the beginning of the planning process, regardless of the finding of human remains during the excavation works at this site*.[24] [Emphasis added in all the above excerpts.]

In sum, three facts created obstacles for the plaintiffs' case:

1. In the past buildings had been constructed over other plots in the same cemetery without Muslim objection (a school and the Agron House).
2. The same plot contained a parking lot that operated for two decades, and the museum building only replaced the parking lot.
3. The fact of the delay, namely, that there was no objection to the plan to build a museum during the planning process.

Qadi Ahmad Natour responded to the claim of delay when he appeared before the Knesset Committee of Interior and Environment by stating the following:

> Regarding the sophisticated formal questions, it was said that everything was conducted legally, as if there were no law and no judge.

> When the District Planning Committee published an announcement inviting objections, and we are asked why we did not object, the answer is – who will object? The State of Israel abolished the Supreme Muslim Council, abolished the waqf, abolished every Muslim institution and destroyed the infrastructure for religious support services for Muslims in the country. So there is no institution that can be expected to respond to announcements or monitor the actions carried out throughout this state. Therefore you cannot use the argument that nobody objected. It is the responsibility of the state that expropriated these places and transferred them to these people. Therefore, the state has to be responsible for the outcomes of these actions. Although the Absentees' Properties Law gave the Custodian this responsibility, and the Custodian handed these rights over, the state institution should say, 'you received the property, but you are not allowed to do these things.'[25]

Qadi Natour is correct regarding the responsibility of the state, but he is wrong regarding the responsibility of the Muslims. Indeed, the state does not recognize a supreme Muslim institution, but the Muslim society has developed strong civil society organizations that protect Arab minority rights, including two Islamic movements focused primarily on Arab rights. Civil society organizations in Israel make use of public advocacy for many citizens' issues, such as planning and construction in non-recognized villages. For example, Adalah, the Legal Center for Arab Minority Rights in Israel, filed petitions with the High Court against the state regarding discriminatory funding for Muslim religious support services, including funding for the preservation of cemeteries. Yet neither this organization nor any other complained about the Mamilla Cemetery. Many other Muslim cemeteries were also neglected by the local and national institutions of the Arab minority. Presumably the reason is the location of Mamilla in West Jerusalem, relatively out of sight of Israeli Arab residential areas.

The Purpose of the Construction Project

In addition to significantly reducing the weight ascribed to the offense to sentiments (because of the delay), the High Court attributed greater weight to the competing interests, particularly the purpose of the construction project. The court held that "a purpose is found to be worthy if it serves objectives that are important to the state and society and are aimed at establishing a basis for coexistence and for a social framework that seeks to protect and promote human rights".[26] The justices added:

> The case before us involves a plan to construct a public facility with special municipal and national importance. Its aim is to construct a public building that will embody highly important social and cultural

> qualities, which can make an important contribution to the public at both the national and international levels. The construction of the Museum of Tolerance as a spiritual and ideological center is aimed at attracting visitors from Israel and abroad. Its aim is to boost the development of Jerusalem as the capital of Israel, and constitutes part of a comprehensive plan to significantly change the urban center of the city and to transform it into a cultural, commercial, and tourist center. The execution of the plan involves implementation of the property right of the entrepreneurs and reflects their freedom of artistic and conceptual expression through the architectural plans of Frank Gehry. In all of the above aspects, implementation of the plan accords with the state's values and aims to achieve important and worthy purposes.[27]

The court did not address the question of whether a structure built over Muslim graves and aimed at promoting the value of tolerance indeed reflects the purpose for which it was built, even though this was a central argument of the plaintiffs and the group of academics and civil society organizations.

Maintenance of Consistent Planning and Construction Processes

In its balancing equation, the High Court also considered the maintenance of consistent planning and construction processes to be a public interest favoring resumption of the MoT project:

> This reality underscores the existence of a public interest in the certainty, constancy, and finality of construction and planning processes, which should be ascribed proper weight in the balancing of interests. Given that during the relevant planning process, no claim was raised asserting any restriction based on the presence of remains of graves in this site, and given that the planning process was conducted legally and concluded without objection, there is a clear public interest in attributing weight to the finality of the planning process and to the importance of implementing the plan, not only in terms of land utilization, but also in terms of the value that should be ascribed to certainty, to constancy, and to public trust in the planning and construction system.[28]
>
> [. . .] The Building and Planning Law holds . . . that the designation of land for development and construction will not be affected if remains of ancient graves are excavated during the works. The law assumes that such exposure should not negatively affect a plan even if certain modifications are needed in order to reduce as much as possible infringing on the constitutional principle of the dignity of the dead. *This is different when in a planning context the case is of a recognized cemetery that*

> *was designated as such in the plan that applies to the site.* In the case of a site that was designated as a cemetery, any development or construction in this area that conflicts with the designated purpose is usually not permitted.[29] [Emphasis added.]
>
> [. . .] In our case, the land was not designated as a cemetery or declared as an antiquities site.[30]

The High Court framing of the dispute as an issue of planning and building laws actually dictated the fate of the legal dispute. The court justices attributed less weight to the offense to the dignity of the buried than to the benefit that emanates from the planned project of the MoT. According to the court, the current status of land in the urban planning processes overrides the previous status of the land as part of a historically designated cemetery.

The High Court was aware that its ruling would create a legal precedent. The MoT entrepreneurs warned the court that if it ruled against construction of the museum it would set a precedent for similar cases in the future:

> The Honorable Court is not exempt from considering the consequences of its verdict: accepting the claim of the plaintiff – that it is eternally prohibited to transfer bones or even the remains of bones of anonymous deceased to an alternative and respected graveyard, and that building over these remains is prohibited – would set a difficult precedent and create a foundation for severely undermining planning and development possibilities or implementing important projects in Jerusalem. Indeed, the long history of the city is directly proportionate to the number of remains of graves therein (as in other parts of Israel). As the Court of New Jersey in the United States said, before long the deceased will not leave space for the living . . . [31]

This argument is appropriate for graves incidentally unearthed during excavation works. The relevant question is whether it also applies to a known historical graveyard such as Mamilla.

Summary of the High Court Position on Mamilla

The following are excerpts from the conclusion of the verdict by Justice Ayaliah Procacca.

> In our case, proportionality in its narrow sense is used to question whether there is an appropriate relationship between the benefit in establishing the MoT in the existing location, as planned, and the extent to which the basic right of dignity of the dead is thereby undermined. Is the offense to public sentiments that results from

implementing the plan in the "purple section" of the Museum compound proportional to and reasonable in light of the benefit that might derive from establishing the museum in the planned compound, both in terms of the general public interest, as well as the property rights of the landowners? My answer to this question is that under the given circumstances *there is a proportional and reasonable relationship between the benefit to be expected from actualizing the purpose behind establishment of the Museum of Tolerance, and the extent of the expected damage that would result from building the "purple section," assuming that special measures will be taken to limit the damage in accordance with one of the alternatives proposed by the entrepreneurs . . .* [32]

[. . .] *The overall benefit of implementing the museum plan*, subject to measures to protect the integrity of the graves, overrides the potential undermining of the principle of the dignity of the dead, as well as the basic right that derives from this principle . . . [33]

[. . .] In the tension that exists between the needs of the living for development, construction, progress, and promotion of human welfare [on the one hand] and respect for the dignity of the dead in historical gravesites that are hidden from view [on the other], the former tends to prevail, subject to the obligation to take measures to the limit the degree of disrespect to the dignity of the dead as much as possible in every case.

[. . .] In certain exceptional cases, an offense to public sentiments beyond the threshold of tolerance needed in a democratic society could justify infringing a human right or undermining a public interest . . .

[. . .] In our case, for all of the reasons presented in the constitutional analysis above, it should be said that *given the presence of human remains at the site, the offense to sentiments that might result from implementing the museum plan, subject to the utmost measures to minimize damage to these graves, does not cross the threshold of tolerance that is needed for coexistence in a democratic society that respects human rights*. Therefore, such offense to sentiments does not breach the required administrative reasonability and constitutional balance between the needs of social progress a*nd the obligation to preserve past heritage, including respecting ancient burial sites that were hidden from view throughout many generations . . .* [34]

[. . .] In light of the above, implementing the museum plan, subject to measures to treat the remains of graves in the "purple section" as detailed in one of the proposed alternatives meets the test of constitu-

> tionality and administrative reasonability, and may be granted approval.[35] [Emphasis added in all the above excerpts.]

In conclusion, the High Court verdict appears to present the following difficulties:

1. The verdict referred to the excavated graves as having been hidden from view and incidentally exposed. In fact, however, the Mamilla Cemetery is an important historical graveyard and the disputed plot contained about 1,000 graves.
2. The High Court did not address the fact that the fatwa permitting removal of the cemetery's sanctity, on which the administrative decisions relied, did so for the purpose of developing a public park, not for construction. Unlike construction, creating a public park does not entail deep excavation.
3. The verdict emphasizes the Muslim plaintiffs' delay in filing their objection to the project; apparently it was unaware of three previous objections by Muslims to development projects in the cemetery or neglect of the cemetery: a 1950 Jordanian complaint, a 1958 complaint by an Israeli Muslim official, and petitions to UNESCO by the Palestine Liberation Organization (PLO) and Jordanian Waqf during the mid-1980s.
4. Unlike cases involving the re-designation of cemeteries for development of vital infrastructure, the MoT project could be located in an alternative site.
5. One of the main justifications for resuming construction of the MoT in Mamilla was the specific quasi-sculptural architectural plan of Frank Gehry. This argument is invalid, as Gehry withdrew from the project in 2010.

The High Court verdict sets an important precedent, which reflects the values of Jewish society as a Zionist society, on the one hand, and a Western society, on the other hand. The High Court viewed the offense to the dignity of the dead – or, more precisely, the infringement upon the collective right of Muslims to have their heritage represented in West Jerusalem's public space – as proportional and reasonable damage. Yet the importance of the Mamilla Cemetery to Muslims is equivalent to the importance of the cemetery on the Mount of Olives to Jews. One can only imagine how an Israeli court, as well as state and municipal authorities, would react in a similar case resulting from construction on the Mount of Olives. One might also wonder how the Mamilla case would have been handled had the plaintiff not been a corporation affiliated with the Northern Islamic Movement, but a politically neutral Muslim entity, such as the Organization of Muslim Clerics in Israel, who are civil servants.

Notes

1 *HaShofet* ("The Judge"), television documentary by Ram Landes. See http://www.mako.co.il/tv-doco/f4b18258fc298110/Article-58b658406237221006.htm (Hebrew).
2 HCJ 547/84 *Piskey Din* 40(1) 113, 141 quoted by Menachem Mautner, *Law and Culture in Israel at the Beginning of the 21st Century*, Tel Aviv: Am Oved, 2008, p. 165 (Hebrew).
3 R. Segev and M. Kremnitzer, *Shiklul 'Arachim ve-Izun Interesim*, Jerusalem: The Israel Democratic Institute, 2008, p. 7 (Hebrew).
4 Z. Segal, "The High Court of Justice in Israeli Societal Fabric after 50 Years," *Mishpat U-Mimshal* 5:1, 1999, 235–80 (Hebrew).
5 Segev and Kremnitzer, op. cit., p. 10.
6 Segal, op. cit.
7 Ibid.
8 Opinion expressed by Member of Knesset Michael Eitan in the documentary *HaShofet*.
9 Article 131 of HCJ 52/06 (Hebrew).
10 Article 254 of HCJ 52/06 (Hebrew).
11 Article 101 of HCJ 52/06 (Hebrew).
12 H.C. hearing of file 52/06 of 3 October 2006 (Hebrew).
13 Article 5 of HCJ 52/06 (Hebrew).
14 Article 183 of HCJ 52/06 (Hebrew).
15 Article 12 of HCJ 52/06 (Hebrew).
16 Article 124 of HCJ 52/06 (Hebrew).
17 Article 248 of HCJ 52/06 (Hebrew).
18 Article 176 of HCJ 52/06 (Hebrew).
19 Article 135 of HCJ 52/06 (Hebrew).
20 Article 152 of HCJ 52/06 (Hebrew).
21 Articles 173–175 of HCJ 52/06 (Hebrew).
22 Article 92 of HCJ 52/06 (Hebrew).
23 Article 210 of HCJ 52/06 (Hebrew).
24 Article 92 of HCJ 52/06 (Hebrew).
25 Protocol 566 of the Knesset Committee of Interior and Environment meeting of 15 February 2006, available at: *www.knesset.gov.il/protocols/data/rtf/pnim/2006-02-15.rtf* (Hebrew).
26 Article 222 of HCJ 52/06 (Hebrew).
27 Article 224 of HCJ 52/06 (Hebrew).
28 Article 184 of HCJ 52/06 (Hebrew).
29 Article 216 of HCJ 52/06 (Hebrew).
30 Article 221 of HCJ 52/06 (Hebrew).
31 Article 151 of the response of the MoT to the petition to issue a decree to stop works, 3 January 2007 (Hebrew).
32 Article 238 of HCJ 52/06 (Hebrew).
33 Article 247 of HCJ 52/06 (Hebrew).
34 Article 250 of HCJ 52/06 (Hebrew).
35 Article 251 of HCJ 52/06 (Hebrew).

CHAPTER

9

The Role of Judicial Tribunals in Resolving Conflicts over Holy Places

The dispute over the plot of Mamilla designated for construction of the MoT took place mainly in the High Court. Even the attempted mediation initiated by the court with the aim of avoiding adjudication of this sensitive and emotionally charged issue was conducted within the confines of the court by its former president, Meir Shamgar. However, the plaintiff rejected any compromise that would legitimize construction over even a small part of the disputed plot. The Northern Islamic Movement carried out an ideological and uncompromising struggle. It was the Islamic Movement that initiated the legal struggle and insisted on transfer of the dispute for resolution specifically in the High Court. The other party to the dispute – the MoT Corporation – also rejected any solution that would involve building the museum in a substitute location because such change would involve enormous financial loss (the $15 million that had already been invested when the hearing began) and create a risk of losing donors (as apparently happened) as well as the time and money required for a new plan. Moreover, the location of downtown West Jerusalem is more attractive than a substitute site. Hence, when all attempts to mediate between the disputing parties failed, the case reverted to the High Court.

This chapter addresses the question of whether a court procedure is an appropriate and effective venue to resolve conflicts involving religious and cultural values related to holy places. In addition, we will discuss various options for resolving conflicts during the initial planning stage of a development project in places that have cultural and religious significance.

A judicial tribunal, whether a court or a commission of inquiry established within a legal framework, is an autocratic method for resolving a conflict. Indeed, once a dispute is transferred to the legal domain, its adjudication and consequences are no longer negotiable but imposed from above.[1] The process is also autocratic in the sense that one of the parties involved, whether a litigant or a ruling authority, has unilaterally determined the particular venue of the legal procedure. There is always one party that is upset by the choice of the tribunal, which might negatively influence its willingness to accept compromise solutions during court hearings. Moreover, even if the court hearing entails a process of mediation or arbitration, the final adjudication will be perceived as an imposed solution and will not necessarily bring an end to the conflict[2] despite the legal framework within which the decision was reached and the obligation incumbent upon the parties to respect the rule of law.[3] Another shortcoming of judicial treatment of a conflict over religious sites is that a court process is usually limited to specific legal questions and does not address the broad spectrum of relations between the parties to a dispute; hence a court decision will not resolve the conflict at its root.[4]

Choosing a judicial theater to address or resolve a conflict has advantages and disadvantages. In some conflicts, a legal tribunal would be the most efficient process, while in other cases such a tribunal would further complicate and prolong the conflict. A legal forum restricts the parties to a particular framework of procedures and laws; it frames the boundaries of the conflict and limits the directly involved parties, preventing the possibility of broader public involvement.[5] At times, however, a court ruling could impose a quick solution to a dispute and enable governing authorities to control and enforce the law if there is a risk that the dispute will lead to bloodshed or provoke mass protest and potential violence.[6] In such a case, legal treatment is not expected to resolve the entire the dispute, only to contain the danger of outbreak of violence.[7]

Another weakness of the legal process is that its efficiency depends on an authoritative body to enforce its verdict.[8] In other words, the need for enforcement indicates that an autocratic solution by a legal tribunal does not bring an end to a conflict, but is only one stage of it.[9] One can only expect that sometime in the future the original conflict will once again erupt. However, a temporary situation of tranquility resulting from a court verdict may endure for a long time, in which case legal treatment could be advantageous. Nonetheless, a conflict over holy places will be permanently resolved only if the parties reach an agreement without the imposition of a solution by a third party. Hence, a judicial decision is part of conflict management, not of conflict resolution.[10]

In 1929, when a conflict erupted over the rights of Jews to worship at the Western Wall, the British Mandate Government established an international commission of inquiry, which operated as a judicial tribunal and achieved a very successful outcome.[11] Its success emanated from two reasons: First, the inquiry was limited to resumption of the status quo situation that prevailed before World War I, an issue that was relatively easy to investigate and resolve. Second, throughout the entire Mandate period, there was a strong ruling power that could impose a decision and prevent its violation. However, when this power left in 1948, and after the balance of power shifted in June 1967, the dispute reemerged and intensified to encompass the entire compound of the Temple Mount/Al-Haram al-Sharif shrine.

A dispute similar to the Mamilla case erupted in 1988 in the Israeli Muslim town of Umm al-Fahm between two Muslim parties, the municipality and the Islamic Movement, but here the court ruling differed from the ruling in Mamilla case. In Umm al-Fahm, the Islamic Movement opposed the paving of a road and construction over a local Muslim cemetery. The president of the High Court at the time, Meir Shamgar, succeeded in bringing the two parties to an agreement according to which the issue would be decided by the then president of the Shari'a Court of Appeals, Tawfiq Asaliya, who was also a resident of this town.[12] The fact that the court ruling had been agreed upon rather than imposed is what enabled resolution of the conflict even though the eventual verdict was in favor of the municipality.

In light of the above-mentioned limitations of the legal framework, the question that arises is: Why did the Islamic movement choose the High Court as a venue for legal remedy? The answer to this question has two aspects: the expected remedy and the other alternatives for achieving the same end. From the perspective of the Islamic Movement, the High Court was the appropriate tribunal because it has the authority to overturn administrative decisions. More importantly, this court can issue an injunction suspending work until a case is decided and has often done so in practice. The Islamic Movement regarded the cessation of work as creating new facts on the ground that would allow it to organize protests and forge coalitions with other civil society entities. In addition, delaying the construction could result in withdrawal by donors when they learn about opposition to the project. For the Islamic Movement, compromise with the MoT project representatives was a nonstarter because of the nature of the plot on which the museum was to be built, that is, a holy place that, according to their belief, must not be subdivided.[13]

However, when the leaders of the Islamic movement realized that the High Court was not in a hurry to issue an injunction to suspend construction, they understood that the venue they had chosen was not in their favor. Perhaps at this point they also realized that although the High Court is known for its liberal approach regarding minority rights, it is still a Jewish and Zionist tribunal. As we saw in the previous chapter, despite its impartial liberal tradition, the High Court is not exactly "home court" for Arab Muslims who are struggling to preserve their symbolic identity in a holy city such as Jerusalem, which is in the eye of a political storm and at the heart of a dispute between two nations. Indeed, the High Court was found to be an unfriendly venue for the Islamic Movement not only because of the national identity of the court's composition, but also because of the imbalance in the legal representation of the disputants. The museum project, supported by institutions of the state, was represented by leading advocates, while the Islamic Movement was represented by Arab advocates who did not have a comparable level of experience. The plaintiffs' advocate, Durgham Sayf, expressed this imbalance in the following way:

> We see a link between money and power. These people have a fortune and they have invested a lot of money in this project. This is evidenced

> by the fact that when they suspended work for a day or two after the Shari'a Court issued an injunction, they exerted pressure on various authorities in the ruling system and suddenly the police retreated from its position and refrained from enforcing the injunction.[14]

Moreover, the possibility that the High Court would reject their petition – as it eventually did – could create a legal precedent that would put an end to their ideological struggle against construction over Muslim cemeteries and prevent them from returning such cemeteries to their original use. Moreover, their attempt to transfer the case to the Shari'a Court failed, as we saw in chapter five.

The Northern Islamic Movement and the Shari'a Court used the Mamilla controversy to challenge Israel's laws and policy regarding the religious rights of Muslim citizens of Israel. The Mamilla dispute was an opportunity for them to accuse Israel of having an illegal and discriminatory policy and to use this claim in order to reach out and influence the local, regional (Arab-Muslim), and the international public opinion. From their perspective, the dispute involved the following questions: Does a Muslim minority have a right to preserve its heritage by maintaining its cemeteries and other holy places? Does the Shari'a Court in Israel have independent judicial standing? Do religious Muslim figures have the right to determine what is a holy site and to decide what the state and government institutions are allowed to do in a Muslim cemetery? Does a Muslim community have the right to administer waqf properties and religious institutions? All of these questions remained unanswered even after the High Court issued its verdict.

Every judicial issue that the Al-Aqsa Corporation raised in its petition represented an attempt to fundamentally revise the rights of Muslims in Israel and to reinstate the rights and power that they had prior to the establishment of Israel. This was the reason that the Northern Islamic Movement chose the High Court. Its leaders presumably believed, at least initially, that this venue provided a golden opportunity to expose an extremely unreasonable initiative, and that the High Court as well as Jewish public opinion would side with them. This was my personal impression from conversations with Muslim functionaries during the court hearing. They viewed the Mamilla case as the best test case for this purpose. They believed that the public would view the construction of a monument representing the value of "tolerance" over land belonging to a Muslim cemetery as clearly unreasonable. This was precisely the position of the group of seventy Jewish academics and seven Israeli organizations that participated in the court hearing and opposed construction of the MoT over a historic Muslim cemetery. Moreover, the Islamic Movement's activists apparently believed that the discovery of hundreds of skeletons beneath the ground – as well as the status of this cemetery as one of the most important historic cemeteries of Muslims in Palestine – would speak for itself, and that consequently Jewish and international public opinion, and perhaps even the High Court, would side with them. They also believed that Jewish justices, who were aware of the potential threat to Jewish cemeteries throughout the world, would seek to avoid granting legitimacy to action that damages a Muslim cemetery because such legitimacy could be used by anti-Jewish elements to justify damage to Jewish cemeteries abroad.

Sheikh Raed Salah formulated the strategy and action plan of the Northern Islamic Movement. He regarded media exposure as a goal in itself. Apparently he believed that news of the court hearing would reverberate throughout the world, generating publicity, popularity, and support for him and his movement. For the Islamic Movement in Israel, the Mamilla affair was indeed an opportunity to challenge the system and win an important precedential case. However, it also entailed enormous risk. A negative verdict in the High Court might reaffirm the legitimacy of the system and set a precedent that could prevent the Islamic Movement from implementing its strategy of preserving and reviving abandoned Muslim holy sites in the future. Their challenge to the legitimacy of the system, including its legislation and policies, was thus a double-edged sword: the principled and precedential strength of their strategy was also its weakness. Once the official Israeli establishment realized that the Mamilla dispute entailed not only the specific issue at hand but also an attempt to undermine the legitimacy of the entire system, it adopted a firm stance in favor of the MoT. The civil society organizations and the group of 70 academics who opposed locating the planned museum in Mamilla could not attract enough support within Jewish Israeli public opinion or in the High Court to counter the official stance.

The Museum entrepreneurs were aware of the possible damage to the image of the project resulting from its focus on the principle of tolerance while being built on an old cemetery and causing hundreds of skeletons to be uprooted, thereby offending Muslim sentiments. Yet according to them, they were confident that they had acted in good faith and that, under the circumstances, their decision to resume the project was correct. They believed that even if their image suffered in the short term, once the project was completed the public would forget the controversy. The MoT entrepreneurs had succeeded in recruiting donors on the basis of a specific plan designed for Mamilla, and they were afraid of losing financial support, as well as the involvement of the MoT's renowned architect and planner, if they were to relocate beyond the city center. They viewed the Islamic Movement's opposition as politically motivated, not as a sincere grievance. They pointed to the following facts in support of their position: First, no Muslim opposed the plans during the planning and zoning process. Second, the specific location had been used as a parking lot for at least two decades, during which time nobody questioned how many people were buried underneath or who they were; thus there are no direct relatives whose sentiments would be offended by removal of the skeletons. Third, when the petition was filed before the court, most of the skeletons (about 400) had already been removed. Fourth, a vast amount of money had already been invested in the project, and every delay in its implementation or change of location could cause significant financial loss. Finally, they claimed that reburial of the uprooted human remains and construction of the MoT would actually honor the dead in a way that the previous situation – when they lay buried and unacknowledged beneath a parking lot – did not. Now, with the possibility of reburial, one could also build a memorial to them and to the entire cemetery. Even though they believed in the strength of their case, the entrepreneurs consulted experts regarding a possible compromise with the Al-Aqsa Corporation, but the plaintiffs rejected any compromise.

The Northern Islamic Movement's mode of operation with respect to Islamic holy places relies primarily on the use of force and protest rather than dialogue and lobbyism, as illustrated by the following examples: renovation of abandoned mosques without informing those who currently possess the property (such as the Sarafand Mosque); demonstrations that involve praying at mosques located in predominantly Jewish localities (such as Tiberias); and organized demonstrations at the construction sites of projects located on Muslim burial grounds, which sometimes result in violence. In the case of Mamilla, the movement could also have organized public demonstrations and a media campaign, but it opted to pursue legal recourse through the High Court. By so doing it took an enormous risk because once it petitioned this court it had to accept the legitimacy of the High Court of Israel and commit itself to its final decision.

We can gain some insight into the Northern Islamic Movement's mode of operation by comparing it to its sister organization, the Southern Islamic Movement. The southern faction of the Islamic Movement also acts to preserve Muslim holy places in Israel, but they try to maintain a low profile, relying on quiet field work, persuasion, and dialogue with state institutions and Jewish rabbis. For example, between 2005 and 2008, the head of the Southern Islamic Movement, Member of Knesset Ibrahim Sarsour, and his colleagues cooperated with MK Rabbi Michael Melchior (Meimad-Labor) and other rabbis to promote two legislative bills. The first bill listed ten abandoned Muslim holy sites that would be declared holy places to be renovated and administered by Muslims; the list could later be expanded.[15] The second bill proposed that an authority be established to preserve and develop Muslim holy sites, to be jointly run by the government and the Muslim community, with government funding.[16] These two bills were drafted during a long series of meetings between the movement and rabbis, with the participation of Knesset members, and were discussed in Knesset committees and other government fora, but they never materialized.[17]

One can further analyze the mode of operation that the Northern Islamic Movement used in its struggle against the location of the MoT in Mamilla by comparing it with two possible alternatives: first, a compromise that would permit construction of the museum while preserving the visible burial site in Mamilla in good condition and perhaps even erecting a special memorial to the cemetery and those buried there. This alternative was suggested to the Muslim plaintiffs during the mediation process, and they rejected it. The second alternative was mass protests at the site itself. The Northern Islamic Movement's leader, Raed Salah, attempted this approach in 2007 with respect to the Mughrabi Ascent affair, but it was ineffective because Sheikh Salah was unable to recruit enough supporters within his own Islamist constituency. If this was the outcome when a central and sacred site such as Al-Haram al-Sharif/Al-Aqsa was involved, it would be all the more ineffective in the case of a neglected Muslim cemetery that had been used as a parking lot for two decades.

It is also instructive to compare the strategy of the Northern Islamic Movement to that of Jewish Haredi groups that struggle for control of the public space in their residential areas, such as the Bar Ilan Street affair and the Karta parking lot in Jerusalem. In both these cases, as in many others, mass demonstrations achieved their goals. In contrast, however, mass demonstrations by the Islamic Movement cannot provide the crucial leverage sought for two reasons: First, the Islamic Movement has not been able to inspire the masses to demonstrate over low-level holy places, only over the Al-Aqsa compound. Second, state institutions view the Northern Islamic Movement's activities as a provocation against the Jewish-Zionist nature of the state, and therefore they have ruled out negotiation and compromise. Their only response is to dispatch the police to contain these demonstrations.

We can draw additional lessons from another dispute over the use of land in which the same Sheikh Salah actually succeeded in mobilizing many people and accomplishing his goal. In 1998, when Israeli military authorities designated a piece of land in Wadi 'Ara known as Al-Rouha as military training zone number 107, mass demonstrations organized in Umm al Fahm and its vicinity impelled the government to compromise and change its plan. The dispute resulted in the government acceding to the demands of popular Arab groups to reduce the training zone significantly and to reallocate large tracts of Jewish-controlled lands to the jurisdiction of nearby Arab towns and villages.[18] Perhaps the Al-Rouha struggle succeeded despite its violent nature because it involved tangible interests, namely, privately owned lands slated for development purposes, and because the Arabs had framed the issue as "land expropriation." Partisan politics also favored the residents of the Al-Rouha area because the government of Ehud Barak (1999–2001) sought Arab support at the ballot boxes.

Considering the favorable results that the Islamic Movement was able to achieve when it chose to use public protest or create facts on the ground, it is surprising that in the case of Mamilla it opted for a judicial procedure before the High Court rather than the Shari'a Court. The choice of a civil judicial venue – the High Court – turned out to be a major strategic error on the part of the Islamic Movement because the outcome has the effect of barring any future attempts by the movement to preserve old Muslim cemeteries rendered for other purposes in the past. The movement only succeeded in delaying the construction project by several years and in causing some financial loss to the MoT entrepreneurs – resulting in a smaller museum building – but it failed in its principal objective of relocating the museum. Even after the verdict issued, however, opponents of the MoT continued to take action against the project, which indicates that the judicial decision did not put an end to the conflict. The autocratic decision leaves the party that lost the court case alert and poised for another opportunity to reopen the dispute through alternative methods such as mass demonstrations, slander, and violence. Indeed, a few months after the verdict was issued an initiative opposing the MoT by Rabbis for Human Rights (in cooperation with Shas party activists and the Atra Kadisha Haredi organization) was announced, declaring the future museum religiously "impure" because it was built above graves. The initiative was unsuccessful, but future developments are unpredictable. In May 2010 the newspaper *Haaretz* published a series of articles criticizing the MoT initiative in Mamilla. A broad media campaign appears to be the most effective approach. Indeed, the publicity that challenged the rationale of the project seems to have deterred potential donors and possibly led the museum's architect to resign (although he denied that he withdrew from the project for this reason).

Another mode of struggle that Muslim opponents to the MoT in Mamilla employed was to open a new front at the international level. A group of Palestinian organizations and individuals appealed in February 2010 to the UN and the International Court of Justice in The Hague. This new initiative could subject Israel's policy and its High Court verdict to a moral and legal test. If the MoT Corporation does not change the location of the museum building in Jerusalem, it appears that the conflict will revert to its point of origin, that is, the ideological struggle of Muslims to have an impact on the symbolic landscape of Jerusalem. Such a confrontation could embarrass Israel and galvanize those who challenge the legitimacy of its policies and its very existence as well as its standing in Jerusalem. At the time of writing, the campaign has already started.

Notes

1 S. LaTour et al., "Some determinants of preference for modes of conflict resolution," *The Journal of Conflict Resolution* 20:2, June 1976, 320; Y. Maley, "From adjudication to mediation: Third party discourse in conflict resolution," *Journal of Pragmatics* 23:1, January 1995, 96, 101.
2 A. Tidwell, *Conflict Resolved?* New York: Pinter Press, 1998, p. 22.
3 Tidwell, p. 22; M. Hudson, *International Tribunals, Past and Future,* Concord: Rumford Press, 1994, p. 236.
4 Maley, op. cit.; Hudson, op. cit., 233.
5 LaTour, op. cit., p. 320; Hudson, op. cit., p. 236.
6 Manley, op. cit.; Hudson, op. cit., p. 238.
7 C. R. Mitchell, *The Structure of International Conflict*, New York: St. Martin's Press, 1989, p. 276.
8 L. Kriesberg, *Constructive Conflict: From Escalation to Resolution*, Lanham: Rowman & Littlefield Publishers, 1998, p. 323.
9 Mitchell, op. cit., p. 276.

10 B. Hill, "An Analysis of conflict resolution techniques: From problem-solving workshops to theory," *The Journal of Conflict Resolution,* 26:1, 1982, 115.
11 Great Britain, Colonial Office, *Report of the Commission Appointed . . . to Determine the Rights and Claims of Moslems and Jews in Connection with the Western Wall or Wailing Wall in Jerusalem*, London, 1930.
12 HCJ 593/86 Islamic Assoc. vs. Umm al-Fahm Municipality (unpublished verdict, dated 14 February 1988).
13 R. E. Hassner, "'To halve and to hold': Conflicts over sacred space and the problem of indivisibility," *Security Studies* 12:4, Summer 2003, 1–33.
14 Protocol 566 of the Knesset Committee of Interior and Environment meeting of 15 February 2006, available at: *www.knesset.gov.il/protocols/data/rtf/pnim/2006-02-15.rtf (Hebrew).*
15 *Haaretz*, 26 December 2007. http://www.haaretz.com/hasite/spages/938577.html (Hebrew).
16 http://www.melchior.org.il/viewpage.asp?pageid=328 (Hebrew).
17 http://www.pmo.gov.il/PMO/vadot/hakika/2008-2009/11/des4251.htm (Hebrew).
18 Y. Reiter, *National Minority, Regional Majority: Palestinian Arabs versus Jews in Israel*, Syracuse University Press, 2009, p. 181.

Conclusion

Among disputes over holy places, the dispute over construction of the MoT on a plot of land that had served as a burial site in the past is unusual in that it results from a one-time entrepreneurship rather than an enduring intercommunal conflict over rights regarding a holy place. Yet from the point of view of the Islamic Movement, which strives to preserve and rehabilitate Muslim holy sites throughout the country, the Mamilla affair is only one link in a chain of confrontations with state institutions and planning authorities in Israel. From a broader perspective the Mamilla case represents a conflict over the right of an indigenous minority to be represented in the public space and to preserve its holy sites, regardless of their physical condition or the extent of their attachment to it. Moreover for the Northern Islamic Movement, *appropriate* representation in the public space is not enough. It aspires to revive the indigenous landscape of the public space, namely, the landscape of the Arab homeland that existed before the takeover by Jewish immigrants who established the State of Israel and constitute its dominant majority.

This dispute has highlighted several questions of principle regarding the relationship between Israel as a Jewish state and its Arab citizens, who constitute a predominantly Muslim national minority. At the immediate level, the dispute relates to the tension between preservation and urban development in the heart of West Jerusalem, but more broadly the Mamilla dispute represents tensions and conflicts that relate to a range of subjects. The first of these touches on the essence of the struggle between the Zionist and Arab nationalist movements in four spheres: the regional Israeli–Arab sphere, the religious Jewish–Muslim sphere, the particular national Israeli–Palestinian sphere, and the intra-ethnic sphere comprising a Jewish majority and an Arab-Muslim minority.

The government of Israel and the Jerusalem Municipality gradually and continuously encroached on the Muslim cemetery that remained in West Jerusalem after 1948, rendering parts of it for other public uses. The Northern Islamic Movement struggles against this precise trend in its efforts to preserve the partially erased landscape, an Arab Muslim landscape of cultural identity.

The Mamilla dispute has powerful symbolic and practical implications for the Israeli–Palestinian struggle over the future and character of Jerusalem. The establishment of the MoT in the center of Jerusalem is aimed at reinforcing the image of the city that Israel seeks to project, namely, a united city under Israeli sovereignty – living proof that under Israel's control, coexistence among peoples and religions is possible. The Muslims' demand for preservation of the Mamilla Cemetery directly challenges Israeli policy by attempting to revive the Arab Muslim fabric of Jerusalem, even in the heart of the west side of the city.

The Mamilla Cemetery is among tens of Muslim cemeteries that the State of Israel almost completely obliterated for modern development purposes. The state and municipal authorities carried out the above policy in cooperation with qadis and other Muslim activists. Yet this "cooperation" occurred at a time when leading Muslim figures were subject to pressure by the martial regime or personally motivated to engage in corrupt real estate transactions. At the same time the State of Israel and international Jewish organizations were striving to preserve Jewish cemeteries in Europe as a living memory of entire Jewish communities that had been wiped out by the Holocaust.

The High Court of Israel repeatedly asserted that Israeli law does not discriminate against Muslim cemeteries, as development projects have also been carried out on plots of land where Jewish human remains were discovered. This High Court determination is correct regarding incidental exposure of graves during infrastructure and construction work, but it is incorrect in reference to designated and well-known cemeteries. In most of the cases in Israel and abroad in which judges and Jewish clerics permitted the paving of roads or construction over burial sites, the presence of human remains was an unexpected discovery that occurred during the course of the work. The Mamilla Cemetery is a well-known historical and important cemetery, part of which was obliterated and rendered for use as a public park in 1964 with the permission of a senior Muslim judicial cleric.

The following question arises in this context and remains unanswered: Did the state authorities and Jerusalem Municipality know in advance that they were granting the MoT entrepreneurs a plot of land that might contain hundreds of Muslim graves? If the museum entrepreneurs had known about the graves in advance, the High Court ruling would probably have been different. The Muslim plaintiffs failed to prove that the official authorities and museum entrepreneurs had had prior knowledge about what lay beneath the land designated for the MoT. Such knowledge is usually not documented. The MoT entrepreneurs' contention that they did not have such prior knowledge was partially challenged by Anat Hoffman, a member of the Jerusalem Municipality, who stated that once they discovered the first grave, they should have immediately ceased work and sought an alternative location for the MoT.[1] A similar view was expressed at the High Court hearing by one of the plaintiffs' advocates, Durgham Sayf: "The museum representatives are trying to scorch the land; they come from abroad and attempt to establish their own private museum over a Muslim cemetery, and they know it [that this is a cemetery]. The archeological findings prove it."[2]

The High Court drew a distinction between an ancient, designated cemetery and graves that were incidentally discovered, having been "hidden from sight." This distinction is morally, emotionally, and pragmatically correct.

However, the Mamilla Cemetery is an exception because it belongs to both categories at the same time. It is a renowned historical Muslim cemetery, designated as such in the past, which was gradually and ironically encroached upon by Muslim entrepreneurs for urban development purposes, such as construction of the Palace Hotel by Mufti Haj Amin Al-Husayni. A similar process continued after the establishment of Israel in 1948, enabling among other things the construction of a parking lot and the subsequent allocation of this plot of land for a museum. Hence, categorizing the disputed land in Mamilla is a matter of interpretation.

It cannot be denied that the Mamilla affair represents a troubling trend of encroachment upon Muslim cemeteries in Israel. I know of no comparable process in which Israeli authorities permitted encroachment upon a known and demarcated Jewish or Christian cemetery for purposes of development.

If the Mamilla dispute had involved construction of an emergency room, for example, the public interest would most likely have overridden the Muslim religious interest. But the nature of the construction – under the heading "Museum of Tolerance and Human Dignity" – created a difficult moral and educational problem.

An Israeli educational program initiated in 2005 (under Minister of Education Limor Livnat from the Likud Party) and titled "One Hundred Concepts in Heritage, Zionism, and Democracy" defines the value of tolerance in the following way:

> Tolerance is among the basic values of democracy. It shapes the attitude toward the other. Each of us is obligated to respect the other as a human being and respect his or her opinions and his or her right to express an opinion even if we disagree with these views or they disturb us.

Anyone who disapproves of locating the MoT in Mamilla would say that the above definition of tolerance was not given due weight in the High Court verdict, a court with an international reputation for protecting democracy, liberalism, and tolerance. The verdict in the Mamilla affair attributed less weight to tolerance and liberalism than to other values.

The Mamilla affair reflects a clash between human dignity (specifically, the dignity of the dead) and the economic interests of contemporary society. It also reflects the tension between the needs of the Jewish state, on the one hand, and the sentiments of the Arab-Muslim minority and its need for identity symbols, on the other hand. Two factors caused the High Court to devalue the extent of damage to the dignity of the dead and to the sentiments of Muslims: the long delay of the Muslim plaintiffs in submitting a complaint and the many precedents presented to the High Court according to which Islamic law and practice permit the removal of graves. Hence, the High Court gave more weight to other public interests such as the need to insure consistency in planning and construction processes.

We saw in chapter 5 that the shari'a indeed permits construction over old cemeteries, as occurred more than once in Arab localities in Israel. However, the shari'a insists that any development over cemeteries serve the public interests of the Muslim community, not those of a non-Muslim community. This condition was not met in the Mamilla case.

Another question of principle question raised by the Mamilla dispute is: Who is authorized to interpret the Muslim religious law in Israel? Is it appropriate for an Israeli court and Jewish judges – who base their opinion on reports submitted by Jewish experts on Islamic law – to rule in such a dispute? Or should such issues be decided by Muslim judges of the shari'a court system, an official judiciary system of the State of Israel?

The State of Israel grants shari'a courts relatively broad autonomy in matters of personal status, such as issues pertaining to gender and equality between the sexes, but the question of jurisdiction over waqf assets differs because it touches on national interests, namely, territory, land tenure, representation in the public sphere, political power, and economic independence. Moreover, the Shari'a Court of Appeals and its president unequivocally support the radical approach of the Northern Islamic Movement, which opposes the national interests of Israel. One cannot expect that the High Court of Israel would be objective and neutral regarding a legal party whose point of departure is deliberately anti-Zionist, particularly when the legal dispute has an impact on the public space of Jerusalem, the capital of Israel, as well as the character of the country. For these reasons the High Court denied the authority of the Shari'a Court to rule in the dispute after it attempted to intervene. My impression is that if the opponents of the MoT had been moderate Muslims or if they had family members buried in Mamilla and could identity their graves' location, then the High Court might have issued a different verdict.

The Mamilla affair touched an open wound in Israel and caused the issue of General Waqf properties in Israel to resurface. Israel's 1965 amendment to the Absentees' Properties Law, enabling the state to take over waqf properties, was a blow to the country's Muslim community. In their struggle against construction of the MoT in Mamilla, the Shari'a Court and the Northern Islamic Movement were attempting to revive the glory and authority of the waqf institution. The Shari'a Court briefly deluded itself that it still had jurisdiction over land disputes involving what had been "general waqf" properties before Israel was established. The High Court verdict, however, reaffirmed that the 1965 amendment had voided the special status of waqf properties, and thus their fate was no longer subject to shari'a court jurisdiction, nor was it in the hands of the Israeli Muslim community.

In conclusion three factors distinguish the case of the Mamilla Cemetery dispute from other cases:

1. In all other disputes the burial sites were intended for development and infrastructure, whereas the Mamilla enterprise is devoted to the concept

of "tolerance." The very fact that a dispute erupted and reached the courts casts a shadow over the project and its goal.

2. None of the comparable cases discussed in the High Court involved a large historical cemetery in a city that is holy and important to the three monotheistic religions.
3. None of the other cases cited for comparison had as many graves as were discovered in Mamilla, where the human remains of 400 deceased were already unearthed at the time of the hearing, and – according to the estimate of an IAA archeologist – another 600 remain under an unexcavated part of the museum plot.

At the same time, the following factors also had an impact on the High Court verdict:

1. For decades the Muslim community neglected the cemetery and did not act to preserve the site, even taking into account the unfortunate political circumstances. Years of neglect, abandonment, and passive acceptance of continuous encroachment upon the cemetery cannot be counter-balanced by the two-day clean-up campaign that the Northern Islamic Movement arranged in 2006.
2. The Mamilla affair epitomizes a struggle of identity and ideology between a national and religious minority and the state's hegemonic culture. When the minority challenges the majority on such a highly charged issue, it is not surprising that the majority reacts.
3. Senior Muslim clerics themselves contributed to the encroachment upon the Mamilla Cemetery, beginning with the British Mandate Supreme Muslim Council and concluding with the president of the Shari'a Court of Appeals during the 1960s, Qadi Tahir Hmmad.
4. The MoT project was not the first to change the designated use of this burial ground. On the same plot of land stood a multi-story parking lot, which the museum building was intended to replace. The construction of the parking lot in the mid-1980s did not give rise to significant protest, with the exception of a complaint submitted by Jordan and the East Jerusalem Waqf Administration to UNESCO.

Notes

1 Minutes of the 566 meeting of the Knesset Committee for Interior Affairs and Environment, 15 February 2006 (Hebrew).

2 High Court hearing of 3 October 2006.

Epilogue

Local disputes in which one of the parties fails to achieve its end at the local level frequently result in the losing party shifting the confrontation to a higher level – usually the international arena. In the literature of political science this process is known as "scale shift" and in our case as "upscale" from the state to the international level.[1] In the Mamilla dispute such a process has been underway since 2010.

After the Islamic Movement and the group of academics and Israeli civil society organizations lost the case in the High Court, the struggle against the MoT in Jerusalem was picked up by Palestinian civil society organizations, including Israeli–Arab organizations. Fifteen Palestinian organizations recruited sixty East Jerusalem dignitaries whose families are buried in Mamilla and launched a media campaign via the internet. During 2010 thousands of people signed the online petition against construction of the MoT in Mamilla. On 10 February 2010 the Palestinian organizations appealed to five senior officers of the UN and to the government of Switzerland (in its capacity as trustee for the Fourth Geneva Convention). They demanded that the issue be investigated and that Israel be ordered to stop the works, preserve the cemetery as a site of antiquities, and rebury the human remains that had been removed. The petitioners emphasized that West Jerusalem had come under Israeli control in 1948 in contravention of the 1948 UN partition resolution, which regarded Jerusalem as part of a *corpus separatum*, and that Israel had violated its commitment to protect holy places. The international campaign accuses Israel of continuous long-term activities aimed at erasing non-Jewish heritage and landmarks from the country's landscape. These charges are accompanied by pictures of the human remains that were removed in order to build a museum that they view as Jewish in nature. The campaigners also claim that Israel discriminates against Muslim holy sites, as exemplified by its maintenance of 136 Jewish holy sites and absolutely no Muslim holy sites. In addition the campaigners assert that the High Court verdict is based on a misleading presentation of IAA findings, which ignored the report of its own archeologist, Gideon Suleimani, and his affidavit as well as the declaration by the US-based Congress of Reform Rabbis against construction of the MoT in Mamilla. They go on to claim that the High Court is biased in favor of Jews and against Muslims, that Israel violates human rights and international law on the issue of Mamilla, and that consequently appealing to the international legal system is their only recourse.

The media campaign generated dozens of critical articles in the world's

Al-Khassaf, *Kitab Ahkam al-Awqaf*. Cairo: Ministry of Awqaf, 1902.

Khalidi, Walid *All That Remains: The Palestinian Villages Occupied and Depopulated by Israel in 1948*. Washington D.C., Institute of Palestine Studies, 1992.

Khamaisi, Rassem. *General Survey The Islamic Waqf; Land. Mosques and Cemeteries within the Green-line*. Kufr Barra, Al-Aqsa Association for the Protection the Islamic Waqf, 2002.

Kong, Lily. "Ideological hegemony and the political symbolism of religious buildings in Singapore" *Environment and Planning D: Society and Space* 11 (1993), pp. 23–45.

Kramer, Martin. *Islam Assembled: The Advent of the Muslim Congresses*. New York: Columbia University Press, 1986.

Kriesberg, Luis. *Constructive Conflict: From Escalation to Resolution*. Lanham: Rowman & Littlefield publishers, 1998.

Kroyanker, David. *Halom BeHakitz: Yerushalayim HaLo-Bnuya*. Jerusalem: Migdal David – The Museum for Jerusalem's History, 1993 [in Hebrew].

Kupferschmidt, Uri M. *The Supreme Muslim Council, Islam under the British Mandate for Palestine*. Leiden, New York, Copenhagen and Köln: E.J. Brill, 1987.

Layish, Aharon. "The Adaptation of a Religious Legal System to the Modern Period in a Foreign Surrounding: The Shari'a in Israel", Proceedings of the Israel Academy (Hebrew Series), vol. IX, no. 2 (2005), pp. 13–51.

Layish, Aharon. "The Muslim Waqf in Israel", *Asian and African Studies*, vol. 2 (1966), pp. 41–76.

LaTour S. et al., Some Determinants of Preference for Modes of Conflict Resolution. *The Journal of Conflict Resolution*, 20(2): June, 1976.

Lefebvre, Henri. *The Production of Space*. Oxford UK and Cambridge (Mass.): Basil Blackwell [1974] (1991), pp. 401–416.

Lefebvre, Henri. *Writing on Cities*. Oxford: Blackwell, 1996.

Levy, Andre. "Towards Politics of Identities," *Panim*, 10 (1999), pp. 31–40 [in Hebrew];

Luz, Nimrod. *The Arab Community of Jaffa and the Hassan Bey Mosque*. Jerusalem: The Floersheimer Institute for Policy Studies, 2005) [in Hebrew].

Luz, Nimrod. "Islamization of space and society in Mamluk Jerusalem and its hinterland", *Mamluk Studies Review* 6 (2002), pp. 135–155.

Luz, Nimrod "Metaphors of Resistance – Holy Places in the Palestinian Society of Israel: The Case of Maqam Abu al-Hija" [Hebrew]

Maley, Yon. "From adjudication to mediation: Third party discourse in conflict resolution." *Journal of Pragmatics*, 23(1) (January 1995), pp. 93–110.

Makdisi, Saree. "The Architecture of Erasure," *Critical Inquiry*, 36:3 (Spring 2010), pp. 519–559.

Mautner, Menachem. *Law and Culture in Israel at the beginning of the 21st Century*. Tel Aviv: Am Oved, 2008 [in Hebrew].

Mitchell, Christopher R. *The Structure of International Conflict*. New York: St. Martin's Press, 1989.

Mitchell, Don. *Cultural Geography. A Critical Introduction*. Oxford; Blackwell, 2000.

Natour, Ahmad. "The Battle for the Muslim Cemeteries in Israel" in Marshall J. Breger, Yitzhak Reiter and Leonard Hammer (eds.), *Religion and Politics: Sacred Space in Palestine and Israel*. London and New York: Routledge, 2012. pp. 168–192.

Nave, Emanuel. "Implementation of Shari'a in 20th Century Civil Courts: A

Comparative Study of Adjudication in Personal Status and Waqf Issues of Muslims in a Muslim Country (Egypt) and a Non-Muslim Country (Israel) (PhD Dissertation, Hebrew Universuty, 1997) [in Hebrew].

Or Commission Report, *Commission of Inquiry into the Clashes between security forces and Israeli civilians of October 2000*. August, 2003.

Ory, S. "Makbara", *Encyclopaedia of Islam*, 2nd ed., Leiden: Brill, 1991, IV pp. 125–128.

Pile, S. (1997). "Introduction: opposition, political identities and spaces of resistance", in S. Pile and M. Keith (eds.), *Geographies of Resistance*. London, New York: Routledge, pp. 1–32.

Reich, Roni. "The Cemetery in the Area of Mamilla in Jerusalem", *Qadmoniot* 26 (1994), pp. 103–109 [in Hebrew].

Reiter, Yitzhak. "The Administration and Supervision of Waqf Properties in 20th Century Jerusalem" *Varia Turcica* (Istanbul: Institute Francais d'etudes Annatoliens) 26 (1994), pp. 169–182.

Reiter, Yitzhak. *Islamic Endowments in Jerusalem under British Mandate*. London and Portland OR: Frank Cass, 1996.

Reiter, Yitzhak. *Islamic Institutions in Jerusalem: Palestinian Muslim Administration under Jordanian and Israeli Rule*. The Hague, London and Boston: Kluwer Law International, 1997.

Reiter, Yitzhak. *Islamic Awqaf in Jerusalem 1948–1990*. Jerusalem: The Jerusalem Institute for Israel Studies, 1991 [in Hebrew].

Reiter, Yitzhak. "Judge Reform: Facilitating Divorce by Shari'a Courts in Israel", *Journal of Islamic Law and Culture*, 11:1 (March 2009), pp. 13–38.

Reiter, Yitzhak. *National Minority, Regional Majority: Palestinian Arabs versus Jews in Israel*. Syracuse University Press, 2009.

Reiter, Yitzhak. "Qadis and the Implementation of Islamic Law in Present Day Israel" in Robert Gleave and U. Kermeli (eds.), *Islamic Law in Theory and Practice*. London and New York: I. B. Tauris, 1997, pp. 205–231.

Reiter, Yitzhak. "A Twofold Barrier – The Case of Religious Services for the Muslims in Israel" in Shlomo Hasson and Michael Karayanni (eds.), *Obstacles on the Development and Equality of the Arabs in Israel*. Jerusalem: the Floersheimer Institute for Policy Studies, 2006, pp. 166–182 [in Hebrew].

Reiter, Yitzhak. "Waqf in Israel Since 1965: The Case of Acre Reconsidered", in Marshall J. Breger, Yitzhak Reiter and Leonard Hammer (eds.), *Holy Places in the Israeli–Palestinian Conflict: Confrontation and Co-existence*. London and New York: Routledge, 2009, pp. 105–128.

Rozen, Yisrael. "Pinuy Kvarim LeTzorkhey Tzibur" [Removal of Graves for Public Purposes], *Tehumin* 18 (1998), pp. 254–273 [in Hebrew].

Rubin Peled, Alisa. *Debating Islam in the Jewish State*. New York: SUNY, 2001.

Sandberg, Haim. *Land Title Settlement in Eretz-Israel and The State of Israel*, Jerusalem, The Harry and Michael Sacher Institute for Legislative Research and comparative Law, Faculty of Law, The Hebrew University of Jerusalem & Land Use Research Institute, Israel National Fund (Keren Kayemeth LeIsrael), 2000.

Scott, James. C. *Weapons of the Weak*. New Haven, London: Yale University Press, 1985.

Shahar, Ido. "Legal Reform, Interpretive Communities and the Quest for Legitimacy:

A Contextual Analysis of a Legal Circular" in R. Shaham (ed.), *Custom, Shari'a, and Statute in the Muslim World: Studies in Honor of Aharon Layish*. Leiden: Brill, 2007.

Segal, Ze'ev. "High Court of Justice in the Israeli Societal Fabric after 50 Years" *Mishpat U-Mimshal*, vol. 5 (1) (1999), pp. 235–280 [in Hebrew].

Segev, Re'em and Mordechai Kremnitzer, *Shiklul 'Arachim ve-Izun Interesim*. Jerusalem: The Israel Democratic Institute, 2008 [in Hebrew].

Al-Sharbasi, Ahmad. *Yas'alunaka fi al-Din wal-Hayah*. Beirut, Dar al-Jil, 1977 [in Arabic].

Shehadeh, Raja. *Palestinian Walks: Notes on a Vanishing Landscape*. London: Profile Books, 2007.

Shitrit, Bekhor Shalom. *The Supreme Muslim Shari'a Council*. n.p. [Jerusalem: Government Press] 1949 [in Hebrew].

Skovgaard-Petersen, Jakob. *efining Islam for the Egyptian State: Muftis and Fatwas of the Dar Al-Ifta*. Leiden: Brill, 1997.

Al-Shawkani, Muhammad. Al-Fath al-Qadir. Cairo: M. al-Babi al-Halabi, 1349–1351/1930–1932.

Tarrow, Sidney. *The New Transactional Activism*. Cambridge: Cambridge University Press, 2005.

Tidwell, Alan C. *Conflict Resolved?* New York: Pinter Press, 1998.

Tilly, Charles and Tarrow, Sidney. *Contentious Politics*. Paradigm Publishers, 2006.

Tuan, YiFu. "Thought and landscape", in Meinig, Donald. W. (ed.), *The Interpretation of Ordinary Landscape*. New York, Oxford; Oxford University Press, 1979, pp. 89–102.

Al-Ulaymi, Mujir al-Din. *Al uns al-jalil bi-tarikh al Quds wa'l-Khalil*. Amman: Maktabat al-Muhtasib, 1973 [in Arabic].

Vilnai, Zeev. *Sacred Gravestones in Eretz Israel*. Jerusalem: Ahiever, 1996 [in Hebrew].

Zahalqa, Iyad. *The Shari'a Courts between Adjudication and Identity*. Jerusalem: Bar Association, 2009 [in Hebrew].

Al-Zayla' ī, Fakhr al-Dīn' Uthmān ibn 'Alī. *Tabyīn al-'aqā'iq: Shar' Kanz al-Daqā'iq*. Cairo, Būlāq: al-Matba' ah al-Kubrá al-Amīrīyah, 1313–1315[1895/6-7/8] [in Arabic].

Index

Printed and bound by CPI Group (UK) Ltd, Croydon, CR0 4YY

13/09/2026

14961103-0001